UNCOMMON SENSE

FATHER HOMER F. ROGERS

· ·

UNCOMMON SENSE

HARPER COLLINS RELIGIOUS
An Imprint of HarperCollinsPublishers

HarperCollins*Religious*
Part of HarperCollins*Publishers*
77–85 Fulham Palace Road,
Hammersmith, London W6 8JB

First published in Great Britain
in 1992 by HarperCollins*Religious*

An earlier edition of this book was published
in the USA by Mrs Dorothy Rogers under the title
The Romance of Orthodoxy

1 3 5 7 9 10 8 6 4 2

A catalogue record for this book is
available from the British Library

ISBN 0 00 599323-7

Printed and bound in Great Britain by
HarperCollinsManufacturing, Glasgow

CONTENTS

INTRODUCTION

Our world is full of people who honestly think they believe in God, but ask them to describe the God they believe in and they're like the warden who confessed to his vicar that his idea of God was a kind of oblong blur.

There is no such thing as a person who has no religious beliefs. We either have right opinions about ultimate reality and the meaning of things and people, or we have wrong opinions. It is not that a person can know nothing about religion – as I know nothing about celestial mechanics or even automobile mechanics. We may have no formal instruction about religion, but we do have religious beliefs.

We live in a world containing ultimate mysteries such as birth and death and free will and loneliness and creative impulses and community and conflict. These are the raw data of religion, and we must react to them. Our reactions reflect our basic assumptions about the nature of things, and these are our dogmas. Our theology, if you will. These assumptions are either in accord with absolute reality or they are false. And if false, they will increase our pain and suffering and our capacity to hurt others and destroy peace.

In one sense, because we are the heirs of a Christian civilization built slowly and painfully by the labour and sacrifices of our remote ancestors, we are about Christianity like a fish must be about water. But we have taken it for granted for a long time, and during that time it has been eroding and disappearing, and Christian beliefs and practices have been replaced by pagan beliefs and practices which we, unconsciously, suppose to be Christian.

We look around us and see such grief and injustice: people are scared and despairing, and we can't make sense of it. This is the human problem. The Christian religion is the answer. If we cannot accept the Christian explanation we leave the problem unsolved. The world and the human predicament either makes Christian sense, or it makes nonsense. Christ is the answer or there is no answer.

Creation is a sacrament of the presence of God, a veil over His face, for what really terrifies us about God is not His wrath but His love. All that we see in the world reveals something about its Creator: the gentle water of baptism is the same waters of chaos upon which the Spirit of the Lord brooded at the moment of creation, which parted to let the Israelites pass dryshod and returned to overwhelm the armies of Pharaoh, which drowned the world in the days of Noah, and which is added to the chalice of the Blood of Christ. You can see all that in the sparkling drop on the ivy leaf. Look through a microscope at a drop of pond water, and ask yourself is not the drop on the leaf terrible. It is terrible because each drop of water, each grain of sand, is a word, an utterance, a self-donation of the Word of God in His relentless outpouring of His love and power. The howl of the wolf in the night is his brute response to the music of the spheres in a key pitched too keen for human ears. We are allowed to listen to the child's singing because the angel choirs would deafen us: we are given the beauty of the rose because the beauty of the face of God would strike us blind.

God's nature as truth confronts us in the fact that life is a series of problems to be solved and questions to be answered, and inevitably we develop a habitual attitude toward truth. God's nature as love confronts us in our situation as a communal creature, and we are forced to learn His way to avoid strife and conflict. God's nature as joy and beauty confronts us in the wonder and splendour of creation. Every choice we make, however trivial, moves us closer to God or farther away from Him. At our death we step out of time and space and into eternity and recognize God as that which we have been longing for all our lives, or that which we have been avoiding all our lives.

At the judgement God asks us one question: "Do you love me?" But we have to give an honest answer. In order to love Him, we have to know Him, and know what He does, and why He does it. This is the proper study for all Christians, and it will take the rest of our lives.

1

. . . .

REALITY

This book is not intended to explain Christianity, for that isn't the problem. A person coming to this planet from Mars and landing among us, wouldn't ask, "Why do you believe in the Trinity?" or "What do you mean by transubstantiation?" He would ask, "Why do the good die young? Why is there many a slip 'twixt the cup and the lip? Why do the best laid schemes of mice and men gang aft agley? Why is the best puppy in the litter the one that gets run over? Why does a man's reach exceed his grasp? Why is there so much pain, sorrow, grief, misery, and ugliness in human life and human society? Why is everybody homesick, even when he's at home? Why does the happiest married man still scan the faces in the crowd?"

Let me carry the matter a bit further. Why should there be people on earth in the first place? Or, for that matter, why should there be an earth? Why should there be anything? These are the things that need explaining. The Christian religion seeks to explain them. Sooner or later you will make up your mind, if you haven't already, that the Christian religion is true or false, not in terms of how persuasively I explain to you the doctrine of the Trinity, and not even in terms of whether or not the Christian religion makes sense, but whether or not the Christian religion can answer any of these questions.

The Church, for example, has a theory of creation found

11

in the Book of Genesis. In the beginning God created the heavens and the earth. There aren't any other alternative theories of creation. All of the non-theistic theories of the origin of the universe begin with the universe already there. We either accept the explanation that God created everything or we do without an explanation.

That brings us to a distinction and a couple of definitions before we really get started. There are two kinds of believing, which a certain tradition of philosophers distinguish from one another by calling "doctrines" and "dogmas". Interestingly enough, those two terms are really synonymous; one is Latin and one is Greek. But they denote the same thing, a teaching. The word dogma has unfortunate connotations. We don't like people who are dogmatic because that means they are going to shove their beliefs down our throats whether we like it or not. However, the word "dogma" simply means a teaching.

Everyone's got doctrine, and everyone's got dogma. Doctrines are those beliefs that we have as the result of evidence and reasoning. We defend our doctrines in argument. When someone disagrees with our doctrines we say that he is mistaken. That Atlanta is east of Dallas is a doctrine. I can take a compass and start out in Dallas and head east all the way and wind up in Atlanta. There is evidence for that particular doctrine. If someone can show you that your doctrine is wrong, you will say, "I'll be darned," and you'll change your mind. We frequently change our doctrines throughout the course of our lives.

Our dogmas, however, are in a different class. They are those deep, profound, fundamental assumptions that we make about the nature of reality. We don't try to prove them. And yet these are the fundamental categories that give shape and structure to all our thinking. The difference, for example, between medieval times and modern, can be found in their dogmas, that are basic assumptions about the nature of reality, and these are things that we take on faith. Everybody does this.

For example, a child asks her mother, "Why does water run downhill?"

The mother replies, "Well, honey, it obeys the law of gravity."

"Well, Mama, what's the law of gravity?"

Mama: "It's the fact that water runs downhill."

"I know, Mama, but that's what I asked. Why does water run downhill?"

And Mama says, "Well, honey, it just does."

Whenever you get to the "Well, honey, it just does" stage of an argument, you have arrived at one of your dogmas, things that we accept without challenge because everybody else in our culture accepts them. When you find somebody who doesn't accept your dogmas you don't say he's mistaken, you say he's crazy.

We want a set of dogmas that explains more things than any other set of dogmas. For example, for a long time astronomers were satisfied with the Ptolemaic system of astronomy. It solved many problems and answered many questions. It left some questions unanswered. The Copernican system came along and it was adopted, not because it was more logical but because it explained more of the facts. But there are some facts it does not explain. Until we can find another set of assumptions that explains more of the facts than Copernican astronomy, we'll stay with that. What I am proposing about Christian dogmas is that they explain more of the facts than any other set of assumptions. But we are not going to explain the explanation, we're simply going to make it clear so you can understand it.

13

Now I said that these are dogmatic assumptions about the nature of reality. The first question I would like to raise with you is "What is reality?" This is a question which was first asked seriously some centuries before Christ in the Greek-speaking cities of Asia Minor. If you asked the ordinary person today, "What do you mean by reality?" the chances are he would reach out and touch something tangible. This paper is real. This chair is real. This floor is real. Because you can see it, touch it, taste it, feel it, it's real. If we wanted to give a name to this philosophical position, we would call it naïve materialism. I don't mean to denigrate it by implying it's a silly or inadequate theory. By golly, that chair *is* real. It's there. The opposite of "real" in that sense is "imaginary". Notice that this opposition establishes a dichotomy between what you can see and what you can't, between what you can know through your bodily senses and what you can know only by means of your intellect. Mental things to most people have a degree less reality because to most people, the word "real" is synonymous with "sensible", something you can apprehend with your bodily senses.

According to this theory, that which is intangible has a sort of quasi-reality. That view of reality is quite workable. It will pass the pragmatic test. If I see that chair and don't really believe it's there and try to walk through it, I'll bump my shin and knock it over. If you sit me down in front of a dish of bacon and eggs and I am hungry, I'll eat it and it will disappear down my throat and hunger pangs will go away. That was a real plate of bacon and eggs.

That view of reality has one disadvantage. Material things are constantly changing, becoming something else. Most of the time this change is slow and it doesn't bother people. However, some things change very rapidly. If you sit a plate

14

of bacon and eggs in front of me and I am engaged in a fascinating conversation and don't eat them for about fifteen minutes, when I return to my breakfast they are cold.

In order to illustrate further, let me pose a hypothetical laboratory test. I'll take a radio and set it on the shelf, plug it in, and let it play. Again let's assume the hypothetical, that there are 100 parts to the radio. It will play and play, and one day it will stop playing. I take it to the shop and they find a part that has worn out, and replace it. I bring it back and put it in the identical spot, plug it in, and it plays again.

Now, is it the same radio? Sure, it's got a new part, but it's the same radio. So year after year, one by one, the parts wear out until all hundred of the parts have been replaced. Is it the same radio? Most people would say no. When did it cease being the original radio and become what it is now? I don't know that it did.

Let me take that radio and disassemble it and drop the pieces one by one into a bushel basket. All the pieces are there. And the whole is equal to the sum of its parts. Is it a radio? It won't play. Most people would say, "No, it's not a radio. You've got a lot of disassociated parts, but you don't have a radio." If I put them back together, I'll guarantee you it still won't play. Is it a radio? No. Before those parts become a radio you have to have all the parts plus a strange intangible thing we will call the Put-Together-Right.

To get that radio to play, I'm going to have to call in somebody who knows something about the thing called "radio". It's a term that applies equally to any and all radios. He knows the principle and the theories. You can't see, hear, touch, or taste a theory, but unless that theory is somehow embedded in the parts, you don't have a radio.

One of the reasons that we think things are changing so rapidly these days is that we are so close to them. You know that when you are driving down the highway, the fence posts are whizzing by, but the telephone poles a quarter of a mile away are going by very slowly. So our sense of being involved in rapid change is psychological, and we can get really nervous about it. As a result, some folk begin to yearn and search for something permanent and unchanging. This evidently is what happened 2,500 years ago in the Greek cities of Asia Minor. The Greek civilization found its way into Asia and had settled in a number of colonial cities in Asia Minor. Then the Persians came along and reconquered all of this territory. Consequently, things weren't as they used to be. All of a sudden there were new ideas and new customs, new manners and new things to eat, new ways of dressing. New political forms crowded in upon people and they became nervous about how rapidly things were changing, so they began to search for something that didn't change. And this search went on for three centuries until we get to Plato.

Plato was a schoolteacher who taught his students that ideas don't change. He reasoned like this: you've got an apple tree in the back yard. In the spring of the year you find an apple blossom. The petals of that blossom fall off and then what you have is a teensy-weensy, little, hard, bitter, green nubbin thing about the size of a match head. It's not an apple, but it's going to be an apple. The weeks pass. It gets larger, rounder, fuller, and begins to look like an apple. It's still hard and green and bitter, but after a while the green coloration on the skin begins to turn yellow and finally red, and the molecules turn to sugar and are sweet and juicy, and now it's an apple. But watch out. After a while it begins to turn brown and soft. Then it's a gooey, slushy mess which finally dries out and becomes apple dust.

Every apple goes through the process of becoming an

apple and ceasing to be an apple. How do you know it's an apple and not an orange? Well, everybody knows what an apple is. You have in your mind an idea of an apple, and when that hunk of matter conforms to and expresses the idea "apple", then it's an apple. It's put-together-right. The idea "apple" is the same year after year. But concrete, individual apples, the apples you can see, taste, touch, they are only apples fully and completely for a matter of a week or two at the most.

For that matter, it is doubtful if there ever has been any apple which has perfectly expressed the idea of an apple. The idea of apple is in our mind and has this great advantage: it doesn't change. You can't destroy it. Every concrete particular apple is destined some day to cease to be. You'll either eat it or make a pie out of it and eat that, or the worms will eat it, or it will rot. But the idea of "apple" goes on for ever.

And so the Greeks discovered with Plato a level or dimension of reality which made them happy. Where the materialist will say that mental things are less real, the idealist – that's what Plato and his followers are – will say that material things are less real. The idealist looks at the chair and sees in it the process of decay. It won't have the same reality for him that it does for a materialist. As a matter of fact, he may transfer this notion to his own body. Plato did indeed say that man is a soul unfortunately imprisoned in a miserable hunk of matter. Salvation is when he can escape from the body into a realm of pure spirit. A genuine contempt for material things, a belief that matter is evil, is found among the Puritans and in certain oriental religions like the Hindus. As a child I shut my eyes when I prayed, and I was told I did this to shut out the world. Prayer was "spirit to spirit". Such an attitude derives in some measure from Plato.

But Plato had a very bright pupil who could ask embarrassing questions that the teacher couldn't answer. His name was Aristotle, and one day Aristotle said to Plato, "Mr Plato, I'd like to comment on this theory of yours about real apples. I grant you that the concrete particular apple is destined to have a short life. Appleness goes on for ever. The idea of an apple is indestructible and eternal and immutable, but professor, it isn't a real apple."

What had happened? There had occurred not a philosophical but a psychological shift in his point of view. This whole search for an unchanging reality began at a time when men were anxious about the rapidity of change and were groping around for something that didn't change. Aristotle wasn't bothered by that. And he wasn't satisfied with an unchanging apple that he couldn't eat, though he was unwilling to deny the reality of appleness. So he began to teach that reality is a two-layered thing, a duality. You have "matter" and "form" (the blueprint or the idea). True reality exists, he argued, when the two come together. You never have any matter except in connection with some form. And forms don't exist up in the air, they only exist in connection with some matter. If you take one of the bricks in the church, it ceases to be part of the wall and has its own form as a brick. Take a grain of sand out of that brick and it ceases to be part of the form of the brick and has the form of a grain of sand. Matter nowhere exists by itself. Form doesn't exist by itself. There is the material and the non-material, and true reality exists when these two things come together.

Now in a sense, everybody takes one of these three views. The human intellect is the kind of thing that seeks consistency and uniformity. Most people don't ask themselves, "What is reality?" and identify themselves as a realist, an idealist, or an Aristotelian. Nevertheless, people do fall into one of these three categories. This determines all kinds of important decisions such as who you marry and what kind of clothes you wear. So the decision on this question of reality is perhaps the most important we ever make.

At the time Christ began His Church, the chief rival to Christianity was not polytheism. Not many of the educated people still believed in the gods of the early Greek civilizations. The rival to Christianity was a religion which had been imported from Asia, and whose adherents believed, strangely enough, in two gods: a good god who made the spiritual things and an evil god who made material things. This is a central explanation of existence, because we find good and bad things in our experience, and we can explain this phenomenon by saying that there is an ultimate principle of goodness and an ultimate principle of badness, and that these two are in conflict. The Church resisted the temptation to accept this easy explanation and blame matter on the devil. This is why most Christians recite the Creed, because the Church was saying no to this fashionable religion of the first century. The Church decided once upon a time not to be relevant by saying, "No, we do not believe in two gods; we believe in one God who is the maker of heaven and earth and of all things visible and invisible." Thus we make claim against the gods who only make spiritual and heavenly things, and the gods who only make material and earthly things. What we find in the world is sin and mosquitoes and ants and broken bones and rotten apples, but one God is going to have to take the blame for all that. It's harder to explain, but nevertheless, the Church was unwilling to accept this dualistic version of experience. That was shocking and offensive to a great many urbane and educated people of the first, second, and third centuries. "The God you worship made bugs! Ugh!" But the Church said, "Yep, God made bugs. Like it or not."

So the view of reality you choose determines your religion. Let's take a look at what religion is. William James defined religion as an uneasiness and its solution. That's a good definition as far as it goes, but it doesn't go far enough. Historically and individually, both as a cultural phenomenon in history and as an experience in one's individual human life, religion begins in awe. Awe is a compound of interest and apprehension. Interest alone does not create awe, nor does apprehension. But when you are in the presence of that which both fascinates and disturbs you, you have the experience of awe and the ground out of which religion grows. When people experience awe, they want to do something. You might say religion is that which man does in response to awe, to that which excites in him the experience of wonder.

In order to understand this idea more fully, we are going to take as examples two kinds of religion: that of the ancient Greeks and that of the ancient Jews. I've chosen these not because they are the best, but because everybody knows a little about Greek religion, since we've studied Greek mythology in school, and everybody knows a little about the Hebrew religion, since we've studied it in Sunday School. Let's start with the Greeks.

Five thousand years ago, about the dawn of history, a people lived in that land which we call Greece. Greece is a mountainous country, habitable and arable only in the valleys. Let's assume that in one of these little Greek valleys there lived a farmer named John Smith. Once a week he took a basket of eggs on his arm and went to market. (We know he really didn't do that, because chickens hadn't yet been imported from India. But he took something in the basket over his arm and went off to market). He went down the valley following the little stream that opened up onto the coastal plain. There stood a little fishing village where people in canoes went up and down the seacoast bartering for sea shells and pottery. He traded his eggs for things which he could buy at the market, and went back in the afternoon.

Now, one of the things we know about prehistoric man is that he was a man, which means he had something in common with us. His dogmas were different from ours, but his basic experiences weren't so different. At the place where his mountain valley opened out onto the coastal plains there was a bottleneck formation where the ranges of the hills sort of turned and pinched together and the land sloped rapidly and was rocky, so that it had not been cleared for cultivation. There was a stand of virgin forest of perhaps a few hundred acres. John Smith had to go through this forest on his way to market. We've all been in places like this. The trees grew tall and their branches laced together so thickly overhead that you couldn't see the sky. The light of the sun filtered through these branches rather dimly, so that down there in the forest it was always a sort of perpetual twilight. You looked off in any direction and your vision was limited because of the trees and the undergrowth. Underfoot the ground was covered with a spongy carpet of decayed vegetation so that your footfall was muffled. In there, in this particular grove, it was damp and dank and rather gloomy, and John Smith's reaction to this place was much the same as yours and mine. That is to say, it gave him a sort of creepy feeling, but it was a good feeling. He liked it there, just as I like that sort of place. But it also made him kind of uncomfortable.

21

As he analyzed his feelings, he came to the realization that he felt as if there were somebody watching him, that he wasn't alone. It wasn't a bad feeling, but it was a spooky, haunted feeling. And he rather looked forward to the feeling that this place would have on him, yet he didn't want to stay there too long. He would pause, look around him, and rather enjoy the creepy feeling the way you rather enjoy the roller coaster – you're not getting your money's worth unless it scares you. This place sort of scared him, but it didn't *really* scare him. It was that sort of feeling.

One day he mentions this strange feeling to his neighbour. "Yes, I know exactly where you felt it, it's right there where the stream makes a sharp right-angle bend and there's a great, flat, moss-covered rock that juts out into the stream." And John says, "How did you know?" "I feel the same thing when I go through there." And they start talking about it as if there were some spirit that dwelt in the forest.

Let's stop and consider what the primitive Greek meant by the term "god". He did not mean "God" in the sense that we mean "God". To the Greek a god was halfway between what we understand by an angel and a fairy, a little more exalted than a fairy and a little less exalted than an angel. The primitive Greek, in common with you and me, distinguished between the living and the non-living thing (notice I did not say *dead*; the word *dead* suggests having been alive). We distinguish between these two by a very simple test. The living thing moves itself. The non-living thing, if it moves, has to be moved by something else. That chair is non-living. If you don't touch it, it's going to sit there for ever until it disintegrates. But if it moves, somebody has to move it.

The Greeks knew that certain things moved themselves and were alive, and other things were not alive, and yet the non-alive things sometimes moved. Water sometimes moved, and the wind moved. The grain of wheat doesn't move, but if you put it in the ground, up comes a little green shoot, and it grows and becomes wheat. If the non-alive thing isn't moved by something you can see, it must be moved by something you can't see. It's the things that you can't see that cause things to move that are the gods. They were those invisible beings that made eggs hatch and beer ferment and wind blow and fire burn and water run and the wheat to grow, and all those mysterious things that go on in the world around us that excite wonder and awe, and are a part of the mystery of existence. Today our dogmatic assumptions have deprived most of those things of their mystery. Yet they are, in fact, quite mysterious.

Back to John Smith. Something was in the air in that place. He felt a presence. This wasn't something good or bad, it was just alien and different and Other. What was being moved by this was his own viscera, his own blood pressure. He was being affected by this presence. He and his neighbour discussed it. They were very interested in this phenomenon. Then one day his neighbour says, "Hey, do you suppose whoever lives in the forest minds our using it as a passageway to and from the market?" And John says, "My God, I never thought of that."

The next day when he takes his basket of eggs to market and he stands right in the middle of the most dense part of the forest, he looks overhead and sees nothing but this leafy canopy of trees. At that moment, though he doesn't realize it, the sun goes behind a cloud, and that dim light that filters through is perceptibly dimmer. By a coincidence at that moment there is a chilly errant breeze that blows across him, and he discovers that he is perspiring though he is not really hot. Way off in the distance an owl hoots. He jumps inside his skin and goose bumps appear on his arm. He does an impulsive but very natural thing. He takes an egg out of his basket and tiptoes (because you tiptoe in places like that) and lays his egg on the big flat rock. He looks up into the dimness overhead, and he says, "You, whoever you are that lives in the forest, this egg is for you and it is to show you that I appreciate being allowed to use your forest." He has had an uneasiness, and he has solved it. He has solved it by offering the first sacrifice and uttering the first prayer. Notice that his prayer isn't, "Dear God, please don't let it rain and spoil our picnic."

What he is doing with the prayer is explaining the egg.

This response to mystery always involves Something Done and Something Said. He has offered the first sacrifice and he has uttered the first prayer.

John Smith tells his neighbour what he has done, and his neighbour immediately sees how proper this is, and it becomes customary when passing through the forest to leave an offering on the flat rock. A couple of thousand years later a fine marble temple has appeared over this big flat rock, and John Smith's great-great-grandchildren are members of the priestly class. People come from all over the valley to make their offerings and say their prayers, for this is a holy rock. Long ago the trees were cut down for sacrificial fires, but the rock is still there. The rock has in time acquired a numinous quality of its own. The rock excites awe, wonder, and reverence.

The same thing was happening in the neighbouring valley. They too had a forest and a spooky feeling in the forest, a "you, whoever you are who lives in the forest". If you were to climb up on the mountain and finally come out above the timber line where it's barren and the wind blows all the time, there, too, you feel strange and your guts churn. There is a god that lives on the mountain top. Halfway down the mountain there's a big box canyon, and you stand in the middle of that and say, "Ohohoh," and something at the end of the canyon will go, "OHOHOH." You search and search and can't find who it is. He seems to be mocking you, but if you get too close, he stops. You have to stand back at a distance.

There was also a big waterfall halfway up the mountain and you would stand and look up and the water would spray and roar in various ways. It must have felt strange being attacked by this stream of water. So you get a god of the waterfall, a god of the mountaintop, a god of the forest, and a god of the canyon. Eventually you had a god that made beer ferment and a god that made the crops grow. As the Greeks grew more sophisticated and began to compare notes, they discovered that the god of this forest was a lot like the god of that forest, so they merged and became the god of forests. There is a degree of abstraction; one god that makes the crops grow. What the Greeks were in awe of, feared and worshipped, was the personification of the forces of nature. So their ultimate reality was nature.

Now, in some ways, this is a good religion. Here's how they celebrated their religious festivals.

The businesses and banks and schools all closed. Weeks before the holiday they had selected a prime Black Angus ox and had fattened it so that it was juicy and tender. A few days before the festival the Women's Auxiliary and a couple of vestrymen got out fingernail polish and tinted its horns and hooves, and they gathered garlands of flowers to hang around its neck. Then they washed it and curried it. On the day of the festival they had a parade complete with the high school cheerleaders in their pretty little costumes and the mayor in his limo. At the head of the parade would come someone leading the ox. The animal was taken out to a meadow at the edge of town, and the local preacher was called upon to say grace. (You do something, so you have to say something.) They had prayers, and then the ox was slaughtered. They put it on a spit over a big bed of coals and took turns turning the spit all day. While waiting for the ox to roast there were contests, foot races, baseball games, square dancing, speeches, and someone brought beer. There were wrestling matches and they drank the beer, and the first thing you know they were kind of drunk. Finally the animal was cooked and carved up and everyone ate barbecue until they had had enough, and then they went out and drank some more. There was more dancing, and finally about midnight everyone ended up fornicating in the bushes with someone else's wife.

Marvellous religion. You can see why it was so popular. Lots of food, lots of drink, lots of fun. However, one thing is wrong with that kind of religion; it never has and never will and never can produce and sustain a morality, and for a very obvious reason. If nature is that which is ultimately real and ultimately good, then the best thing that man can do is to be natural. To have a morality implies that you prefer one situation to another situation. You ought to do this instead of that. You ought to tell the truth instead of lie. You ought to be faithful to your wife instead of committing adultery. Morality implies that some modes of conduct are preferable to others, but if nature is the ultimate norm, then everything that is, is natural. So there is no basis for preferring one mode of conduct to another.

Birth is natural – so is death. Disease is natural – so is health. The cowardice of the rabbit is natural and so, too, is the fierceness of the fox. So there is no way of deciding if one way is better than another. The only commandment that the worship of nature can possible give is to be natural. To be natural means to express yourself, to follow your impulses. Obviously you can't make a moral code out of the single commandment: Do As You Please. For one finds that in those cultures in which nature is the ultimate god there is a gradual, progressive, total, and final collapse of all morality. We find that happening in twentieth-century America, because even among many of us who profess to be Christians, our real god is science, nature, or "what comes naturally". Consequently, there has been an erosion of all standards and values. Finally such a civilization as ours disintegrates into an individualistic chaos.

In such a society, morality never gets off the ground. It's been the universal experience of mankind that communities can only exist when there are agreed-upon norms and standards of behaviour which the community itself regards as more valuable and more important than what the individual wants. Sooner or later, what I want and what you want are going to come into conflict. Unless we can appeal to some standard outside of ourselves, we are going to wind up butting heads. That's what happened with the Greeks.

A few hundred miles away in the land now known as Palestine, there were a people who were going to become the Jews. They were nomads. They had the same experience as the Greeks did but in a different setting. One night a little shepherd lad, bedded down by the fire with his drowsy herd bunched before him, became alert, jolted and startled. He felt a spooky, creepy sensation of not being alone. He mentioned it to his neighbour and the neighbour didn't say, "Yes, I know exactly where it happened." He said, "Yes, I know exactly how it felt because the same thing happened to me last week when we were sixty miles to the east."

Among the Greeks, who were a settled agricultural

people, it was places that became holy. The Jews were not a settled people, and that fact lies behind the story in the Old Testament about Jacob and the ladder. In my Sunday School Bible, there was a picture of this incident. Jacob was a tall, bearded figure wearing a white nightgown, standing in the bright sunlight on the hillside where flowers were blooming. A few yards away you could see a ladder which reached up and disappeared into the clouds, and on the ladder were half a dozen seven-foot-tall men with effeminate faces and long hair, wearing nightgowns and big golden wings. They were ascending and descending.

But that's not what happened. In the first place, Jacob wasn't a tall, bearded figure, he was a boy. I don't know how old he was, but probably about fifteen. He was the younger of twins, but they weren't identical twins. Esau was the older brother, a great big robust hairy-chested two-fisted he-man who was the joy of his daddy's heart. Jacob was a sissy. He followed his mama around the kitchen and learned how to cook. One day Esau came in from his hunting in the fields, starving to death, and Jacob was in the kitchen, making a mess of pottage, probably chilli. Esau said, "Let me have some of your chilli." Jacob said, "Sell me your birthright." Jacob and his mama connived to play a trick on Esau since the old man had gone blind and was getting ready to transfer the leadership of the clan to his eldest son. He sent what he thought was his son out to kill some venison so he could eat and bless him and offer sacrifices. But Jacob went out and killed a kid and put enough chilli peppers in it so the old man couldn't tell the difference between *cabrito* and venison. Then Jacob got his older brother's blessing, which meant he really supplanted his brother as the head of the clan. When Esau came back he was furious. He was really mad.

28

Jacob decided that the smart thing to do was to go visit grandmother, which is what he did. Grandmother lived a long way away. He was inexperienced and he was travelling light and hurrying. He took a bottle of olive oil and he ran, fearing the wrath of Esau. Nightfall overtook him and he settled down on the warm hillside, scooped out a hollow, and went to sleep, and had a nightmare. In his dream he saw in the darkness before his face big shadowy figures weaving up and down, and he said, "Woe is me, for there is a god in this place and I knew it not."

When he awoke in the morning, he didn't have any eggs, but he had the bottle of olive oil, and he poured the oil out on that particular rock as an offering to the god of that place. He named the place Beth-El, the place where a god lives. Then he went on to Heran and stayed there for fourteen years and came back with two wives and two concubines and many sons and daughters and a lot of cattle. But he went to that particular hillside to say his prayers. If Jacob had been a Greek, that would have been a holy shrine and a temple would have been built. But like all nomads, he didn't stay put. They have a god who comes to them out of the air and follows them around.

So the Jewish notion of God is a sky god. All nomadic peoples worshipped the sky god, and all agricultural people worshipped the earth god. For some reason the sky god was masculine and the earth god was feminine. This sky god is seen as something different and distinct from nature, something outside of nature. He enters into nature from time to time, but essentially he dwells on the other side of what we can see, touch, taste, or smell.

If our notion of the Mystery is inside creation, we say that God is immanent. The Greek god was immanent. The God who dwells beyond the sky is transcendent. The Jewish god was transcendent. The Jewish idea was that if you can see it, taste it, smell it – it isn't God. This is why they prohibited idols and images to represent God. To do so, they believed, was certainly to misrepresent Him because God is a spirit. God is not identifiable with anything that He has made. He is other than and different from His creation.

This God and this religion certainly produced a morality, consisting largely of don'ts. Because it is man's inherent impulse to want to identify with and become one with that which he regards as ultimately worthwhile, and if the worthwhile is spiritual, I must manage to quell and suppress all of my interest in material things. I don't smoke and I don't chew and I don't go with the girls who do. The Jews became strict, even ruthless, moralists. The rules were multitudinous pettifoggery. However, this kind of religion isn't much fun. You have the worship of nature which is fun but not very moral, and you have the god who is moral but not very much fun. At the time of Christ, you could take your pick. You could believe that God was immanent and have a world of fun and let morality shift for itself, or you could believe that God was transcendent and be very moral and not have much fun. For example, the Greek nature gods can't be much help to man because they are involved in the same sort of natural problems and conflicts that man is. On the other hand, the Jewish god became so remote and distant with so little in common with the people that they didn't expect him to understand or sympathize with their problems. Thus again you have the old dichotomy between materialism and idealism.

Plato was looking for unchanging reality, and he found it in a spiritual world. The Jews had a god, the high and lofty one who inhabited eternity, who was unchanging between the cherubim, be the earth never so unquiet. Plato and Isaiah would have understood each other. They had the same identical viewpoint.

Into this dichotomy came a little baby, and as He grew older and developed into maturity, men came to believe He was somehow or other the incarnation of God. If God had become incarnate among the Greeks, He would hardly have been noticed. Half-god and half-man? They had Hercules. Their gods were always falling in love with humans and sleeping with them, and having phenomenal children who were part god and part man. What the Greeks didn't have was the high and lofty one who inhabited eternity. And it was such a God who came to the early Christians, born of a virgin and laid in a manger. No one had seen God at any time to represent Him or to make a picture of Him, according to the Jews. All of a sudden some people were saying, "I saw Him. I saw Him wrapped in swaddling clothes. I saw Him at the Last Supper take bread and wine and break it and give it." Strange words. "I saw Him hanging on a cross."

Thus, because of his belief in the Incarnation, the Christian is forced to take a third view of reality. The Christian says that the Greek and the Jew are both wrong because they are both right. What John Smith felt in the forest was the God of Abraham, Isaac, and Joseph who communicated Himself in His presence by means of His creation. The Christian believes that God is both transcendent and immanent: transcendent in His nature and immanent in His activity. The Jew is right: God is transcendent, eternal pure spirit. But the Greek is also right: God enters into His material creation in order to communicate His reality in His presence to men. So the Church has to say. "I believe in one God, the Father Almighty, maker of heaven and earth." Spiritual things *and* material things. "And all that is visible and invisible." The implications of that are endless.

Yet there is a constant temptation to oversimplify experience. If we simplify it in the direction of matter or in the direction of the spirit, we leave out some important things for which we ultimately become very hungry. For man himself is a body and a spirit. He is not a spirit imprisoned in a body, or a spirit riding piggyback on a body, nor a body with a spirit. He is a spirit-body. He is one creature compounded of these two things. Both aspects of man and both aspects of human experience have reality and value.

2

. . . .

ABOUT GOD

Two thousand years of Christian history and man wants things to be simple. Any time someone says, "Christianity is really only . . ." what follows is sure to be a heresy. Human affairs are complex, and if religion is the key that fits the lock, it is going to be as complex as the lock. If not, it's the wrong key. "Salvation in six easy lessons" just doesn't work.

In the early Church, martyrs were popping up all the time. You literally had to renounce this world in order to participate. The Church was, by and large, an underground organization opposed by the government. The world had very little to offer the Christian. He lived a disciplined, puritanical life. Nevertheless, God created the world and called it good. He loved it enough to inhabit it in His own flesh. We must not condemn the world.

Imagine a seesaw, with materialism on one end and idealism on the other, with Christianity as the fulcrum. So long as the Church was in the middle, accommodating both of these extremes, it was flexible enough to survive intact.

About 300 A.D. Emperor Constantine decided to join the Christians. With the consequent influx of thousands of members since the Church was now respectable, the Church's morals went downhill. Its message was still otherwordly: "I know it is good to be alive in God's world, but don't forget, you were made for more than this. Your home is in Heaven."

Then the barbarians overran the Empire (500–800 A.D.) and the Church went underground again and started producing martyrs and saints again. This was also a period remarkable for its production of monasteries. Then, in about 800 A.D., Charlemagne accepted the Church and the masses joined up again, and down went the morality. These new members were uninstructed and just members in form. This period ended about 1000 A.D. with what the church historians call the period of the Pornocracy, because every archbishop had a harem. Then came Pope Hildebrand who reformed the Church because the Moslems were threatening to take over Europe. So Christianity rolled up its sleeves and we went to war and had the Crusades.

In 1517, Luther, an Augustinian monk, tacked some papers on the door and started the Reformation and something happened that hadn't happened before. The change in men's tastes had always been accommodated within the Church because the centre of the Church had always been the Incarnation. The fulcrum stayed in the middle. But in the sixteenth century the theologians decided to become relevant. They moved the fulcrum out to one end of the seesaw. The Protestant reformers did not deny the Incarnation but they did deny its implication. Theology was adjusted to fit the mood, the temper of the times. The reformers failed in their primary prophetic mission, which was to swim upstream, to run counter to the popular will.

So we had, for 300 years, even in Roman Catholicism, a period of renouncing material things, of asceticism. After about 300 years, man grew tired of being so goldarned holy. The world wasn't so bad when they looked around at it with open eyes. But, because the fulcrum was not in the middle any more, and the Church was inflexible, those who rebelled against the Church's stuffiness had nowhere to go within Christ's body, so they had to leave it altogether. This defection gave rise to the so-called nineteenth-century quarrel between science and religion, which was not really science and religion at all, but rather between a radical materialism and a radical idealism. So we have had for the past couple of hundred years a tug of war for the allegiance of men between a religion which was predominantly otherworldly, or puritanical, and a science which has been primarily materialistic.

The early Protestants had Old Testament names like Benjamin, Jonathan, and Daniel. Protestant theology is quite at home in the Old Testament, and fairly uncomfortable in the New. The New Testament is the story of God's dramatic invasion of the world of time and matter, setting up a religion of crucifixes, candles, bright vestments, statues, as if people were not afraid of matter. And, horror of horrors, people behave reverently toward bread, and what's worse, wine.

The idea that material things can have lasting spiritual value is the Christian ideal that keeps the fulcrum in the centre and prevents mankind from going from one oversimplification to the other, from heresy to heresy.

When I graduated from seminary over thirty years ago, the primary task of a teacher was to answer the challenge of rationalism, to prove that a person could believe in God and retain his intellectual integrity. This is no longer the issue. Most people today are not impressed by reason, but they are impressed by magic. They want charisma, power, mystery. They want not to be enlightened but emotionally stirred. Religion is on the rise. Back when everyone was a rationalist, I went around trying to convince people that there was a mystical side that was real. Now I am finding it hard to convince folk that they can trust their reason, that it too is real.

Listen to your friends. Nine times out of ten people will say, "I feel" when they mean "I think". The balance and fulcrum idea not only means that reality is both material and spiritual, but it also means that our approach to reality is both rational and intuitive. If you don't use both sides of your brain to know God, you are not practising Christianity.

Now let's examine the idea of God. It is impossible to prove the existence of God. It is equally impossible to prove the existence of Fr Rogers. Try to devise a scientific proof that you are not dreaming. There are only two ways to prove anything: the inductive method and the deductive method. The inductive process proceeds from the examination of specifics to the making of a generalization. The only way to do that is to make sure you have examined all the evidence.

Example: how many legs does a man have? In my experience he has two, but I cannot say with certainty unless I see all men. So to prove God this way I'd have to know all things. I'd have to keep looking until I ran into God.

Conversely, to prove that there is not a God, I'd have to know all things and know that God wasn't one of them. So if there isn't a God, only God would know it for sure.

The reason I believe is that the evidence allows me to believe, and because I want to believe. There is considerable evidence for the existence of God, and absolutely none against. There hasn't been a single new atheistic argument presented for the past thousand years. There isn't enough evidence to coerce belief, but there is enough to allow it. Essential to the question is whether or not I want to allow God to exist. If someone says, "There is a moral God who demands our allegiance," you don't ignore it, you go around looking for evidence. If there is such evidence, you'd better start acting as if it were true. In the first analysis you believe because you have found enough evidence to justify it, and you are willing for there to be a God who is bigger and smarter than you. If there is a God, I am not my own boss. If I am my own boss, and there *is* a God, I'm in trouble.

We already know God is a concrete thing. But what does that mean? Here I have a penny. I want to find out what "matter" is. I have heard that there are atoms, and I want to see one. So I make this penny grow until it is the size of a slice of the earth. As it grows, it will get paler and paler and eventually be transparent. The surface of the penny is really a trajectory of atoms. So let's catch one. Now, I've got it in my hand, but I can't see it. So let's expand the atom until it's the size of the state of Texas, and catch an electron. So here it is, and I can't see it, either. Apparently, an electron is a measurable centre of a field of force. It extends until it establishes a relationship with another field of force. So we begin to find that mass equals energy. The difference between a copper penny and a rose petal is a different organizational form of energy.

So, all creation is organized energy. When God began to create He didn't find the matter and say, "I think I'll create something." The source of all the power there is comes from one source: God's energy, which he "othered". God knew antelopes before He gave them a semi-autonomous existence outside His intellect. Creation is to God as the song is to the singer. He didn't do it once upon a time in a land far away. It is an ongoing relationship between God and Otherness. The old rabbis knew what they were talking about when they used "God said". Where does a song go when the singer stops singing? It just goes. And if God were to stop creating, creation would just go. Creation is made out of nothing. I did not have to be. I might not have been myself at all; if a different sperm had fertilized the egg, I'd have been my brother. Considering the odds of our grandparents and great-grandparents getting together, it's a wonder any of us are. That quality of "need not be" strongly implies the existence of a Creator. Created things like us are contingent beings; we depend on something else for our existence. This is the Christian doctrine of creation. It is an ongoing continuous relationship. Therefore everything that exists in creation is something that is in the mind of God eternally.

The existence of the chair implies a creator, a progressive chain of causes, each cause implying the existence of a pre-existing cause. If you set up a line of dominoes to fall over, what makes the first domino fall? My finger – and it didn't have to. The observable universe is like that. If there ever was a nothing, there still would be nothing. You can't imagine a nothing rolling up its sleeves, flexing its muscles, and creating something. This is why we are afraid of dying. We logically conclude that something has to have been always and must continue always.

Rejecting the infinite series of insufficient causes, we arrive at the first cause. We know several things about it. It needs nothing to account for its existence, otherwise it would not be the first cause. We know that the first cause caused, and that it didn't have to. If it had to, then something was causing it to cause, and that thing would be first. So it had a choice to cause or not to cause. Therefore it had something resembling personality or intellect. Therefore God is at least an eternally, existing, personal being who caused.

Let's look at a couple of these attributes. God is eternal, for example, which doesn't mean a long, long time. To be

eternal means to be outside time and space. Suppose the
universe shrank uniformly, exactly, in all its parts. We
wouldn't know whether the universe is big or little. If all
perceptive motion stopped – cigarette smoke, the passage of
supper through the digestive tract, the heavenly bodies – we
wouldn't know whether we'd been sitting here five minutes
or five thousand years. Time is only our awareness of
motion in space. What's happening in Fort Worth is just as
real as what's happening in Dallas, but to get there we have
to go through time and space, since we can't be in both
places at the same time. What happened in the first century is
just as real as what is happening here. We get our reality a
little bit at a time. Time is a limitation on our ability to
comprehend reality.

To be outside of time and space is just to be unaware of
time and take reality all at once. I could smell yesterday just
as surely as I can smell today. The only difference between
the two is that today I know reality by my external senses,
and yesterday by my memory. God knows reality in the
second way, not through bodily senses. God can hear
everybody's prayers because He doesn't have any ears. A
great many religious problems are the result of a failure to
understand this. God doesn't foresee the future. He just
knows it all at once.

God is infinite. That means to have no limits. He is not
great in the sense that He is "great big". He is everywhere,
but He doesn't occupy space. So the scientific concept of
space measurement doesn't apply to Him. The kinds of
limits I have, God doesn't. I think discursively. I examine
bits of evidence and come up with conclusions. God doesn't
do this. Everything He knows, He knows all at once. God is
simple-minded. Everything that he knows is perfectly
harmonized with everything else and it all makes sense.

He has always had just one thought, which is everything.

God is omnipotent. This doesn't mean that He can be inconsistent. He can't make 2 and 2 equal 7, or kiss His elbow and turn into a girl, or cease being God. He can't make an irresistible force meet an immovable object. He can't think nonsense. What it means first and foremost is that all the power there is comes from God. One more thing – He cannot create a moral being incapable of sin. Why did He allow the existence of such a fiend as Hitler? Because you and I had to be allowed to tell a lie yesterday. God must give me free will in order for me to be virtuous. So God had a choice: either a universe which was both good and evil, or one in which there was neither good nor evil. There has to be at least the possibility of good and evil. The possibility of sadism, greed, and all the horrible things we can do is also the possibility of heroism, self-sacrifice, and all the wonderful things we can do.

So, then, God is transcendent, immanent, eternal, non-material, personal, infinite, and omnipotent.

3

THE DOCTRINE OF MAN

To the civilization in which the Bible and the Church appeared, the word "soul" meant rather what we mean by "life". Proving the existence of the soul is like proving the existence of life. It's not easy to do as you might suppose. No one can prove that you are not dreaming while I am standing talking to you. You have to take it for granted, as an act of faith, the validity of sense experience. There is no way you can prove that what you see and hear is really there.

A spirit is an immaterial thing which is not located anywhere inside the body. While I am aware that I and my mind are different things, I do not say, "My will wills," I say, "I will." I do not say, "My memory remembers," but I say, "I remember." What does the *I* stand for? It is that strange, curious, spiritual reality which is referred to by the letter *I* in a sentence: *I* think, *I* will, *I* decide, *I* choose, *I* grieve, *I* love, *I* rejoice. That *I* has no size, shape, or location. Clearly it is in some mysterious fashion associated with my body and I use my body to communicate with you. But I am not the same thing as my body, not even the same thing as my consciousness. You run across such expressions in the English language as, "to possess my soul in peace". Now the soul is the same thing as *I*; how can I possess my soul, or how can I lose my soul? The word "soul" refers to all of those psychic faculties which distinguish a living human being from a dead human being.

Your soul and my soul have an identical nature. You and I are distinguished from one another by principles of differentiation. One is matter: my body doesn't look like any other body that ever lived. That's the way you recognize and distinguish me from Tom Selleck. We might be the same size and shape, and from a considerable distance someone might mistake one of us for the other, but when you see us side by side you will have no doubts.

There are other differences between one human being and another. My *I*, my spirit, is an individual substance of a rational nature. In respect to my consciousness of myself, you and I are as different as an antelope is from an alligator. The difference between you and me spiritually is not the difference between one alligator and another, although the difference between us physically is the same kind of difference. Spiritually there is a substantial difference. The substance is a unique kind of thing. This spiritual nature which is in man is the basis of his freedom.

For the past twenty years or so there has been an enormous amount of noise about liberty and freedom. It dates back to the beginnings of this country when we fought a revolution for "freedom and liberty". The French also fought a revolution to establish *"Liberté, Egalité, Fraternité."* But unfortunately, today people who make the most noise about freedom really don't have the foggiest notion what the word means. They begin by pointing out that although man is free, there are psychologists who claim that freedom is an illusion, that we are not really free. But tell me I'm not really free and I'll laugh at you, because I have this self-consciousness, this connatural awareness of my internal freedom. However, I will admit that there are limitations on my freedom.

1. I am not free to do what I cannot imagine.

2. I am not free to do what is intrinsically impossible. I can't sprout wings and fly. Not even God can make a square circle. However, the limitations of freedom are even more subtle.

3. Every exercise of freedom is a limitation of freedom.

Only an old bachelor or old maid is free to decide whether or not to get married. I am a married man and can no longer choose to be married or single. I had a childhood dream to be a cowboy. But when I became a priest I gave that up for ever and ever. The exercise of our choice when we come to the close of our lives becomes narrower and yet this is the result of free choice. We use up our freedom by making choices. We finally run out of choices, though I don't think that will really happen until the day of our death. The time will come when we will have the choice of giving our lives over to God willingly or unwillingly. That's our last choice. I might add that in a great many situations, refusing to make a choice is making a choice. If I can't decide to stay home or go to a movie, and spend the evening just refusing to make the choice, I choose to stay home.

Now another way our choice limits freedom is by its own exercise. That is to say, choices tend to harden into habits. Let me explain by first noting that we are conscious of freedom most when we have a strong pull in two different directions. "To be or not to be, that is the question," or go to a movie or stay home. If my desire is just about equal and I can't make up my mind, that's when I am aware of my choices. On the other hand, we make choices every day which, though real, are so habitual that we are hardly aware of them. Sometimes we get so in the habit of eating the same thing for breakfast every morning that with each passing day, some other choice becomes less and less likely. Particularly if the choice, the first time, is gratifying and results in pleasure, we tend to repeat it. This is especially true if these choices are morally good or morally bad, considered objectively. Theoretically, nothing at all is preventing me from pulling out a derringer and murdering someone right now. Why don't I do it? Well, I don't want to. But I am free to do it. However, it is against my religion. I am out of the habit of murdering. This is not to say that by easy stages, by losing my temper, by violent cursing, by fisticuffs, I could not work up to the point where I could murder someone. But the longer I repeat a particular choice, the more likely I am to make the same choice the next time when it is offered to me, and the harder it is to make a different choice. The adoption of these patterns of choice is what people refer to as "character".

Normally we make these choices without even being aware of the fact that we are exercising our freedom. Theoretically, there is nothing that prevents people in hell from walking out and going to Heaven, and nothing prevents the people in Heaven from walking out and going to hell. They just don't want to.

Next, I want to distinguish between two kinds of freedom. First, there is initial freedom. Initial freedom is a choice which is followed by freedom of action upon which there are no external restraints. I can sit down or I can stand up. I can light my pipe or not light it. This is the kind of freedom that most people have had in mind over the last twenty years when they use the word freedom to mean "do your own thing". I discovered early in my life that this freedom produces a dilemma. Either I had a job and was making money and had no time to do a lot of the things I wanted to do, or else I had a lot of time to do what I wanted to do because I wasn't working but I had no money to pay for them. Most of the things I wanted to do cost money, so I had to sacrifice one or the other, and that brings us back to the idea that every choice is a rejection of some alternative. In summary, then, initial freedom is the freedom to act, the freedom to do whatever I want to do.

Initial freedom is important because without it there would be no significant human action. That is to say, what I cannot help, I cannot be held accountable for, either to my credit or my discredit. It has been said that there is no great merit attached to a life of service, like that of Albert Schweitzer, because he wanted to live in that fashion; that someone who commits murder, rape, and theft does what he wants to do, and that Albert Schweitzer is no better morally than the criminal because both are merely doing what they wanted to do. But of course there is a difference. It is the moral difference in what they wanted to do. One kind of wanting is much better than another kind of wanting. Nevertheless, without the freedom to do good or evil, no action of ours would have any moral significance whatsoever. It's very important in that sense to remember that when you make a choice you have eliminated a lot of other choices. Your initial freedom tends to diminish as you go through life. Having chosen to be a priest, for example, I have given up the exciting career of mariner or forest ranger or wilderness trapper. I can't do it all. However, let's suppose that I want to go to Finland and hold conversations with Finnish people to find out how they live and how they think. I want to make that journey and talk with those people, and there's no law that says I can't. Nevertheless, there is a problem that prevents me from fulfilling my desire. I can't speak Finnish. So I am not as free as I thought I was.

I want to play tennis and no law says I can't. Playing tennis involves standing behind a little white line and hitting a ball so that it goes over a net and hits a spot on the other side of the court. I want to do that, but I discover that I can't, because when I hit the ball it goes everywhere except where I want it to go. I am not free to play tennis.

What I am pointing to here is something called terminal freedom, the freedom to achieve or accomplish something which requires skill or knowledge or expertise. Let's say I really want to play tennis, I want to enter a major tournament. I see these guys play and come away with a $25,000 first prize, and I want that. So I want to enter and win. How do I go about doing that? I start about thirty years ago, and go out and spend three hours or more a day on the tennis court practising. And even though I practise, I may not make it. Not everyone who enters a tournament wins first place. Terminal freedom is the ability to do or achieve that which we want to do in the face of obstacles and barriers.

What is freedom to a fish? It's the freedom to do fishy things. That is, to swim in the water with other fish, to lay eggs and hatch baby fish and turn around and eat them. Freedom to a bird is the freedom to fly through the air, build nests, lay eggs, and sit on telephone poles and sing. If we pass a law which says that birds will not be allowed to paint their houses red, white, and blue, birds wouldn't care. This is not a liberty which perfects their nature, their birdiness. If we pass a law forbidding me to wear a pink bow ribbon in my hair, being perverse, I would probably want to do that. But this is not a freedom that one would fight and die for, because wearing a pink bow ribbon in my hair is not a freedom which perfects my nature as a human being. It is not an infringement of my humanity.

I have the duty to perfect and fulfil myself and therefore I have the duty to strive for and seek my true happiness. Because I have that duty, I have that right. It is a stark naked political fact that I only have those rights which correspond to my duties. I have no inalienable right which is not the right to fulfil a duty. In practice, the only liberties which men will actually fight and die for are those rights which enable them to do their duty. If I tell an atheist he isn't going to be allowed to worship on Sunday, he wouldn't care. If I am convinced that it is my duty to worship God on Sunday and you tell me I can't, I'll fight you. It is my right because it is my duty. These have to do with terminal freedoms.

Now I have this initial freedom, and the misuse of initial freedom can destroy terminal freedom. It can bring me to the end of life unfulfilled as a derelict, a failure as a human being. The only freedoms that are really worthwhile are terminal freedoms.

Here's another aspect of man's personhood. There have been folk who have seen some conflict between Genesis and evolution. I am not going to speak for or against the Darwinian theory of evolution, but I would like to say this. I have been reading in *National Geographic* about people in Africa who have been discovering evidence of prehistoric man. They have now pushed back in time the life of man on this planet some 3 to 5 million years. Where before scientists thought life on this planet was at most 300 to 500 thousand years, now they go back to 3 to 5 million. But all the talk about how old man is is meaningless. The only way we can determine if a creature is a man or an animal is to catch him alive and watch him behave.

The difference between a man and an animal is not a biological or physical difference, because I am all animal. No one has ever denied that. I've got kidneys and a spleen just like a cat. What makes me a human and distinguishes me from the animals is not anything biological or physical. It is a spiritual thing which obviously can't be tested on a carcass or a corpse, and certainly not on a fragment of a jawbone or a kneecap. A fully preserved body doesn't help, either. It is theoretically possible that the creature that was going to become human could have existed for a million years on this planet in no way distinguishable from you and me, and not been in the least human. It is also theoretically possible that a million years before we shed our tails and came down out of the trees we were fully and completely human. What distinguishes men from animals is a spiritual thing, and in that is our humanity. Once upon a time some creature looked up into the sky of the distant horizon and was filled with wonder and said, "Who and what am I, and what am I here for?" And at that moment, he was human. Every human being has asked that question and, as far as we know, no animal has.

An animal is a sentient, bodily, subsistent being. Man is all of these with the addition of rational at the front end. An organic being, whether worm or man, requires a body so long as life is in it. As soon as the life is gone, it begins to regress into decay and eventually stops being. In animals the sentient faculties are supported by the living body, but they also govern it. The animal faculties of smell and sight serve his instinctive drive to seek pleasure and avoid pain. The higher faculties both ride on, and depend upon, the lower faculties, but they also govern it and enable it to continue to be. Take away man's rational faculties and man becomes an animal, not only the most dangerous, but also the most inefficient. He preys on other people, so we lock him up. Animals don't need a mind to know when to sleep, eat, go to the bathroom. Reason is chief of the faculties natural in man, guiding, through the will, the competitive faculties, the emotions and the sense.

So the intellect is governor. But what governs the

intellect? Some time ago there was a movement in Western thought called rationalism. Essentially, rationalists argued that man, through his intellect, could solve his problems and move into a Golden Age. They ignored the fact that the rational animal is not complete. Aristotle said that man is a rational animal, and that's correct, but man is a natural animal with a supernatural purpose. But the human intellect has one great weakness. In the most important respects, Einstein is no better than the idiot. The function of the intellect is merely to pass judgement on the appropriateness of a variety of means toward an end. But it fails miserably at picking where we should be going in the first place. This is true because goals are either arbitrarily chosen, or else they are given from something outside the intellect.

The intellect is a beautiful instrument, if used for the proper purpose. Suppose I'm on the golf course and there is sudden rain. Over here, close by, is a grove of trees offering temporary shelter. Across the course is the clubhouse where I can get better shelter. I look at the sky and judge whether or not the rain will be brief or lengthy. The intellect is great for judging the best course to follow, but the initial decision to do whatever is necessary to be comfortable is not decided intellectually. This goal arises out of my being itself and also out of past experience. On the other hand, if I am prospecting for gold and it begins to rain, then probably the desire for gold will outweigh the desire to stay dry. But my choice of gold over comfort is still not a matter of intellect. When the intellect gives up, the appetites take over, because the body knows what it wants. It wants to be fed, comfortable, satisfied. When the intellect stops directing the body's actions, the emotions take over, and the intellect becomes the slave of the animal goals established by the emotions. Appetites provide the goals to the ends. This is why the medieval artist painted the devil with horns and a tail. When the intellect stops directing the will, we start behaving like animals.

In common with the rest of the animals, we have the built-in objective of bodily needs, and the intellect becomes the servant. In the myth of Adam and Eve, the only difference was that they knew what they were for. They had an experience of God. It is not necessary to prove that a particular man, at a particular place on this earth has had this experience. It is important that man at one point was clear as to his purpose. This he lost, by turning his aim and goal inward upon himself, and he became a purely natural creature, dependent upon his natural devices and incapable of satisfying his supernatural goal or destiny.

The Church says man is fallen. This brings up all sorts of images to us. It is certainly a true doctrine. I know I'm not satisfied with myself. No one is. Something is wrong with the human race. We have an amazing facility for fouling our own nest. There is a story of Midas, the ancient king who touched things and they turned to gold. But that story can't be true, because if Midas had been human, half the things he touched would have turned into . . . you guessed it.

We don't know what we are for, or what we're supposed to be doing. We mess things up and are in constant conflict with one another. Our lives are always unravelling. We have a yearning for something better than we are, for beauty, perfection, rapture. And yet, because we lack direction, we're constantly grabbing at each other's doughnuts and worshipping idolatrous creatures. Man is a fallen thing. He cannot cure his own difficulty. Our domestication comes about when we're brought into contact with God, when we spend a considerable amount of time with Him, and allow

Him to mould us into His likeness. He lets some of Himself rub off on us.

The story of Adam and Eve is the story of you and me. "Adam" is the Hebrew word for "man". It isn't a story of how sin came into the world, it's a story of how sin *comes* into the world. It has been said that God is unfair to punish all the descendants of Adam for the sin of some remote ancestor. Also, it has been urged that there is no known mechanism by which the guilt of Adam could be transmitted to his posterity. But you don't need a biological transmission to inherit something that isn't biological. If I inherit a million dollars and spend it all on wine, women, and song, my children will be poor, so by what biological mechanism do they inherit my poverty? What has been lost by the human race is this mystical union with God. God didn't rub out Adam and Eve and start over again with Joe and Mary, because man is a communal being who lives in a spiritual and psychological world which has a continuous history. It would be inconceivable that in the long generations since Adam and Eve, no one had ever sinned. Man is a social being, and each succeeding generation is produced by the community which preceded it and produced it.

Only rarely can we step out of our time and place to critique our own culture. If, immediately after the Fall, God had started over and created another human being, innocent and sinless, he would be sinning before nightfall. If we're going to create a righteous individual, he's going to have to come out of a righteous society, and where can we find a righteous society? After all, righteous societies are made up of righteous individuals, the old chicken and egg problem. It's a logical impossibility. The sins of the father are visited upon the third and fourth generation not because God gets mad at the parents and punishes the kids, but because our neuroses and bad habits are passed on to our grandchildren. Man is a social being and once sin has been introduced into society, man can't rise above it and shed it.

Notice how Adam and Eve started blaming each other. They were cast out of the garden, where God and man had sweet intercourse, where man had something to guide his intellect. God sent them forth and placed a flaming angel before the gates, to guard the Tree of Knowledge. Man is also forbidden the Tree of Life, that is, eternal life, but if you will note in the Book of Revelation, the Tree of Life is finally given to those who are saved, and under God's terms, it's something worth having.

4

THE FALL

The doctrine of man's fallen state does not mean a fall from some material utopia. What it does mean is that Adam and Eve had something that we've lost, a mystical union with God, an awareness of His presence, which means that they once had a good governor for their intellect. They were achieving their full potential as beings in the created order. Notice here that in the Jewish/Christian mythos, religion doesn't need to be explained. Life needs to be explained. The story of Adam and Eve explains such individual feelings as sadness at beauty and homesickness at home. We are *not* at home, and in our guts we know it.

Now the serpent was more subtle than any beast of the field that the Lord God had made. He said unto the woman, "Yea, hath God said ye shall not eat of every tree of the garden?" I might mention here that the serpent was taken as a symbol of evil by the Jews, who worshipped a sky god, because the snake was a sacred animal to the neighbouring pagans, who worshipped earth gods and regarded the snake, an underground creature, as magical and a sacred totem animal. Since the Jews warred with the neighbouring peoples, they regarded their gods as enemies of the true God and therefore evil. That is probably the origin of the identification of the serpent with Satan. (It should tell us something about the pagan religions, because I expect people felt about snakes then as we do now.)

The woman said unto the serpent, "We may eat of the fruit of the trees in the garden, but of the fruit that is in the midst of the garden God said we shall not eat of it. Neither should we touch it lest we die." And the snake says, "Oh, come on, now. You know better than that. You'll just gain the knowledge of good and evil and be like God."

This is not the story of how sin came into the world, but the story of how sin *comes* into the world, and you and I are Adam and Eve.

Our Lord tells us in the New Testament that Satan is the deceiver. The Christian theologians tell us that Satan never tells a flat outright lie. He finds that half-truth is a much more effective device for tempting, so he distorts the truth and tells a lie in such a fashion that it appears to be undeniably true. Jesus did not come to release us from the law. The real truth is more subtle and complex than that. The truth is that we are not absolved from obedience from the law. What St Paul tries to tell us in several chapters of Romans is, not that we have to obey the law but rather, that the law comes to us free from any external constraints because we *want* to keep it. Suddenly, because we love God, we will keep His commandments. When we are motivated by love we no longer feel the law as a constraint. This business of Jesus freeing us from the law can easily be interpreted as, "Whee! We don't have to keep the law any more!"

Freedom from the law in the best sense is freedom to keep the law voluntarily, out of love. This misinterpretation is a good example of how the devil works. He takes something that is true and asserts it as truth, but notice that it's never quite the whole truth. Heresy is erroneous because of what it leaves out. A religious fanatic is not a man with too much religion, but too little.

Somehow or other, the Catholic has to do justice to a many-sided reality. God is mercy and God is justice, and God's justice without mercy becomes the harsh face of a tyrannical God, and God's mercy without justice becomes the face of a sentimental, wishy-washy God. Somehow or other you have to have both. So the devil's approach to Eve is typical of this limited and distorted truth. And in a perverse sort of way, she did gain the knowledge of good and evil. Eve was the first person to say, "I have my own ideas about religion." We've all heard that many times in our lives, and we've also heard it this way: "Isn't it nice that there are so many denominations so that we can choose a church that suits us?" Dear people, it's because of that kind of thinking that we have so many denominations. If I select a Church that suits me, that means I am the judge of God's revelation, and that God is obliged to tailor His revelation to my taste. Heaven forbid that I should have a religion that suits me any more than I should have a chemistry that suits me. People who have their own ideas about chemistry blow themselves to kingdom come. People who have their own ideas about religion frequently wind up in spiritual confusion. What I want and pray for is God's ideas about religion.

The second promise of Satan to Eve is that Eve will become as God. What she did, and what you and I do, because remember, this is a story about how sin *comes* into the world today, was to make herself an exception to the general rule. It's like saying, "I know that convention says you shouldn't have sex until you are married, but after all, Charlene and I are very much in love, intending to be married in the spring, so why shouldn't we?" Or, "I am a bank teller and I know that convention says one should be honest in handling other people's money, but after all, I have a sure thing in the fifth race and can put the money back on Saturday." In these examples, the rules don't apply to me; I am an exception. And in a very real sense this is making oneself into one's own God. In the first three or four centuries of Christianity, people like Ignatius and Augustine were fond of saying that God became man in order that man could become like God. The Eastern Orthodox Church emphasizes this teaching, and their theologians speak of the process of sanctification as the "divinization of man". Another phrase which has been used to describe the phenomenon is "ingodding". Charles Williams speaks of "mutual indwelling" or "co-inherence". In the Anglican Prayer Book it's "that He may dwell in us, and we in Him."

Clearly, to "be like God" is what God wanted Eve to do. Why, then, would it be sinful for her to want what God wanted for her? Or for her to try what God intended for her to do? Because this being like God is not something that one can *do*. It's only something that one can receive, as a gift. Eve decided that she wanted to do it herself. What the snake really offered her was a short cut, an easy salvation in a few easy lessons. She had found a do-it-yourself religion. She wanted what no one can have, which is Easter without Good Friday. Sanctification without sacrifice. Deification through self-indulgence.

Now not only did Eve strive for God-likeness, which she ought to have had, but in doing so, she usurped the place of God in the scheme of things. She said, "I'll make up my own rules and I will be my own God." She read the lines in the script written for God. This is a kind of adolescent rebellion, which seems right and reasonable when you're fifteen years old, but looks ridiculous when seen from a more objective point of view. "Only God can really be trusted with other people's lives, but I will try it myself. Just give me half a chance. I know what's good for you, so I will manage your life and tell you what to do." I have tried in the course of my ministry to avoid that sort of meddling, but lots of people want me to tell them what to do. It's a lot easier than coming to a decision and making up your own mind. But my task is to help them see clearly what are the consequences of their various choices, and then to let them decide. Only God lives in eternity, and I must live in time, which is a passing present moment. Yet I will try desperately to cling to the past and control and dominate the future. Only God can really be self-sufficient, but give me half a chance and I'll make a stab at it.

The next thing that happened is that the eyes of Adam and Eve were opened and they knew that they were naked. That's interesting. I'm sure you have had this experience when contemplating some course of action which your intellect or the Church or society says is sinful. You will rationalize, justify, and come to believe your own lie, which finally seems good to you. That is, you will do so until you have actually done the deed, and then at that moment there is an element of reality in the commission of the act itself that destroys the illusion of goodness.

When God said, "How come?" typically Adam blamed it on the woman and she blamed it on the snake. One thing we will discover is that sin is any act, either internal or external, which results in alienation or isolation of man from God or from his fellow man, or from nature. You have here the immediate first fruits of original sin, in a family quarrel.

Adam and Eve are looking at each other and both are saying, "It's your fault. I wouldn't have done it if you hadn't tempted me." The consequence of this alienation is that Adam and Eve, who had been living in paradise, suddenly found themselves out in the cold, cruel world where they had to work for a living. "Accursed shall be the ground on your account. With labour shall you win your food from it all the days of your life. It will grow thorns and thistles for you, none but wild plants for you to eat. You shall gain your bread by the sweat of your brow until you return to the ground, for from it were you taken."

Finally the Lord God said, "The man has become like one of us, knowing good and evil; what if he now reaches out his hand and takes fruit from the Tree of Life also, and eats it and lives for ever?" And God drove them out of the garden of Eden and placed east of the garden cherubim with flaming swords.

And ever since, man has been struggling to find his way back to paradise. Ponce de Leon searched for the fountain of youth. The Knights of the Round Table searched for the Holy Grail. In fact, romantic literature has as its central theme the Quest, and whatever the search, it really represents man's effort to restore or recover in the future that which he dimly knows he once had and lost in the past.

We speak of the Fall of Man and we speak of Original Sin, but these should not be confused. First let me tell you in terms of theology what the Fall is *not*. First, remember that theology is the explanation; let's see what the question is. The doctrine of the Fall and the doctrine of original sin seeks to answer the question that underlies all the great works of art; it has been expressed by all the poets. *Why* are things not as they should be? *Why* are we dissatisfied with ourselves? The philosophers whose work lay behind the French Revolution were unwilling to conclude that anything was wrong with *man:* he wasn't fallen, they said. This argument gave rise to the myth of the Noble Savage, because their notion of what was wrong with man was that he had been corrupted by civilization. If he could return to a state of natural innocence, like the American Indians or the Pacific Islanders, then all would be well. This idea also underlies the thought of Karl Marx, who argued that the thing really wrong with man is capitalism. If we do away with capitalism, we will have a kind of paradise, a state of innocence in which man will naturally and spontaneously do good, and the State will just wither away. We could ultimately eliminate all law. And Jesus came to release us from the law.

You find this same idea underlying the extreme form of early American Whig political philosophy in the proposition "that government governs best that governs least". Behind that is the "natural goodness of man". Man really desires to be good, but has been prevented from goodness by bad institutions and bad laws. Every society has some explanation of why things aren't like they used to be, and probably never were. Something is wrong with man. The newspapers highlight stories of rape, murder, chicanery, and all kinds of misconduct. To translate this into personal, individual terms, I am not pleased with my own performance, and neither are you. Perfection, which every man demands of himself, in one way or another, is an illusive and unattainable goal. Every man has a conscience which accuses him. Nobody performs up to his capabilities.

But it's more than that.

After three years of work between high school and college I scraped together a little money and a lot of courage and went off to Baylor University in Waco, Texas. I hardly had a dime. I lived in a rooming house on 5th Street and paid $8 a month for rent for an upstairs room in this Victorian house. One summer I managed to buy a little radio with a red plastic case. Many nights I would sit by the window, fighting off the green midges, dripping in perspiration, and listen to a station in Mexico playing rancho folk music at one or two in the morning. It was plaintive and wistful, songs like "Marie Elena", and I would want to cry. That kind of music plucks a chord somewhere in your consciousness, evoking a strange and curious feeling of yearning and wistfulness. What is it about man's condition that makes him sad when there's nothing to be sad about?

Why is it that you can sit in a rocking chair on the front porch of the house in which you were born and lived all your life and look at the landscape you have seen every day of your life and be homesick? You can, you know. What is it that we want, the lack of which makes our hearts break? I am the most happily married of men, I love my wife and wouldn't trade her for Solomon's harem. She's wonderful and we have an absolutely perfect marriage. I have known this for over thirty years, yet in my old age, tired and worn out and much too beat up to have sex on my mind, why is it that I will still wistfully scan the faces in the crowd looking for I know not what? Why is it that all the classical love stories are about unrequited love? An artist like Shakespeare knew too well the truth about the human condition to allow Romeo and Juliet to marry and set out on the impossible task of living happily together ever after. It would have spoiled the love story if Romeo and Juliet had degenerated into the typical suburban couple who quarrel and squabble and can't communicate. To prevent that, he simply killed them off, which is the only way you can end a romantic love story.

What are we searching for?

Keats says that there is always an element of sadness associated with the perfection of the beautiful, and it's the fact that the beautiful never lasts. One of the charms of an open fire is that it is always a dying fire. What is it about the season of autumn that makes it almost everybody's favourite season? There is a sort of cosmic feeling that comes with autumn that we don't get in spring or summer or winter.

An old Baptist revival hymn has the line, "I am a stranger here within a foreign land." This idea is taken from St Paul, and it is a true saying; we *are* strangers here in a foreign land. This is not our home. We are exiles. We belong in paradise. It is the universal human situation that man is never quite satisfied. It is as though he were looking for something and didn't know what he was looking for, but knew he would recognize it if he ever found it. Somehow there is something which we know we ought to have and don't have; it has to do not only with what we want but also with what we ought to be. For this reason human life is like a quest, a search, a yearning outward. This is what the Church means by the Fall of Man, and the Adam and Eve story is the way in which this truth is mythologized. It is told over and over again to keep us in mind of the fact that whatever it is that we want, we haven't found it yet. Man was created to know God, to love God, and to enjoy God for ever. Man is a natural being with a supernatural destiny.

We are told in Genesis that God walked in the garden in the cool of the evening, and God and man communicated with one another in a free and intimate fashion. This is the analogic way of saying that Adam and Eve had as a constant condition of their being something the greatest saints and mystics achieve imperfectly and fleetingly only for brief moments in their lives. They had that profound, intuitive, and mystical awareness of their relationship to God that gives a sense of perfect being, of knowing one's place in the cosmos and being in that place.

Everyone knows by the age of fifteen that they were created for bliss. You don't have to be instructed in that. It comes to you at the beginning of adolescence when you are suddenly open to the profundities of existence and you start reaching out to them. Man discovers his finiteness, and in this sudden awareness of his fallen state discovers the same thing in others. This has happened to everyone at one time or another. It happened to the caveman, to the American pioneer, to the medieval peasant, to the slaves under the pharaohs of Egypt. It is out of this experience that one begins to believe in God. As C. S. Lewis says, the appetite, the fact of human hunger, is no guarantee that I'll ever get anything to eat, but it is a strong suggestion that there is such a thing as food.

Now I want to call your attention to an interesting insight. I don't raise my kids right because my parents didn't raise me right, and *their* parents didn't raise them right, and one of the insights of the old Jewish rabbi who put Genesis together was to blame it on our first parents. This isn't an effort to duck individual responsibility. What it does state is the solidarity of mankind in both good and evil. I cannot sin without damaging others, because it is this solidarity which makes it possible for me to benefit from other people's virtue and other people's sacrifices. And if I am going to benefit from other people's virtues, I have to be willing to suffer for other people's sins.

What then is original sin?

Well, it's not the fact that God is angry with you and me because of the sin of Adam and Eve. It's not that the sins of the fathers are visited upon the children, even beyond the third and fourth generation. That's just a statement of demonstrable fact. "Original" doesn't refer to Adam and Eve. Rather, it means that I was in sin from the moment of my own origin. I was born to sin. Sin, when we come to discuss it more explicitly, is an alienation from, an isolation, a separation.

Again, this is not something that needs proving. From the beginning, man is in the habit of acting exclusively to seek his own pleasure and avoid his own discomfort. If someone walks through here and steps on all our toes, I would feel my toes hurt worse than I would feel your toes hurt, which is natural. But unless I'm careful, I might conclude that my toes really do hurt worse, that no one has suffered as I have suffered, that no one has loved as I have loved. It is this tendency to regard myself as unique or special that is the essence of original sin. If you pass a friend who doesn't speak to you, you are liable to get your feelings hurt, feel like he's cutting you cold. It might never occur to you that he had a headache. It might never occur to you to speak to him first. If I have a headache, I am aware of it. If you have one, you have to tell me, or I am liable to think you're just being grumpy. I am different. I am special.

Man is a natural creature with a supernatural destiny which he can only attain with supernatural aid and assistance. Mother Eve's problem was that she tried by her natural equipment and endowment to accomplish the goal which could only be attained by supernatural means. Let's use an analogy with which we're all familiar: the domestic dog. God is to man as man is to dog. Not a perfect analogy, but close. If man has a universal longing for something he knows not what, the same thing is true of the domestic dog. Man has the capacity for divine fellowship. A dog certainly has awareness of need for the companionship of man. Speculate how the first dog became domesticated. There was a wild dog hanging about on the fringes of the camp and finally crawled in on its belly with its tail wagging to eat the scraps. It finally identified and associated with man, using its canine nature to help man herd his sheep or track his game, though this probably came later. I think the chances are that primitive man saw a dog lurking about the camp, creeping in to steal food. He thought the dog was interesting or cute, but he saw that the dog had a natural instinct for human company. If you've ever been followed home by a stray, wet, half-starved puppy, you know what I mean. You go into the house, and he stands outside the door whimpering, yearning to be let in. Dogs frequently prefer the company of people to that of other dogs.

Now, until a dog finds a person, he obviously has this emptiness in his life. I don't know what it's like to be a dog, and I can't judge reality from inside a dog, but I know how he behaves. I know I am committing what the literary critics call the pathetic fallacy by reading human feelings into a dog, but he looks and acts like he wants to belong to people. Until he finds people, he probably has this vague emptiness. However, he wants to belong to people on a dog's terms, and we can't allow that. Jesus said, "You have not chosen me, but I have chosen you." When Mama and Daddy think it's time for their child to have a pet they go to the kennel and select a puppy and bring it home. So, in terms of the analogy, the dog can only be domesticated when man reaches out to include the dog into his own society. That is, the initiative has to be with man. The dog's part is to be hungry for this relationship, to yearn. But if we allow the dog to enter our society on his terms, we haven't accepted him into human society, we are turning human society into a kennel.

The dog must become obedient to man. This is a long process by which he is changed and altered. When at long last the dog is thoroughly domesticated, we will say of a dog that he is almost human. He will know his place, which is to be loved and accepted in my home. Notice, under the influence of the nineteenth century, we made the mistake of supposing that the wild dog is the natural dog, and that domestication is some kind of perversion of his true nature. Not so. We don't really know dogs if all we have seen are puppies. We don't really know chickens if all we have seen are baby chicks. We don't really know oak trees if all we have seen are seedlings. Only when all the potentialities of the dog have been actualized is its nature complete. Since obviously the dog has the potentiality, the domestic dog is more doggy than the wild dog, which exists in a state of imperfection.

Applying that analogy to man, just as the dog seems to have an innate capacity for and a desire for the companionship of man, we want God to accept us on our own terms, which, if He did, would not be admitting us to divine society but would be God descending to our society. When Jesus became man, He became like us in all things except sin. You see, I don't want to have to give up all of my gross animalities, those parts of me in which my animal nature dominates over my rational nature. My doctor and my intellect tell me I ought to lose some weight. But put a piece of chocolate cake in front of me, and somehow or other my animal appetite takes over. I want to be Godlike without giving up all my imperfections. But I can't do that. First of all, I can only fulfill this desire and satisfy this yearning if I am brought into contact with God. No dog ever domesticated himself. A dog becomes domesticated when he's brought into the camp, or into the house, and made a member of the family by the action of the family. God takes the initiative. We can want it, and we can yearn for it, but we can only achieve it if, first of all, we are brought into contact with God, and become obedient to God. Finally, after a long time, we become almost divine – Christlike. God became man in order that man might become like God just as the dog becomes almost human.

There are limitations to this analogy. In the first place, man and God are both persons, and the dog is not a person. But there are other points at which the analogy holds. My dog and I can communicate. It's not natural for man and dog to talk, so for a dog to converse with me is supernatural. And yet, oddly, it is only as the dog achieves this supernatural ability that he becomes fully natural. I have a dog at home, about fifteen years old, that probably has an English vocabulary of 300 words. I can say to her, "Want to go outside?" and she runs to the door and sits there wagging her tail. This communication between man and dog is sometimes only learned slowly and gradually. Similarly the communication between God and man is slowly and gradually learned. God knows what I am thinking. My problem in communicating with God is a problem of my listening.

Another interesting and valid extension of this analogy is that we may think of our relation to God as if we were God's house pets. This tells us two things. First, it corrects our pride and arrogance in thinking that God needs us, as if the Father and the Son two thousand years ago started a Newcomers' Club. Poor old God, we want to say, unless we get in there and help Him, He's not going to get what He wants. It's not like that at all. God could run this parish a hell of a lot better if I were not helping Him. But out of His mercy and condescension, He has stepped back and given it to me.

It's kind of like this true story. Forty years ago when I was first discovering this religion. I was spending a Saturday afternoon visiting Fr Lewis who was curate at St Matthew's

The Fall

Cathedral in Dallas. I was just pestering the daylights out of him, and he was patiently sitting and talking with me on a kindergarten level about theology. He was married and had a two-year-old son named John. His wife came in and said, "Ed, would you go to the grocery store for me?" and handed him a list. Fr Lewis and John and I went to the grocery store and when we came home and got out of the car, Fr Lewis had a sack of groceries and in this bigger sack was a smaller sack which contained six limes. Fr Lewis reached into the big sack and got the little sack and very solemnly handed it to John, saying, "Son, will you carry this into the house for me?" John swelled with pride, took off for the kitchen steps, stumbled, fell, and spilled the limes all over. He looked at Daddy. Fr Lewis picked up the limes, put them in the sack, and handed it to John, and turned and walked into the house. John looked at Daddy and looked at the sack. Then he pulled himself up on his feet and carried the sack into the house. John put the sack on the kitchen table, and Fr Lewis said solemnly, "Thank you, my son." The kid beamed and smiled.

This parish church is my sack of limes, and I will often stumble and spill it in the yard, and God in His infinite mercy will give it back to me without saying a word. And unless I'm awfully careful, I will say, "See what I have done! I have helped God!" Fr Lewis could have carried that little sack in with the big sack and never even noticed the weight of those six limes. But John needed to be needed, and Fr Lewis in his infinite mercy said, "My son, would you carry this in for me?" God says, "My son, would you run this parish for me?" I make all kinds of stupid blunders as the rector of this parish, and somehow, because of God's divine grace, the good people of this parish pull themselves together and keep on going. We are God's pets. This is a wonderful corrective of any sense of arrogant pride that might let us suppose for a moment that God needs us. He doesn't.

Another thing it does is correct the activist notion that God has sent us into the world to accomplish something.

In 1970, I spent my vacation in San Miguel de Allende in Mexico where I had been asked by local Episcopalians to be their summer supply priest. They had just become a parish and gained the right to call their own rector. Evidently they liked me, because they called me. I turned them down and said that I was happy with the job I had at St Francis in Dallas. They met once a week and kept issuing me a call. I said no, but they said, "Why don't you go home and pray about it?" I said all right.

Now I loved the place and the people very much. I was very happy with the Mexican language, culture, and people, but I also loved St Francis. This is my home and its folks are bone of my bone and blood of my blood. I was torn; I wanted to know what God wanted me to do. I prayed earnestly. After about six or eight weeks of this constant prayer, one Thursday I offered the Mass with this intention: "Please, God, tell me what to do. Shall I go to Mexico or stay here?" As I was uttering those words I heard God say in a tired and exhausted voice, "Homer, I don't care!" Of course I laughed out loud. But I immediately knew that if someone else had had that problem and had asked me for advice, that's what I would have told them. What God wants me to do is be a good priest wherever I am, but He has given me free will to make a choice. I chose to stay. I don't know whether I did right or not. But what do I mean, "did right"? Right in the sense of choosing which place I would enjoy the most? I'm afraid that's what I meant when I was asking God to tell me what to do. God doesn't need me at either place, and He doesn't need you. But He, in His mercy, allows us to carry a sack of limes.

Besides correcting our pride and our vanity, it also tells us something about God and the way He loves us. He really does cherish us. You know when you go to the kennel and buy a puppy and bring it home, you expect it to pee in the middle of the living room rug, but this doesn't make you hate the puppy. You expect it to chew up your slippers and dig up the flower bed and be a bit of a nuisance until it's domesticated. But until that happens, you don't stop loving it. On the contrary, you think it's cute. You have a fondness for it and you cherish it. That's the way God feels about us. This too should make for our humility and help us avoid that grim business of either thinking that God needs our help or thinking of God as a sort of taskmaker who is waiting to give us grades on our performance. You only develop a dog's capacity for domestication by being very patient with it, by recognizing its limitations and working within those limitations.

I can well remember when Fr Lewis first told me that God doesn't need me. I felt almost hurt, and yet, in reflecting on it throughout the years, I've come to treasure this notion. If God doesn't need me, it means that His love for me is totally unselfish love. He loves me the way I love my dog, with an affection and tolerance, with a kind of delight and pleasure. My dog is a lot more trouble than she's worth, and I am sure that I'm a lot more trouble to God than I'm worth. As a matter of fact, the trouble I am to God sent Him to the cross – that's how much He loves me.

There is another point I want to make about the difference between moral and natural good and evil. In Genesis, at the end of each day of creation, God looked at his handiwork and said, "That's good." All the whales and fish and winged fowl and beasts of the world, each after its own kind – it was all good. Being and goodness correlate exactly. Everything that God made is good to the extent that it is, that it has its perfections. Evil is not a positive quality in things but rather is the absence of a good that ought to be there but is not. It is not evil that my car can't have baby cars. But if I decide to go into the pig business and buy a sow and discover that she can't have little piglets, that's natural evil, because it pertains to the perfection of pigs to reproduce. The fact that a stone cannot see is not evil, but the fact that a man cannot see is evil – not morally evil, mind you. Moral evil is the intentional knowing and deliberate evil choice of a lesser good.

For evil to exist, it has to inhere in something that is good. For example, an apple is good, and you can't have a rotten apple unless you have an apple first. The attractiveness of evil lies in the good in which evil inheres. Another example: it's good for a little boy to go fishing. Every little boy ought to go fishing at some time in his life. But to play hookey in order to go fishing is evil, not because fishing is evil, but because the boy is enjoying this good at the sacrifice of a greater thing. If I strangle my mother-in-law because I can no longer stand her infernal yak, what I am seeking is peace and quiet, and that is good. But I am seeking it at the cost of a greater good, which is human life. No one ever chose evil for its own sake. Sex isn't evil, it's good, naturally good, always, everywhere, and in every circumstance – that is, depending on how expertly it is performed. Adultery is evil not because it is seeking sexual pleasure, but because sex takes precedence over a better thing, which is family loyalty and the solidarity of the clan. The ancient Jews thought that they had a tribal relationship with God. Therefore, when they snuck off and partook of the rites and ceremonies of

Baal, god of the Canaanites, this was adultery. They went "whoring after strange gods".

If evil ever becomes so complete an evil that it destroys the good in which it inheres, it destroys itself. If the rotten apple becomes so rotten that there is no appleness left, then there is no rottenness left, either. But there is always in that case a residue which is good. An apple that is rotten falls to the ground. Even if all appleness is gone, all being is not gone. What is left is humus which returns to the soil and makes fertile the soil to make another crop of apples next year.

God will win in the long run. There is no way that evil can finally become triumphant. An automobile which is absolutely no good as an automobile is still good as scrap iron. Evil in the long run cannot triumph, though in the process of its career, it may destroy a great deal that is good. But you can't have evil unless you have good. Last autumn I dumped ten wheelbarrow loads of manure mixed with straw on my flower bed. It sat there and rotted over the winter. This spring I went out and dug my hands in it and it smelled like nice, clean, moist, fresh dirt. It was good. Evil can't win in the long run, and this is the basis of Christian optimism.

5

MYTH AND MAN

By way of getting your attention, I'll begin by saying that the Bible is all myth. Myth doesn't mean fairy tales and falsehoods, so I'd better explain first what a myth is, and in order to do that, I must introduce you to my grandmother.

My grandparents on my mother's side were very much a part of my childhood. My grandmother lived next door to us for a while. Before that she lived in McKinney, and we would travel back and forth to see her. After the Civil War, my grandparents moved to west Texas and homesteaded in Jones County, south of Wichita Falls. They lived in a dugout sod hut. Grandpa failed at farming, so he took off and tried to make money using teams of mules to dig stock tanks for ranchers, leaving Grandmother and several small children at home way out miles from nowhere in woolly country where Comanche Indians were not entirely pacified. Grandmother would entertain me when I was a small boy with hair-raising tales of life in the Old West. I was impressed, and if I were to repeat the stories that she told me, you would be impressed too. But let me tell you what impressed me the most.

When she was getting older and it was felt that she'd better be where we could keep an eye on her, she moved from McKinney to Dallas and lived next door to us. In the back yard she raised chickens. The neighbourhood cat would get after her chickens. When I was ten or eleven years old, visiting her, outside in the back yard one day Grandma

saw the black cat in the chicken yard. She sent me into the
house to get her double-barrelled breech-loading twelve-
gauge shotgun. I tore into the house and brought it to her.
(I've still got the shotgun. I've taken it dove hunting. It's got
a kick like a blind mare mule.) Grandma was a little bitty
thing, didn't weigh a hundred pounds wringing wet. She had
defended herself and her bairns from range bulls and
drunken cowboys and Indians with this shotgun. So I
brought the gun. About that time the cat jumped up on the
fence and started running along the fence as fast as a cat can.
My grandmother, seventy-five years old at that time, picked
up this heavy double-barrelled twelve-gauge shotgun, took
an appropriate lead on the cat, pulled the trigger. The cat
took a double backward somersault off the fence and fell on
the ground, all nine of its lives gone at once. I was impressed.

Anything Grandmother told me from then on, I'd have
believed her.

I was impressed by my grandmother. Other people had
grandmothers and grandfathers, and great-grandmothers
and great-grandfathers who pioneered this country, just like
mine did. They were remarkable people. How do you tell
the story of the settlement of this country, of the conquest of
the wilderness? I don't know that you can. Just to tell the
story of my grandmother would take a whole book. To tell
the stories of everybody's grandmothers would take a vast
library. The pioneers were rough, hardy, great, and
resourceful people. I am impressed by those people. You
can try to debunk heroes, but it's going to take a lot of
debunking to erase from my memory that running black cat.

The reason to tell that story is to distil the impression that
we all have of our grandparents. You select one pioneer
character like Paul Bunyan, Pecos Bill, Davy Crockett, and
tell a story about them that is characteristic – not necessarily

true in all particular details. One legend about Davy Crockett is that he shot a bear when he was three years old. Now I rather doubt that, but I know that my grandmother killed her black cat when she was seventy-five. And if it turned out that Davy Crockett really did kill a bear at three, I wouldn't be surprised. We keep the memory of those heroic people alive in movies and television series, when we invest John Wayne with all the imaginary virtues of Davy Crockett and my grandmother and your grandmother. We tell the story of the West over and over again. It never seems to lose its appeal. That is a myth.

The telling of a myth may take ten thousand different forms as to detail, but it's the same myth, the same story. Human courage and ingenuity faces great odds and comes out victorious. What is the point in telling this story? Because you and I, as we sit and hear the story or watch it on television, will identify with the characters. Something of the ideals and the moral courage and the integrity will rub off. Something of the ethos of those we tell about in myth will become a part of our thinking, of our very being. Thus myths have the effect of shaping our character and ultimately of shaping our culture. By and large, the thing that forms a culture is the stories that are told to the children generation after generation.

In a way, myth errs by understatement, because it gropes to tell a story that is too big to tell. The value or truth of a myth can't be measured by whether or not its incidents actually happened, but by whether or not it distils the essence of those cultural values and ideals which we are seeking to inculcate in present and future.

Also, for a myth to be a myth, you have to have a public forum in which the myth is told over and over again. The great stories of Homer, the *Iliad* and the *Odyssey*, were originally sung around campfires by professional bards who were not just poets, but were more like medicine men. There was a magic in their stories, which were retold around other fires of other warriors. It was the telling of these tales which taught the young what it meant to be an Achaean. It taught how one should behave in different situations, and what one's truths should be.

So, when you consider the purpose of the myth, it makes no difference whether the story is a true account faithfully and historically rendered, or whether it is a total fabrication. Either way, its value lies in the degree to which it is true to life.

Here is an example of how a myth was devised to explain a large movement in history. The European people about whom Homer wrote in the *Iliad* and the *Odyssey* invaded and conquered a portion of Asia Minor which is now Syria and Palestine. They had invented a military tactic which was irresistible. Up till that time, a bunch of unorganized warriors on opposite hillsides rushed together in the valley to fight. Now, in spite of what you see in the movies, in almost any kind of hand-to-hand combat, any two guys can lick one guy. The way to do it is very simple. While one of them engages the big guy in front, the other goes behind him and runs his dirk under his ribs, and that's the end of the one guy. Now when this bunch of people rush together in a melee at the foot of a hill, no one wants to be engaged against two other guys. If my neighbour in a hand-to-hand fight is dispatched and the guy who fought him comes to join the guy who is fighting me and one looks like he's going to get behind me, I am going to back up. In early primitive battles there were relatively few casualties. One side would lose its courage quickly and take to its heels. So it was critically important to get that initial advantage and start killing a few guys so the enemy can see they're outnumbered, and the next thing you know they are running like crazy.

But this is a rather chancy tactic, and the Europeans invented a manoeuvre that took some of the chance out of combat. They trained soldiers to fight in formation, to line up after putting on heavy armour and carry shields, spears, and swords. They were trained not to break ranks and not to rush madly forward, but to go in slowly, elbow to elbow. If one got killed, they were to close ranks quickly, thus keeping the other guy from getting behind. If the enemy made flanking, encircling movements, they would simply bend the line back. These guys were called hoplites. Asiatics would come running at them, and they would throw spears, engage in close battle, sacrifice mobility and agility for protection. These Europeans captured city after city this way, and seemed irresistible. In battle after battle, the Asiatics lost men and surrendered territory, until they began to think that the Europeans were invincible. They couldn't stand up in pitched battle against these hoplites.

Then one day some clever Asiatic invented a counter-attack: the slinger, or peltast. They took a leather strip about six feet long that was bowed out like a pouch, took a rock the size of an egg, put a knot in the long end and held the knot between the two middle fingers. They looped the other end and held it between the thumb and first finger. They found they could throw an egg-sized rock a good city block and hard enough to break a bone or a skull. These Asiatics, having developed their sling, decided to go into battle without body armour. They sacrificed protection for speed and mobility. They charged the hoplites until they got a spear's throw away, and then they would stand and hurl rocks. Even though the Europeans had body armour and helmets on, if they were hit in the head with a rock the size of an egg, it could knock them out. If they got hit on an arm or leg, it could break a limb. So the hoplites , who had been trained not to break ranks but to advance slowly, were in deep trouble.

Finally, in desperation, they would break ranks and go charging up to these peltasts who would then simply back out of their reach because they weren't heavily armed. The peltasts would shout, "Yah, yah, you can't catch me," and throw some more rocks. When the hoplites were thoroughly scattered all over the field, the peltasts would go in with speed and manoeuvrability and engage them on a two-to-one basis. Next thing you know, the hoplites are running for dear life over the hill. It was amazing. A miracle. The Asiatics had discovered a winning technique. A small, insignificant people who had thought of themselves as hopelessly outclassed, suddenly found themselves victorious over these giants they had feared for so long. It was as if a junior high football team took on the Dallas Cowboys. And it actually happened.

Whether or not the Asiatic who discovered this tactic was a Jewish shepherd named David is really rather unimportant. The important thing is that the Jews believed that their God had come to their aid and had miraculously delivered them from the Philistines. Any time from then on when anybody felt he was facing hopeless odds, he would remember the story of David and Goliath, which was told over and over again, Sabbath after Sabbath, in the synagogue.

Here's another example: England was invaded and conquered by Romans. In the fourth century, because of political and military revolution on the Continent, the Roman troops were pulled out of England, but before that time many of them settled in England in the following manner: a Roman soldier enlisted in the army for twenty years, and he usually signed up when he was about fifteen years old. At the end of twenty years' service, he was mustered out while still in the prime of life. Mustering-out pay was a grant of farm land in one of the conquered provinces. The Roman soldier by the end of his enlistment was usually single, and he would often marry a wife from one of the conquered peoples. He began to produce a mixed breed of citizens who spoke Latin at home and the native language in town. These thirty-five-year-old ex-soldiers would form a military reserve to be called up in time of military need.

When the Roman legions were pulled out of Britain, the land remained to be defended from the barbarian invasions of the Picts, Scots, and Irish by what we would call the national guard, a citizens' militia, partly Roman and partly British. It was customary in the Roman Empire, since the soldiers did not want to leave their farms during harvest or planting time, to hire mercenary soldiers from Germanic tribes. In Britain they hired whole tribes of Angles and Saxons to defend them along with the citizens' militia against the Picts and Scots. However, the mercenary soldiers turned on their employers and began to slaughter, murder, rape, and burn. Finally, they drove the half-Roman and half-British citizens back into the mountains of Wales and Cornwall. The Roman citizens were Christian, but the Angles and Saxons were heathens and pagans. So these Roman-British citizens and militia had to defend themselves against the people that they hired to help them. Possibly the revolt of the Angles and Saxons was because the British couldn't meet the payroll. At any rate, the citizen militia under the command of an officer known as the Pendragon went into the field to defend

Christian civilization against barbarism, savagery, and heathenism.

One of these Pendragons was probably named Arthur. For years and years, for generations and generations, fathers and mothers told their children around the hearth fire of an evening stirring tales of the courage and gallantry of Arthur Pendragon and his bodyguard – the Round Table. And so King Arthur and the Knights of the Round Table have survived in a story embellished, oddly enough, with lots of strange elements derived not from Christianity but from the religion of the land of the Celtic people, with whom these British people had taken refuge – Merlin, black magic, and so on. But the gist of the story is the heart and courage of these men who went out to fight for the cross and for civilization against savagery and heathenism.

So there is a historic core to the myth of Arthur and the Round Table. The thing that makes it a myth is that it was formative of British character.

The Bible has served that same purpose. In medieval times all Christians listened to it, and the invention of printing just made it more available. Among the covered wagons that set out from St Louis to Oregon, the Bible was usually the only book the pioneers had to read. They read it over and over again, memorized big hunks of it, and hence it had a hand in forming the American character. That is the purpose of the Bible: the formation of a mind and character which is finally not American or European, but Christian.

There are two ways we can abuse it: one is to be a fundamentalist, and the other is to be a higher critic. They are a lot alike, in that they err not in believing too much but in believing too little. When everyone began to read and write, they did so in the manner of small children learning their basics. Each word has one literal meaning and only one. If you go back in early Church history to the time of the highly sophisticated and educated people of the Roman Empire, you find that the treatment of the Scriptures was typological and analogical, as well as literal. The medieval Bible commentaries are fascinating because of the different levels of meaning that scholars found in both the Old and New Testaments.

In the Middle Ages, when almost the only people who could read and write were the monks, we find that their treatment was similar to that of the Romans, considering various levels of meaning without distressing the sense of the text. After printing was invented suddenly everyone became literal-minded. A lot of people today who praise the Bible as the Word of God unfortunately believe that it is not only the inspired Word of God, but that every word of it is historical fact. "What was good enough for Jesus Christ is good enough for me." They get into a peck of trouble. When the Bible says that the mountains danced like rams and the little hills skipped like young lambs and the trees lifted their hands, I know what the psalmist meant, and you do, too. He was a poet, not a descriptive reporter.

Let me put it like this. I've mentioned my wife, the best anyone ever had. She and I have fought a good deal over the past years. There have been times I have wanted to strangle her and many more times, I'm sure, she has wanted to put poison in my coffee, but on the whole and by and large, we've had a wonderful marriage, and I am much in love with her. Much more than on our honeymoon. I want to tell you about her, so that you would know her as I know her. I could have biologists write books about her body chemistry, her size, shape, and identify the mole on her left shoulder blade. I could have a psychologist write an in-depth analysis of her personality and how her mind works.

A biographer could write a history of her. An artist could paint a picture and perhaps come a little closer. But there's no way to really know my wife except as I know her. But the closest way of getting at my wife as I know her would be to have a poet write about her, because the essential quality in my wife is not anything material or intellectual or even psychological. It is mystical, and anyone who has ever been in love knows that.

The Bible is a love story. Just as my wife and I have had many a falling out, God and His people had many a falling out. But the love has endured, and this is the story of how it endured. It is better read, then, as an effort of people who were in love to tell someone else about the love they feel and the Person they love. It is inevitable that from time to time they fall into poetry. So much of the Bible has to be read and understood as poetry because you miss the point otherwise.

Now, there is a lot of stuff that purports to be and undoubtedly is solid historical fact. David was king; Solomon became king when David died and left his son an immense treasure of gold and silver. When Solomon died his weak son Rehoboam acted foolishly and alienated the ten northern tribes and the kingdom split. In 723 B.C., the king of Assyria came down and conquered the northern kingdom. In 586 B.C. the king of Babylon came and conquered the southern part. Seventy years later a remnant returned and rebuilt the city, as it is told in the story of Jeremiah and Ezra. This is solid historical fact.

But basically, the Bible is a love story. To fail to see it as that is to miss a vast amount of meaning and depth. One of the things that is very interesting about the Bible is that the people who wrote the Bible also read it. These books were written over a long span of history. Those who wrote the later books were familiar with the earlier books and often spoke of them. This is particularly true of the writers of the New Testament. We tend to think of Matthew, Luke, and John as being sort of rude peasant types without a great deal of education. But let me tell you something about them: they knew their Old Testament just about by heart. Because we don't know it so well, we overlook the fact that an enormous amount of the New Testament is either direct quotation from the Old Testament, or an expression of the ideals of the earlier Scriptures. It's an incredible and amazing book. It is also myth, and I believe that God inspired it. But God didn't go to all this trouble to tell us what kings reigned in Jerusalem in 783. Rather, He wrote the Bible to be used in the formation of our mind and character.

There is a phrase in the New Testament, in St Paul: "Let this mind be in you which is also in Christ Jesus." The mind of Jesus was formed by the Bible. His prayer book was the Old Testament which contained the psalms. When Jesus hung dying on the cross, there came to His mind a line from Psalm 22, "O God, my God, why hast Thou forsaken me?" So two thousand years ago, the Bible functioned as myth in the formation of the human character and personality of Jesus Christ.

We are told in Genesis that God created man in His image after His likeness. The first thing this means is that God and His creature man are capable of personal relations, even though God is a spirit and doesn't have two eyes, two legs, wear a hat and carry an umbrella. One must beware of presuming from human experience the divine attributes, however. When we say Jesus teaches us to call God Father because we all have fathers and therefore know what fathers are, we are confused. It works the other way. Only after we know God in His Fatherhood will we know what human fathers are supposed to be and never quite are.

We can't learn about God by looking at people. We learn about people by looking at what God has revealed to us about Himself. When we say that God and man are both persons, we don't say, "Well, I know what a person is and therefore I know what God is." We have never known personality in that perfection. When we say Jesus was perfect, it doesn't necessarily refer to His moral character, but to the full and complete integrity of His human nature. He was fully and completely human, not partly human or quasi-human, which was one of the early heresies in Christology. Thus the idea that man is made in the image of God means in Christian theology that God and man are enough alike in their personhood to be capable of personal relationships. So, although there are personhoods of God the Father, God the Son, and God the Holy Spirit, it is not so radically different from our personhood. God and man are enough alike in their personhood to be capable of personal relationships. They can communicate with one another. They can identify with the other self by entering into the other's consciousness, by becoming one with him, feeling what he feels, suffering when he suffers, rejoicing when he rejoices.

Now likeness is something else.

Likeness of God implies that kind of agreement in the developed personality which enables two people to share with one another. For example, suppose two men are drafted into the army. One is from a well-to-do, educated and urban family, went to the best prep school and then to Harvard, and had every cultural advantage. The other man, we'll call him Charlie, is a country bumpkin who can barely read and write. They have very little in common. You would hardly expect them to strike up a warm and intimate friendship because, by and large, opposites do not attract.

But what enables us to share in another's life is the sharing of attitudes, values, and common experiences. Now these two men turn up side by side and shoulder to shoulder at boot camp. They go through the same set of experiences, are insulted by the sergeant, and finally graduate from boot camp and go off to war and share a lot of common indignities: the same foxhole, mess, mud, anger, and a whole lot of other things which over a long time develop in them common attitudes. The college graduate is still a college graduate, and Charlie is still a country bumpkin, and there are areas where they cannot share. But now they have a large number of thoughts and feelings they can and do share, and in respect of those, they have a likeness.

We are told that man is *created*. Not only is he given the potential for interpersonal relationships with God, he is also given a number of the common attitudes of God. What man lost at the Fall was not the image of God, but the likeness. The result is that you and I are now born in the image of God, an image that is unimpaired, unmarred. We still have the potential for communion with God. Our task in this life is to acquire the likeness, to acquire enough of the common attitudes of God so that we will simply be like Him, have something in common with Him, and hence some basis for companionship. That's what the Bible is for.

6

ONE, HOLY, CATHOLIC, APOSTOLIC CHURCH

Christ did not come to earth and live for thirty-odd years, die on the cross, descend into the grave, ascend into Heaven to sit at the right hand of the Father in order to provide anything remotely resembling individual and personal salvation. This is the primary error of post-Reformation theology, whereby we in the Western world have confused our Christianity with a late medieval departure in theology known as nominalism, spawned in the brain of one William of Occam in the fourteenth century. Nominalism provided us with a metaphysical foundation for that characteristically European and American idea known as "individualism". Christ, on the contrary, came teaching a concept of the kingdom. The good news was specifically that the kingdom of God had arrived. It was here, in our midst. God had already entered history and made His appearance.

This kingdom of God is a social concept, the individual or personal salvation involved being related to and identified with a redemptive community. What Christ came to do was to renew the covenant, and to establish a new Israel. The Christian Church has, from the beginning, conceived of itself as the Israel of the New Covenant. As a matter of fact, the Church's definition of what constitutes the covenant community is close to the Jews' own. A Jew is a member of the covenant community as one that keeps the law, which begins in the practice of circumcision, whereas the sign of membership in the new covenant community is baptism.

The Church is not an organization, not something that you join, but an organism, an organic thing. If I am a member of the Dallas Sports Car Club, I will be a member in good standing as long as I pay my dues. But that's not the way it works with the Church. It is rather something that you are born into, something you can't get out of. The entrance into this covenant community occurs at baptism. No one is ever born a Christian. You're not a Christian until you are baptized, but once you're baptized, you're a Christian throughout eternity.

The essential definition of an organism involves four points. Let's take, for example, a cocker spaniel puppy. A puppy is organic. He is a head, a backbone, a tail. He is a body, legs, hair, liver, eyes, nose, and ears. Each of those things is separate. Each item is different from the next, yet all together they make one thing. The puppy is a unity in a way that a company of soldiers on parade is not a unity. A company of soldiers can be broken up and dissolved, and each soldier will continue to exist independently. But if you cut off the tail of a puppy, the tail dies. If you dismember the puppy dog enough, the puppy dies. He is a unity of different parts, all of which are necessary and all of which taken together constitute one thing – the puppy dog. The organism, the puppy dog, is alive. This again is a distinction between an organism and an organization. The arrangement of the parts in the motor of an automobile make one engine, but the engine is not alive. The puppy dog is alive.

Again, considering the puppy dog as an organism, there are a certain number of essential elements which make the puppy dog a puppy dog. There is a wholeness, a completeness about the puppy dog, and it is possible to ascertain and describe what are the essential elements that make up the puppy dog. Without a liver, without a backbone, a head, or a tail, he is not that one organic thing.

And finally the organism of the puppy dog exists through time in a continuous unbroken existence, so that the old dog is the same dog as the little bouncy puppy. The dog has a beginning and an end, but in between there was an unbroken continuous continuity, a sameness, and this sameness persists in spite of obvious changes. The puppy grows in size and the hair on its muzzle will turn grey, but it's the same dog. Now these essential notes of an organism, when they are expressed in ecclesiastical terms, are simply those notes by which one describes the Church in the Creed as One, Holy, Catholic, and Apostolic.

The Church is One.

This simply means there is only one Church. I know there are a lot of different denominations; if there's only one Church, which of these is the real Church? That question fails to take into account the definition of the Church. The Church is that social body, composed of all those persons who have been baptized in the name of the Father, and of the Son, and of the Holy Spirit. They're all members of one Church. As a matter of fact, the word "Christian" means a baptized person. We would certainly allow the Boy Scouts to define what a scout is; we would allow the Masons to define what a Mason is. And surely the Christian Church has the same right to define what a Christian is. In the atmosphere of vague humanitarianism that prevails in the world today, the word "Christian" is used by lots of people to mean "a nice guy". I have had people come to me who want to be married but have never been baptized, and I tell them I'm sorry, but a Christian marriage is only for

Christian people. They get real indignant and say, "Well, I'm a Christian." When questioned, they turn out to believe vaguely that Jesus Christ was a nice guy, they believe in what they understand of the ethical principles of the Sermon on the Mount, and they look on themselves as well-intentioned, rather decent people. But the Christian is a baptized person. Now, there may be nice Christians and ugly Christians, heretical Christians and orthodox Christians, Christians who are going to Heaven and Christians who are going to hell, intelligent Christians and stupid Christians, but there are no unbaptized Christians.

A baptized person is a Christian and a member of the one Church. So here's what we make of the different denominations. I have six children. If we had a big family spat, and two of my children moved to Oklahoma City and changed their name to Jones, and two others moved to Houston and changed their name to Smith, and two others moved to Amarillo and changed their name to McGillicuddy, how many families would there be? You'd have one family acting as if it were three different families. But nothing that those kids could do could ever change the fact that they were sons and daughters of the same mother and father. What we have, of course, in the different Christian denominations today is a lot of Christian people acting as if they belonged to different churches, which of course is not true. Because it's not true, the Church is under a rather serious obligation to seek to discover some means whereby the division or schism in the Church can be overcome, and the Church reunited.

I mentioned in the case of the puppy dog that its unity does not consist of an identity between all the parts. You have a puppy dog which consists of a head and a tail and much in between. It is a mistake to suppose that the unity of the Church presupposes some kind of uniformity. This is certainly not desirable, but even if desirable, it is quite impossible. There are some ten thousand Episcopal churches in the United States, not to mention those in England, Canada, Ireland, Australia, and so on. They all use the same Prayer Book. And in spite of this, the worship offered in no two towns is exactly alike. There is room in this uniformity for individuality.

A simple example. There are some 125 families in my parish. It is a part of the discipline of the Episcopal Church that we observe a Friday abstinence. Let's suppose that 125 families in St Francis parish were each observing the Friday abstinence. In your family you have lobster, and we have tuna casserole. It's entirely possible that no two families would serve the identical fish dinner, and yet everybody would be observing the Friday abstinence. There is considerable room for diversity. There is a relatively small number of basic bedrock doctrines and disciplines that constitute the essence of the Christian Church. And within those limits there is room for an enormous amount of individual self-expression, even difference of opinion. What constitutes a breach in the Church is not the difference of opinion but the absence of charity. I'm not saying that if everybody just loved everybody else, all the differences would disappear. There are differences that are real, and there are differences that go to the root of the nature of the Church itself. I am saying, however, that the failure to be able to resolve those differences is the result of lack of charity.

Theoretically, there ought to be some way to unify the Church under one earthly administration. I don't know how to do it, and I'm not about to set myself up as the one who knows how, but it could and should be done. But until the day arrives, if it ever does, remember that despite its seeming diversity, the Church is One.

The Church is Holy.

This corresponds to that aspect of the puppy dog that is alive. You'll see what in a moment, but I need to define the word "holy". It's a word which exists in every language and is a common term in every religion. In Greek it's *hagios*, in German *heilig*, in Latin *sanctus*. The Polynesian word is *taboo*. When the American and British whalers first made landfalls in the South Pacific, they brought back and introduced the word *taboo*, commonly interpreted now as "forbidden". But that's not what the word means. It means "holy". The English sailors would land on some Polynesian island and flirt with all the native girls, and when some man would make a pass at a particular girl, they would all freeze up, become indignant, and say, "No, no. Taboo." The sailors would go exploring on the island and the natives would show them around happily until they came to some particular mountain or cave and want to go up it or in it. Then the natives would say, "No, no. Taboo." So the sailors thought it meant forbidden, but what the natives were really saying was, "You can't go in there. That's holy. You must let that particular girl alone. She's holy." The primary meaning of holy is "to belong to God for His exclusive use". So that particular mountain or cave or girl had been designated and set apart by the natives as the exclusive property of God, and therefore, not for human use.

Recently in popular theology some people have expressed the notion that the distinction between the sacred and the profane is a false one, that after all, the earth is the Lord's and all that therein is. So if everything belongs to God, then it's a mistake to say this girl or that cave belongs to God and this one does not. There is some truth in this idea. Everything does belong to God. However, we have treated the creation as if it belonged to us. We have drawn lines and built fences and said, "Mine." By the time we get through, every square inch of the earth's surface and everything which has been created will have been claimed by some human being as his own and for his exclusive use. Thus has mankind profaned God's sacred creation. So in order for God to reclaim any portion of His creation, He has to move in, build yet another fence, and say, "No, that's not yours. That's mine."

You find in practice that when something has been set apart and designated as sacred, actually the sacred thing has been so designated in order to indicate the true nature of everything else in that class. God has claimed only one day in seven. He blessed the Sabbath day and called it holy. Is it because one day belongs to God and on the other six you can do as you please? No, as a matter of fact, all seven days belong to God, but it's because of the sacred character of one day that we finally learn what the other six are for. Similarly, God has claimed a tithe, a tenth of one's possessions or income, to be turned over to the Church for His use, because I don't have anything that is mine to do with as I please. It is only by putting money in the collection plate that I learn what money is for. It is loaned to me, as is everything else, and it really belongs to God and must be used according to God's purposes. Now as a Christian father, I may spend money to buy shoes for my children. This is spending money in accordance with God's purposes. But the only way I know that God cares how I spend my money is because I take ten cents out of every dollar and put it into the collection plate. Then it dawns on me what the other nine-tenths are for. I don't have *anything* that I can do with as I please.

God has said that about the Church. The Church is holy,

and it belongs to God. In the baptismal service in the 1928 Book of Common Prayer there is a paragraph immediately following the baptism of a child or adult, right after he has been wet three times with living water in the name of the Father, of the Son, and of the Holy Ghost. The priest is directed to make the sign of the cross on the child's forehead and say, "We receive this child into the congregation of Christ's flock, and do sign him with the sign of the Cross, in token that hereafter he shall not be ashamed to confess the faith of Christ crucified, and manfully to fight under his banner, against sin, the world, and the devil; and to continue Christ's faithful soldier and servant unto his life's end."

What soldiers and servants have in common is that they are not their own master. That Jesus Christ is Lord is the first Christian Creed. The rest of the Creed, "I believe in God the Father Almighty, maker of Heaven and earth, and of all things, visible and invisible" – all of that is an elaboration and an expansion of the original baptismal credal confessional that Jesus Christ is Lord. It is an identification of Jesus with Jehovah, with Adonai. But the word obviously and necessarily carries the lesser meaning of "boss". Jesus is Boss.

We are not our own boss. The purpose of the Christian Church is not to aid people in achieving "self-realization" or "self-fulfilment". There is no such thing as that. We are soldiers and servants. Four hundred years ago, when this paragraph in the baptismal service was written, the phrase about being Christ's soldier and servant was based upon biblical phraseology. The original Greek term translated in the King James version over and over again as "servant" is *doulos*, which means slave. We could, without doing violence at all to the source material, sign a person with the sign of the cross as Christ's soldier and slave unto his life's end.

One, Holy, Catholic, Apostolic Church

These days we have lost something very precious, something which has enabled millions of people throughout history to play over their heads. This accounts for the martyrs. There were lots of people who were tickled to death to give their lives for Jesus Christ. This is the kind of attitude you encounter whenever and wherever you find the Christian religion producing saints, the Church's great moral and spiritual heroes. Contrast this with the mentality of most Christians today who move into a new community and go church shopping, seeking to find a church which can provide the most for them. That sort of mentality is so far removed from biblical Christianity that I don't even know how to address myself to it. The Church belongs to God, and the members of the Church are Christ's soldiers and servants. Until the Church produces that mentality in her membership, she will never really attract people in large numbers.

Certainly anything great, noble, splendid, and lasting that has been produced by the human spirit in the arts, in literature, mechanics, invention, warfare, or politics, has come out of that kind of devotion. One thinks of the starving artist in the garret, determined to produce a masterpiece whether or not the world will recognize it. That kind of dedication, that kind of commitment and conviction, is necessary if anything worthwhile is going to be achieved by man. And it is the desire, not just the willingness, but the *desire* to spend one's life, to empty oneself for something that is much greater and more valuable and more important than oneself that provides meaning and value to one's life. If I devote myself whole-heartedly to stamp collecting, then my life has the meaning, value, and richness of my stamp collection. If I devote my life to breeding a better hamster, then my life has all the richness and meaning of hamsters. If I devote my life to Jesus Christ, then my life has something of the meaning and value and richness of His life.

The initial credal statement of the Christian Church was the simple statement that Jesus is Lord. We have been chosen by God in order that He might indwell or inhabit. This is the internal vital principle which makes the Church a living organism, namely, that the Holy Spirit which is God's own life is communicated to the Christian at baptism.

It is nourished in the Christian continually through his communion, prayers, and other worship. God intends and desires to live in us, to look out upon the world through our eyes. The Church has always emphatically believed that when a person is baptized, God begins to live in that person's life through the donation of His Holy Spirit to that person. So there is active within the Christian two centres or principles of volition and choice, the human and the divine. Both are acting together in the life of the Christian. God indwells His Church by indwelling His people. In the Wisdom literature which speaks a great deal about the Holy Spirit, the Third Person of the Trinity, it says, "My dwelling place is in the full assembly of the saints." This means that, having been baptized, having become a dwelling place of the Holy Spirit, the further activity required of us is that we conform our character to the Divine Character, our will to the Divine Will, and that we allow God so to live in us that other people finally, after spending a short time with us, will go away and say, "That's the kind of person that Jesus surely must have been like." I've known some folk like that.

Of course, every Christian manages to achieve this condition every now and then. More and more we are supposed to surrender our wayward and rebellious will to the Divine Will so that in our lives, in our behaviour, in our relationship with other people, God may act in us so that we may become another incarnation, another Christ, through whom God works to redeem His creation. The Church is Holy.

The Church is Catholic.

The word "catholic" is a Greek compound of *kata* and *holos*. *Kata* means concerning, having to do with, according to. *Holos* is that root word which we find in English in "whole, complete, entire, total, holistic. The word *catholic* when applied to the Church does not signify principally and primarily what a great many people glibly say it does, namely, "universal". That's its unity, which we talked about when we said it included everyone who has ever been baptized, when we said the Church is One. The unity of the Church, which includes all baptized Christians, of course includes not only all of those living today, but all of those who have gone into eternity to their reward. They count, too. If we're going to be truly democratic, we are going to have to allow some mechanics for giving them the vote. Their opinions are just as important as yours and mine.

All this being true, catholicity refers to something else. Applied to the puppy dog, it means that all of the essential elements of the organism are present and healthy and operative. A true puppy dog has its liver, spleen, guts, nose, eyes, ears, tail, toenails, and everything that belongs to the fullness and completeness of a puppy dog. A three-legged puppy dog is not catholic. The word "catholic" has a non-technical secular sense and you find it sometimes when it's said that a person has a catholic taste in literature. He enjoys reading drama, fiction, short stories, non-fiction, poetry, biography, murder mysteries, and anything else that can be

95

classified as literature. If a man has catholic tastes in literature, he reads and enjoys it all.

But the word "catholic" in common usage has several additional meanings. To the ordinary person, the word "catholic" means Roman Catholic. The opposite of that is Protestant. Back in World War II, Uncle Sam got into some trouble with his soldiers' dog tags when he labelled everyone as either Catholic, Protestant, or Jewish. He found out after a while that the Greek Orthodox and a great many Anglicans refused to accept the designation of Protestant. It's hardly fair to call the Greek Orthodox Church "Protestant". Occasionally some Hindu, Buddhist, or something else was asked whether they were Catholic or Protestant and replied, "Neither." The recruiting sergeant would say, "Well, you have to be one or the other. Everything that isn't Roman Catholic is Protestant." That's the popular meaning of the word catholic.

There is another sense used by scholars, in which the word "catholic" refers to the kind of Christianity which was in the world, and explosively in the world, from the time of Christ until the sixteenth century, when the Reformation occurred and altered everything. In that sense, "catholic" is the opposite of "reformed". In this sense it refers to the type of Christianity which has liturgical worship, a three-fold ministry of bishops, priests, and deacons; which has the sacraments; which recites the Creeds; and, since the third century, has had monasteries and convents. In that sense, of course, the Episcopal Church would claim to be catholic.

But in the truest sense, the original sense, the word "catholic" simply means holding and practising all those things which Christ commanded to His apostles, and observing all of the disciplines which He commanded. "Go unto all the world and preach the Gospel to all nations, baptizing them in the name of the Trinity and teaching them to observe all things whatsoever I have commanded you." I can't imagine any honest or sincere Christian ever admitting to himself in the wee dark hours of some lonely morning, "Yes, I know that there are things which Christ revealed to His Church, but I don't believe them. There are certain things which Christ commanded, but I think differently."

The root of catholicism is "entire, whole, complete". The opposite of "catholic" in this sense is "fragmentary, partial, incomplete", or in a more common usage, "sectarian". Let's suppose for the sake of a hypothesis, that in the phrase "teaching them to observe whatsoever things I have commanded", Jesus commanded twenty-six different things for us to observe, and you could spread them out and label tham A, B, C . . . for the twenty-six letters of the alphabet. The "catholic" then is the one who practises all twenty-six. The sectarian is the one who says, "Oh, I like A, but I don't want any B and C, and oh yes, I'll take some D." This approach makes me and my judgement and my wisdom the arbiter of what God has revealed. This is essentially the spirit of heresy. The word *heresy* is Greek for "choosing", and the heretic is the person who chooses what portion of the Divine Revelation he shall receive and believe and put into practice.

Now I need to distinguish between material heresy and formal heresy. A man who is honestly mistaken may be in material heresy. This isn't a sin, it's merely a mistake, an error, and I doubt seriously if anyone has ever lived as a practising Christian and gone into eternity and faced God and has not had some of his errors corrected. I, of course, am a great intellect, a wise man, and a marvellous theologian. Nevertheless, when I see God at the Day of Judgement and it's all explained to me, I confidently expect to say about several things, "Oh, I see, I was mistaken!" God created my intellect. He is responsible for the brain He gave me. I'm responsible for how I use it. As long as we are doing the best we can to find and follow the will of God, even if we make errors of judgement, it's no problem for us in the long run.

The formal heretic is the guy who looks the Revelation of God square in the face and says, "No, I think I know better. It's not like that, it's like this." This is the man who chooses his own religion. The sectarian heretical spirit asks, "What is the least I can do to get by on? What is the minimum requirement?" The catholic spirit says, "What more is there that I should believe and do?" The appetite for fullness and completeness and totality, that eager hunger for more and more of God's truth, that is catholicity. I have been an Episcopalian for forty years and a priest for thirty-five, and hardly a day passes that I don't learn something new about my faith. But on the other hand, I have never had to go back and change anything that I was taught when I was confirmed. It's like a mathematician who will learn more and more about maths every year of his life, but never has to go back and ask himself if 2 and 2 really make 4. The catholic mind in Christianity is that which is eagerly seeking to enlarge and increase its grasp of the Divine Revelation.

The Church is Apostolic. This means that the Church has continuity with its own past. We have a record in the sacristy of every service that has ever been conducted in this church, and you can find that every Sunday we had a congregation of people who have come together to worship God. There are only two people who were here when I came. The day will come when I will be no more, when a priest will stand here and ask a group of people how many know the name of the rector before him and no one will know. And yet the Church will go on. Souls are drawn into the Church they die, they move away, but the life of the congregation goes on. This parish has a personality and an identity. Every time a new person comes into this congregation or leaves, it changes a little. But it goes on, and it has been going on for two thousand years.

In the 1920s there was a genius that God raised up in the Church, a man by the name of Frank Gavin. He was naturally brilliant, would have been a genius even if he had been an atheist. He lived in Cincinnati, and knew from grammar school that he wanted to be a priest of the Episcopal Church, and knew he wanted to teach New Testament in seminary. He went to college, graduated, and in order to pursue his ambition to become a professor of New Testament, he enrolled in the Hebrew Union Theological College in Cincinnati and took a rabbinical course. He graduated with high honours and was qualified to be a Jewish rabbi. He had no intention of practising Judaism, but he had this remarkable insight that if you wanted to understand the New Testament, you had to understand Jesus, which meant you had to understand Judaism because Jesus was a Jew. Gavin wanted to get inside Judaism as best he could. He wanted to understand the mind of St Paul, who was a Jewish rabbi, so he decided he would become a Jewish rabbi in order to know what St Paul knew. After graduation, he went to one of our seminaries and took the standard course in preparation for the Episcopal priesthood. Again he graduated with honours. He did graduate work and earned a doctorate in New Testament studies and taught New Testament at General Theological Seminary. He had a short life. He died before he was forty.

A number of years ago when I was fresh out of seminary, the great English liturgical scholar Dom Gregory Dix came to this country and made quite a splash. He brought some insights to the study of the liturgy that were seminal and creative, that turned a corner in the academic world. Someone asked him in a conference here what started him thinking this way. He said, "Well, I suppose it was largely due to one of your fellows, a man who seems to be better known in England than he is in this country. Frank Gavin."

I never knew Frank Gavin, but the priest who instructed me and brought me into the Church was a student of Frank Gavin. And the mind of Frank Gavin is alive in me. My approach to teaching the Christian religion is essentially Frank Gavin's approach, but I never laid eyes on the man. There are people who have left this parish to become priests and teachers, whose method of teaching Christianity has been influenced by Fr Rogers. I don't know who influenced Frank Gavin, but I am sure that he would be able to tell us. Today, he himself is practically unknown. He died in 1936, the year before I was confirmed.

There is an "ongoingness" in the life of the Church that is transmitted from one person to another, to another and another. There is no way I can imagine the number of wise and holy teachers of the Christian religion, both clergy and lay, who have contributed to my education; numberless, holy, hard-praying Christian men and women, right back to the time of Christ. So if you don't know the name of the rector of this church before I came, you don't need to know. There have always been bishops and priests and congregations of Christian people who have, in one way or another, by teaching Sunday School or by the example of their lives, transmitted down through the ages this living heritage which is ours. The Church is continuous with its origins.

One of the things which makes that fact important is that an organism has a memory. I can remember things that happened when I was very small. I can remember a Christmas spent with my grandfather when I was three-and-a-half, though my memory is just a tableau here and there. I can remember his moustache as he stood in front of the fireplace in a house in McKinney, Texas. I remember the pit-bull terrier puppy named Rex my father bought me. I can remember all these things.

I am the same person that did those things. I can remember shameful and ugly things I have done. I can remember some rather lovely and wonderful things I have done. I can remember, and the Church remembers. This memory is embedded in me and in you. It conditions our behaviour in ways that we oftentimes are not aware of. But this organism, this Church, has been going on each year without exception, without interruption, for two thousand years.

There's a rather interesting story about a young priest fresh out of seminary, who went to his first parish, and the first Sunday he got into the pulpit and he really laid it out. He talked about the congregation's vices and problems. He wanted to establish right off how it was going to be. He preached a dogmatic and accusatory sermon, and he understandably offended half the people in the congregation. After the service an old dowager came bristling up and said, "Young man, I will have you know that I was an Episcopalian before you were born." He picked up the end of his stole and fingered it and said, "My daughter, when I am wearing this, I am 2,000 years old."

Of course the guy was an ass. But he was right. People sometimes want to know when this congregation was founded. One answer is 1948, when its name first appeared on the diocesan rolls as an organized congregation. But you might say it was founded 1,980-odd years ago. There is an

101

uninterrupted "ongoingness" that gives the Church a 2,000-year-old memory.

One of the consequences of this is that we are not citizens of the 1980s. We are citizens of eternity. That's what the Bible tells us. When Our Lord says that we should be in the world but not of it, the word He uses there for "world" is difficult to translate. The word "world" is not a precise translation, except in the sense in which we speak of the world of business or the world of art, that total cluster of attitudes and activities that make up the life, values, and mentality of the businessman or artist. The world in that sense is the American way of life in the 1980s. We can be *in* that world but not *of* it. And the most difficult thing for anyone to do is to stand outside of his own time or his own "world" and view it objectively.

A Christian is a sharer of a culture which is two thousand years old, and what we are supposed to do by immersing ourselves in the culture of the Church is to acquire that point of view which would make us equally at home in the first century or the fourth century or the seventh or the twelfth or the seventeenth or the twentieth. Or the twenty-seventh, for that matter.

If St Paul were to be resuscitated and brought back to earth and turned loose in Dallas, there is only one thing that I know of going on today that would make him feel perfectly at home, and it's what I am going to be doing tomorrow over there in the church in front of the altar, wearing those funny clothes. Those funny clothes would be familiar to St Paul because they are similar to the clothes that he and Jesus wore. And if I were to be sent back in time to his place at Tarsus, there is one thing that would be going on there that would make me feel perfectly at home – Sunday Mass.

One, Holy, Catholic, Apostolic Church

A number of years ago I took a course in Chaucer from Dr Clifton at North Texas State University. Of course, he knew more about Chaucer than I will ever know, but I knew some things about Chaucer that he did not know, and I knew these things without ever having read Chaucer. Dr Clifton admitted as a puzzlement that he didn't understand why in the Middle Ages all of the love stories are stories of unrequited love. Chaucer knew, and I know. Chaucer and I share the same identical world view. Dr Clifton mistakenly supposed that Chaucer was opposed to monks and nuns because he criticized them so severely. The reason Chaucer criticized monks was not because he was opposed to monasticism, but because he believed enthusiastically and emphatically in monasticism, and he knew that the monks of his time weren't living up to the ideal. He believed in monks, that's why he criticized the ones he met. Chaucer and I look out upon the world through the same pair of eyes. I can get inside the mind of Chaucer and Dr Clifton couldn't. And this enables me, and it will enable you, to take a look at those things that the contemporary culture regards as absolute and final and sort of grin and say, "No, I've been there before."

You don't have to wear a stole to be two thousand years old. The moment you were baptized you were two thousand years old. You are the heir of a culture that transcends all of the civilizations that will ever rise and fall. The Church was born into the civilization of the Roman Empire and Rome fell. The Church went on. The Church wedded itself to the Middle Ages and the feudal system, and the feudal system came to an end, but the Church went on. The Church allied itself with the eighteenth-century political system in Europe, and that political system collapsed but the Church went on. And the Church has espoused the liberal humanitarianism of twentieth-century America, and that too will disappear and the Church will go on, and this experience will become part of the corporate memory of Christian people a thousand years from now. And some priest will tell the story of a smart-alec priest just out of seminary who said to the lady, "My daughter, when I am wearing this, I am 3,000 years old."

I do not know what civilization will be like a thousand years from now, or which of the institutions will survive. A thousand years ago they had jousting and tournaments, and sport of that sort. I suppose that folk might have thought that jousting and tournaments would go on for ever, but today we have the Super Bowl. Will there be a Super Bowl a thousand years from now? I doubt it. But the Mass will be said a thousand years from now. The Gospel will be read, and the same ancient prayers will be said, and the mind of Christ will go on until He returns to gather us all up and present us to the Father.

7

THE TRINITY

In your schooling you may have run across a professor who made fun of the people in the Middle Ages who concerned themselves with how many angels could dance on the point of a pin. Needless to day, the people in the Middle Ages knew angels can't dance because they don't have bodies, but to answer that question, I would like to test your imagination for a moment by asking you to focus your thoughts upon the point of that pin, and then ask you how many people's thoughts can rest on the point of that pin until it is crowded and some of the thoughts begin slipping off. Obviously, an infinite number of thoughts can come to rest on the point of that pin, because thoughts do not occupy space in the same way that bodies do. Now since this pin is roughly the same shape as the Washington Monument, I will ask you to transfer your thoughts from the point of this pin to the point of the Washington Monument. I will ask you if you went by way of Memphis or St Louis. As a matter of fact you did not, I suspect, pass through any intervening space. One instant you were on the point of the pin and next instant you were on the Washington Monument. Notice what I said – in one instant *you* were on the point of the pin. To be sure, your thoughts were on the point of the pin, yet in a very real sense *you* were.

Now I direct your attention to a number of phrases in common speech that you have heard and used all your life.

"I was a thousand miles away." "I am sorry I can't come to your party but I will be with you in spirit." "I was beside myself." "I lost myself in a book." In a very real sense, you are wherever you are thinking about. The spirit can come and go at will. You can leave your body behind. We all recognize in our common speech that spirit is the kind of thing that is not necessarily tied to the body.

Now God is a spirit with no body. God is personal, spiritual, eternal. Let's notice what is meant by the word "personal". It is exceedingly difficult to conceive of a person except in relationships with other persons. For example, I am who I am because of the family I was born into, the town where I was raised, the schools I went to, the church I belong to. If you don't believe that, just imagine my having been taken at the age of five days and given to a Chinese peasant family in the interior of Communist China. I would not have the same set of memories, would not be talking English, would not have had the education or the same set of experiences. The person is understood in relationship to other persons. So perhaps we can understand God as a person by talking about the relationship of persons called the Trinity.

The doctrine of the Holy Trinity is central to the Christian religion. You may ask any hundred people you meet today what is the essential doctrine of the Christian religion and they will probably say, "To believe in Jesus Christ." But never mind that. Up until about two hundred years ago, if you had asked anybody, Protestant or Catholic, what was the central doctrine of the Christian religion, he would have said the Holy Trinity.

We don't think Trinitarian these days, because we think individually and concretely. In earlier times people were a little more precise and emphatic on the subject. An example of this view is to be found in the Athanasian Creed. This creed is in all of the prayer books in the Anglican communion, though only in that of the American church since 1979. You will see at once why early American Episcopalians looked at this statement and said, "My God, we can't use that. It'll scare people off."

It starts off by saying, "Whosoever will be saved, before all things it is necessary that he hold fast the Catholic faith." Of course, everybody knew that if the American Protestants heard that word "Catholic" they would flick off their hearing aids. That in itself was bad enough, but it gets worse. "Which Faith except everyone do keep whole and undefiled, without doubt he shall perish everlastingly." That means all Protestants go to hell, and we can't have that in our prayer book.

And the Catholic faith is this: that we worship one God in Trinity, and Trinity in Unity, neither confounding the Persons, nor dividing the Substance.

For there is one Person of the Father, another of the Son, and another of the Holy Ghost.

But the Godhead of the Father, of the Son, and of the Holy Ghost, is all one, the Glory equal, the Majesty co-eternal.

Such as the Father is, such is the Son, and such is the Holy Ghost.

The Father uncreated, the Son uncreated, and the Holy Ghost uncreated.

The Father incomprehensible, the Son incomprehensible, the Holy Ghost incomprehensible.

The Father eternal, the Son eternal, and the Holy Ghost eternal.

And yet they are not three eternals, but one eternal.

As also there are not three incomprehensibles, nor three uncreated, but one uncreated and one incomprehensible.

So likewise the Father is Almighty, the Son Almighty, and the Holy Ghost Almighty.

And yet they are not three Almighties, but one Almighty.

So the Father is God, the Son is God, and the Holy Ghost is God.

And yet they are not three Gods, but one God.

So likewise the Father is Lord, the Son is Lord, and the Holy Ghost is Lord.

And yet not three Lords, but one Lord.

For like as we are compelled by the Christian verity to acknowledge every Person by himself to be both God and Lord,

So we are forbidden by the Catholic Religion, to say, There be three Gods, or three Lords.

The Father is made of none, neither created, nor begotten.

The Son is of the Father alone, not made, nor created, but begotten.

The Holy Ghost is of the Father and of the Son, neither made, nor created, nor begotten, but proceeding.

So there is one Father, not three Fathers; one Son, not three Sons; one Holy Ghost, not three Holy Ghosts.

And in this Trinity none is afore, or after other; none is greater, or less than another;

But the whole three Persons are co-eternal together and co-equal.

So that in all things, as is aforesaid, the Unity in Trinity and the Trinity in Unity is to be worshipped.

He therefore that will be saved must thus think of the Trinity.

Now that is pretty raucous. It is much simpler to say you give your heart to Jesus and let it go at that. You believe all that stuff about "one uncreated and not three uncreated"? That's crazy. However, let it be noted that while the Athanasian creed was certainly not the composition of Athanasius, it was nevertheless compiled by some person or persons not long after the time of Athanasius when people in the Roman Empire were well-educated and profoundly interested in philosophy. One of the great errors that people make in religion is to say, "If I can't understand it, it obviously doesn't make any sense." This creed was the product of a highly sophisticated civilization, drafted and approved by people who were not all that different from us today. At one time this creed made sense to people and for good reason.

But they did not invent the doctrine of the Trinity, so if it was not thought up by a bunch of monks on Mount Athos, where did it come from? The first evidence for it is to be found in the Gospels, in the life of Jesus, whom his disciples began to regard as "the Lord" or "Adonai", a word the Jews used to mean Jehovah whose name they could not mention. This man, a carpenter from Bethlehem, made such an impression on the people who knew him personally and intimately, that they came to the conclusion that this man was different. The growing conviction in the minds of the Apostles that Jesus was more than human finally comes to verbal expression in St Peter's confession after the experience on the Mount of Transfiguration: "Thou art the Christ, the Son of the Living God." That in itself does not imply absolute divinity. Superhuman, perhaps, but not yet equal with the Father.

When they got around to writing Jesus' biography thirty years after his death, they quoted Him as having said, "I and my Father are One." And "He that has seen Me has seen the Father." Things like that clearly identify Christ with God the Father. Then He turned right around and said, "I came not to do my will but the will of the Father who sent me," clearly distinguishing himself from the Father. So He both is, and is not, to be thought of as God. That's pretty difficult already. But then Jesus talks about this spirit He is going to send, and the Church has the experience of the Holy Ghost and comes to the conclusion that the Holy Ghost Himself is some kind of personal spiritual being who both is God and is not the Father and is not the Son. So the Church found itself, to its own amazement, believing in three divine persons. However, in the beginning they were all devout mono-theistic Jews, and one of the most horrible things a Jew could do was to believe in multiple gods. Now remember that God cannot accomplish a contradiction in terms. He can't make a square circle, or create a rock He can't lift. Yet here we have the Church believing that God is both three and one, three without ceasing to be one, and one without ceasing to be three. How in the world are you going to do that?

St Patrick came to Ireland with this notion and the Irish said, "You're putting us on." "All right," he said, and picked up a shamrock and asked, "How many shamrocks?" "One," they said. He said, "Now how many leaves does it have?" "Three." "Okay, so there." But of course, you can't explain God in terms of vegetables. If St Augustine were teaching a confirmation class and came to this point, he would strike his cigarette lighter and say, "What's that?" Somebody would say, "Fire." Somebody else would say, "Light." And somebody else would say, "Heat." Then he would say, "Okay, now you understand the Trinity." But you can't explain God in terms of physics, either.

It wasn't until the Council of Nicaea in the fourth century that the Church finally solved this problem and came up with a formula which preserved the rationality of God and allowed intelligent people to believe in a three-in-one God. The principle of contradiction in logic runs "Things cannot both be and not be at the same time and in the same way." Therefore God is Three in one sense of the word and One in some other sense of the word. The formula that solved this at the Council of Nicaea is that God is one *ousia* and three *hypostaesis*. Once you put it like that, you see how it clears things up. It will comfort you to know that those terms have exact English equivalents. We translate them one "substance" and three "persons". But these concepts still need further explanation.

The people who put together the Athanasian Creed were talking about ultimate reality. Remember that your God is whatever you believe to be ultimately and finally real and valuable, that thing for the sake of which, when the chips are down, you would sacrifice everything. When you have peeled away the surface layers and come straight to the heart of the matter, the doctrine of the Trinity will be found to define a *community of persons in love*. Let's put it this way: "Whossoever would be sane, whosoever would keep his sanity before all things, it is necessary that he hold fast to the total scope of reality."

Insanity is being out of touch with reality, thinking I am a bunny rabbit. Therefore, being sane means having a firm grip on every aspect of reality. The whole grasp of reality is "neither confounding the Persons nor dividing the Substance". In the West when we approach the question of man made in God's image, we see God as a random collection of isolated individuals. But everyone has something about him that he shares in common with everybody

111

who has ever lived. On the other hand, everyone has something about him that is uniquely and exclusively his and which he shares with nobody else who has ever lived. Which of those is important? Ninety-nine people out of a hundred will respond without stopping to think, "Well, obviously, that which makes me an individual, of course." But they are wrong. They are "dividing the Substance", the universal, human nature of humankind. There is a substantial reality in our thinking that we can define by the term "human nature", yet when we Westerners look at ourselves in relation to our fellow man we see only differences, overlooking the more important similarities, dividing the substance.

Cross the border into China and there you have the opposite heresy. If we in the West divide the Substance, there they confound the Persons. That is to say, when a classical Marxist looks out at the human race, he sees only collective mankind. There is a tendency on the part of collectivists, whether they be fascists or communists, to see people in a mass, so much so that individual characteristics are lost to their understanding. The reality of the human condition is strange. That is what the Athanasian Creed is talking about. If you are going to be sane in your approach to daily living, you'd better see man in community and recognize at the same time the reality of the individual, neither thinking so exclusively and sharply of the community that the individual becomes blurred, nor thinking so exclusively and sharply of the individual that the community becomes blurred.

As a kind of loose rule of thumb, God the Father is the divine intellect, God the Son is the divine will, and God the Holy Spirit is the divine affection. Man is made in God's image. Thus the doctrine of the Trinity tells us that for a human person to be whole and entire, there has to be a harmonious integration of the relationships among the intellect, the will, and the affections, and these faculties must operate in a certain sequence and order, each proceeding from the previous one. The human act which has its own integrity begins with a rational judgement. In this phase you are unemotional, uninvolved, coldly rational. Judgement is purely intellectual. Then, guided by the intellect, the will makes a commitment and acts, obedient to the intellect. Then the emotions are allowed to come into play, to see to it that you enjoy having done what is right.

Now a human act can be perverse in many ways. Normally acts which pervert human existence begin with an emotional or imaginative enjoyment of some subjective condition. We say to ourselves, "Wouldn't it be nice if . . ." In my imagination I enjoy this fantasy. My will comes along and acts to make the fantasy a reality. Finally, the intellect follows along and we find reasons for having done what we wanted. That's called rationalization, and that's when we get into trouble. Then there are people who are all intellect and no action. Vestries can be like this. They can discuss a problem for an hour or two and then pass a resolution to buy new letterhead stationery. A month later when they read the minutes, they remember that they passed a resolution to buy new letterhead, but no one bought any. We never said who was going to do the job. We just sort of figured that we had solved the problem and that was all there was to it. If we had a good Trinitarian theologian sitting in the presiding officer's chair at vestry meetings he would not let the group just pass a resolution and adjourn without saying, "Now, who is going to do this? We have solved the problem intellectually, but who is going to order the new letterhead?" A great many of our daily problems are a result of having our Trinity confused.

Now I said you can't explain the Trinity by vegetables, flowers, and other finite metaphorical objects. All I can do is present an imaginative notion which will enable you to think of the Trinity and to think about it in some way that is not shamrocks or lighters. If God is a person, and a spiritual person, chances are if we are searching for an analogy, we would be more apt to find that analogy in the spiritual persons with whom we are acquainted – namely, mankind. Man is made in God's image, and if God is a Trinity, it is not unreasonable that there might be in man something like the Trinity.

Let me draw you a picture of a sailboat. You were not thinking about a sailboat, but you know what a sailboat is and you had that image somewhere. When you think of a sailboat you are thinking "subject", and sailboat is the object of that thought. Now you "know" the sailboat, so inside your own mind, without your doing a thing, there exists a subject/object relationship. There is a thing in mind and there is what the mind is thinking about, namely, a sailboat. But not only do you know about sailboats, but you also know about yourself. So that when you know yourself or think about yourself, there is the self that is thinking and the self that is being thought about. So there is a kind of subject/object relationship in our own selves.

The trouble is that you can't think about yourself and about the American Revolution at the same time. We are not simple-minded. But God is, and God has never had but one thought, and in this thought of God's is everything that God knows, all harmoniously related in an integrated fashion. God does not reason to a conclusion as we do. He does not know something and then figure out the implications by what He already knows. He just knows everything He knows, and knows it all at once. He has never had but this one thought.

So in God there is a subject/object relationship that is God the thinker and God the thought. Into God's thought went everything that God knows, including His self-consciousness. God's thought was conscious of itself and of the thinker. Thus the thought became an independent thinker. It was a subject/object relationship which turned around and became an object/subject relationship. God and His Thought thought about each other.

"God the Thinker" and "God the Thought": God loved what He knew, so God the Thinker loved God the Thought, and God the Thought loved God the Thinker; thus we have God the Lover and God the Beloved, and hence a personal God whose personality exists in a relationship. (If that doesn't strike you with its obvious logic yet, perhaps it will when we get through.)

The love we are talking about here is a kind of going out of oneself to get inside the skin of another, to identify with that other and to know what it is to be like that other. In this total donation of the self to the other goes everything which is in the consciousness of God, including self-consciousness; so there is a third self-consciousness, which comes into being, which is the mutual self-donation of the first two. This is the Holy Spirit. Of course, this explanation is simplistic. What I'm trying to do is suggest to you something of the nature of the Trinity.

I have said that a person tends to identify with and emulate that which he regards as ultimately real and worthwhile. If God is to be this Trinitarian thing which we have been talking about, then how can I be like Him? I will never be omnipotent. I will never be infinite. I will never be fully eternal, so I can't be like God in His metaphysical attributes. The only way I can imitate God is in His moral attributes. So I am concerned to know what God is like in that respect, what kind of *person* He is. It is interesting to note that you can only begin to get a notion of what a person is like when that person starts doing something. As long as you sit perfectly still and keep your mouth shut, I will never know whether you are wise or foolish, whether or not you have a sense of humour, or indeed anything about you except what you look like. It is only when you get into action that you begin to reveal your character and personality. For this reason we need to learn about God by finding out what God is doing, what He's up to.

What we have just said about the Trinity means that God was knowing everything there is to know and loving all that He knew and enjoying all truth, goodness, and beauty, and sharing this knowledge and enjoyment in an intimate relationship of three perfect Persons who were perfectly in love. I defy anyone to think of any nicer thing for even God to be doing.

Whether or not one likes truth, goodness, and beauty, most people will spend their lives in continuing curiosity about such ideals. Man is a questing and asking animal. As soon as we are able to talk, we start pestering Mama and Papa with questions. I had an uncle, a Civil War veteran who had a missing finger on his right hand. As a little child I asked him a lot of questions, just pestering him to death. Finally I said, "Uncle Rafe, how did you lose your finger?"

He said, "Well, I'll tell you, only if you promise not to ask me any more questions." I said sure. "It was bit off," he said.

Every time we get an answer to a question it raises another question. All of our probing into truth simply pushes the horizon of truth back further unless there is somewhere an ultimate truth to satisfy the human intellect. Of course, we are doomed to be forever frustrated; it would seem that man's mind has an infinite appetite for truth. There is no truth that we have ever discovered that has stopped us from looking for more truth. Notice that we spend our lives looking for someone to love and to be loved by. We have never found that relationship and nobody has ever found it. Man is not by nature mono-gamous, because we have an infinite appetite for love which cannot be satisfied with any finite object. Unless there is somewhere an infinite object for our love, our hunger and internal yearning is going to be forever frustrated. I think that's what hell is.

Not only that, but we have an infinite appetite for happiness. We have never found what it takes to make us happy. When I was nine years old, I was convinced that all it would take to make me permanently and abidingly happy was a bicycle. One Christmas I got a bicycle. Less than a month later I had discovered that what I really wanted was a Shetland pony. Though I never got the Shetland pony, I next discovered that I really wanted something else. I don't really know what I want.

But I do. I know what you want, what we all want. We want everything. We want God. That is all we ever want. The way I explain it to children – and they catch on rather quickly – is by asking, "Which would you rather have, a toy or a toy factory?" God has everything and has been enjoying it for ever, and God knows far better than we will ever know the tangy goodness of a cold beer on a hot summer day.

Let me explain what I mean by that. Suppose a dozen people go to a symphony concert. One of them is an accomplished technical musician. He will enjoy the symphony concert in one way and another person sitting next to him, who is not a musician but an amateur music lover, will enjoy it in another way. The guy sitting next to him has never been to a symphony before in his life and what he gets out of it will be something else. Someone sitting next to him has just been told by his doctor that he has terminal cancer and has only three months to live – he will react to the symphony in yet another way. The next person has just been told by his sweetheart that yes, she will marry him, and he gets something else out of the symphony. This means that there is an awful lot in the symphony that I don't get. But God could get it all.

God is engaged in the total enjoyment of all reality, the complete understanding of all truth. And He is sharing this experience in the context of a perfect love with Someone Else who can understand it as Man. That is pretty great. That is what we want, too. Since there is no tomorrow for God to enjoy something which He does not have today, God's happiness cannot be increased nor can it be diminshed. God is as happy as He is ever going to be, which means infinitely happy. God doesn't need a cotton-picking thing. Nothing that we can do can increase God's happiness or diminish it. God had everything that even God could possibly want. Why in the world did God create? We are not at one of those "Well, honey, it just does" stopping places. But there are two aspects of creation that I want you to understand.

The first is very important. God creates for the same reason that you sing in the shower. Just for the sheer hell of it. Because it's fun. Creation is not God's labour, it's His play. God took a handful of stars and went "Whee!" like a frisbee out into space, and there was another galaxy. God made the stars for the same reason that you and I shoot off fireworks. We tend to think of God in our own image, and we are most of the time very solemn, very purposeful, very earnest. God isn't. God is playful. God is kind of silly. He made alligators and antelopes and hippos – any God that would make a hippo has got to have a sense of humour. Then why did God make people? Take a deep breath. Here we come. What was He doing? If we had been doing what God was doing, on the analogical human level, we would be sitting up all night long with our two best friends and a bunch of new albums and a keg of beer having an all-night bull session about some very exciting topic of conversation. *God was having a party.*

You think I made that up. Jesus said, "The kingdom of Heaven is like a man who gave a wedding feast for his son and invited guests." Once upon a time, before there was any time, God said to each other, "This is too good to keep. There ought to be someone else to share it with." He said, "I've got it. Let's make a bunch of people so they can come to the party." So in one sense creation is an overflow of the divine love. God was so happy He could not contain Himself. Philosophically, it pertains to the nature of being to communicate itself. That is a demonstrable fact from natural history, and it is also a "Honey, it just does." It pertains to the nature of God to communicate His being in an outpouring, a self-donation. God made man in order that there might be persons with whom He could share His felicity. That's the answer to the Big Question, "What are we here for? What is life all about? What is the final end and purpose of man?"

This is what man is for: to enter into and become a part of and to participate in the essential interior divine activity.

119

To do what God is doing. What is God doing? God is knowing, loving, and enjoying God. Man was made to know, love, and enjoy God in this life and in eternity. Man was made to go to God's party. We're all invited.

The salvation which the preachers have talked endlessly about is nothing more or less than achieving the purpose for which man was created, becoming fully human. You and I are not yet fully human. We are not anteaters or butterflies, but we're not yet fully human. Salvation means to become fully human. Therefore it is not a momentary event that occurs when you give your heart to Jesus. It is the end of a process of growth and development. Damnation, on the other hand, simply means to fail eternally to be a human being.

When Jesus was trying to explain hell to His disciples He took them out and showed them the Jerusalem city dump, and He said, "That's hell." In the city of Jerusalem a donkey went up one street and down the other and gathered all the garbage and took it out and dumped it in the valley of Gehenna and they set fire to it. Because there was a lot of organic stuff and wet trash, it smouldered and burned, and before it was all burned up, another load of garbage came the next day, so there was forever and eternally a smoky pall over Jerusalem coming from the city dump. He said, "That's what hell is like." What do you find in the city dump? Discards, things that are no longer of use to anybody. That's what damnation is. Your whole nature and constitution is designed for the knowledge of truth, the entering into a loving relationship in the same kind of love that God makes, and the ecstatic enjoyment of the beauty of reality. To have all of your faculties designed for truth and to fear, dread, or despise truth is the essence of hell.

The Trinity

When God set about creating companions for Himself in eternity He ran into a problem. He wanted to make people who could love as He loved, but love is not love if it is forced. Man had to be given free will. If I fall in love with a girl and she doesn't like me at all, I can pull out a pistol and point it at her head and say, "Love me or I'll blow your brains out." And she will say, "Yes, I love you." But it's not love unless it comes voluntarily from within a person. So God had to make us capable of not loving. Consequently, He gave us free will.

But it is more complicated than that. Not only is love not love if it is forced, it is also not love if it is bribed. If I had a million dollars and sixteen producing oil wells and a Cadillac convertible and I said to a girl, "Will you marry me?" and she said, "You bet," how would I know whether she loved me or my money? (For that matter, how would *she* know?) There is one way I can find out. I may have sixteen oil wells, but if she doesn't know, she thinks I am poor, then if I said, "Honey, will you marry me?" and she said, "You bet," I would know she loved me and not my money.

Now, as we said, all we have really wanted was everything – that is, God. God, as he exists in eternity, is so dazzlingly desirable that if He were to reveal Himself to us as He is in eternity, this would constitute a bribe. It would make it impossible for us to say yes or no freely.

So, God can't entice us with the joys of Heaven without destroying our freedom. Now God's dilemma is this: He wants us to love Him, not because He needs our love but because loving Him is so much fun that He thought we might like it. But we can't love Him unless we know Him. We can't love Him freely *if* we know Him. So He has to reveal Himself to us while concealing Himself from us.

121

That's quite a trick. The way God solved this problem was through the creation of space and time.

God's nature as a community of persons in love is expressed in the fact that we are placed in a community of persons. We are supposed to learn to love each other the way God loves each other. If we are going to get along without friction, conflict, or pain, our love must be a purely altruistic self-giving love which asks nothing in return. It's not easy – I've tried it. One day, we will step out of time and space and enter into eternity, where we will see reality face to face. Then we will recognize God at that moment as the thing for which we have been yearning and searching for all our lives and will spend eternity enjoying Him. That's Heaven. Or else we will recognize God as that thing which we have been avoiding and running away from all our lives and will spend eternity avoiding Him. That's hell.

This life is a trial run. This life is God taking us through the kitchen on the morning of Thanksgiving with a dip spoon saying, "Taste this. Take a bit of that. See how you like this. Have some of this." He hurries us on from one dish to another when we would rather stay and fill our plate with hors d'oeuvres. But He says, "Wait, just taste." He only gives us a tiny little sliver of this and He pushes us on toward something else, like the pumpkin pie.

Remember the parable in the New Testament about the man who gave a wedding feast for his friends and invited guests and there were some who wouldn't come. They had more important things to do. Yet there is really nothing else more important, because we have never wanted anything else. The drunken bum staggering at the steps of a bawdy house at midnight fumbling for the doorbell is searching for God. Now, he'd be surprised if you told him that, but that's what he really wants. He is seeking God, as we all do, under analogous forms of creation; the commandment against other gods and graven images is simply God's warning that we should not try to be content with anything, because what we really want is everything. Man was made to know, love, and enjoy reality in eternity. God gave me my wife to love, not to satisfy my need for love but to whet my appetite for love. God gave her to me to practise loving on so that I can become a lover, so that when I enter eternity and stand face to face with Him whose very nature is love, I will not be offended by it.

In eternity, you will have forever what you really want. That's the most frightening thing imaginable. Very few of us are saints yet. If I were to die tonight I doubt if I could go clodhopping into the presence of God and feel perfectly at ease and comfortable there. But God loves me and will accept me, and I will be accepted. Not because I deserve it, but because God is loving, can I stay there. In eternity you will have forever what you really want. And what God wants for us is to enjoy the party, in the community of persons in love called the Trinity.

8

. . . .

THE COVENANT
AND ACHAN

Man is a natural creature with a supernatural destiny. The one thing he cannot do by his own powers is to supply what it takes to perfect him. What Adam and Eve had that we lack is mystical union with God, that intuitive awareness of his relationship with God which can prevent man from feeling exposed and vulnerable and lonely in his universe.

Because man is a social being, his redemption must be accomplished in society. Unfortunately, since about the fourteenth century, Western man has tended to ignore the social side of his own nature. There is one thing called humanity and each of us is a concrete particular instance of that. We are bound together on a spiritual level so that whether I know you or not, what is taking place in my soul affects you. What takes place in your soul affects me. You can go further and state that whatever meaning I have as an individual is granted to me and conferred upon me by my community.

Western man may have a hard time understanding this, but the Jews did not. The Old Testament is presupposed to this notion so solidly that the Jewish people thought of themselves in this way but had a very weak conception of the individual person, and practically no notion at all of individual immortality. They did not think of themselves as individuals who were Jews – they just thought of "us Jews".

God selected the Jews out of all the peoples on the earth and gave them a special divine vocation. The Jews were in Egypt a long, long time, some four hundred years, and Jewish history as such really begins with the Exodus. Prior to this time the Jews had had a favoured place in the Egyptian state and in the Egyptian economy. They had been assigned to the Land of Goshen, on the seacoast between the Nile Delta and the Isthmus of Suez. It was a rather fertile part of Egypt, a choice bit of land.

But there was a dynastic revolution and a new royal family came to the throne, and this royal family knew not Joseph. That is to say, the Pharaoh was not in favour of the position which the Jews had held in the previous dynasty, and he began to oppress them. Then along came Moses. The name Moses is not a characteristically Jewish name, but is an Egyptian name. It appears in Thutmoses, and in Ramases, which is Ra Moses. Very probably he was a Jewish child who somehow or other had been placed in the reigning family, and when he was forty years old – that is to say, when he was no longer wet behind the ears – something happened. Early one Sunday morning, after an all-night dance, he was driving his Cadillac convertible home on the expressway and he saw a gang of labourers who were being abused by an Egyptian foreman. He put on his brakes and he stopped his car and jumped out and said, "Hey, my good man, you can't do that!" Thump, thump, thump. The guy fell over and hit his head on the pavement and cracked his skull. He was dead.

The position of Moses at the court was probably not too secure, because he decided that discretion here was the better part of valour and he took off and went east and

125

wound up in the ranch country. He alighted from the stage coach one afternoon and there at the town pump were some beautiful girls who were drawing water, and a bunch of drunken cowboys were teasing them. Moses (this is all in the Bible) had been the light heavyweight champion in college so he walked into the crowd swinging and knocked these guys in the head and then said, "May I draw your water, my dears?" They took the water and went on home and told their daddy what had happened. He said, "Why didn't you invite the nice young man home to dinner?" One of the girls went back to the local hotel and found him and said, "Daddy said we would like to have you come to dinner." So he did, and was hired on as a hand, and rapidly rose to a position of foreman of the ranch and married the boss's daughter. Now it turns out that the boss was the local preacher – the High Priest of Midian who was also a great landowner, a wealthy livestock rancher. So Moses had it made.

One day when Moses was out riding the fence he saw something out in the distance that was definitely of interest to every man in ranch ountry – he saw a fire burning. So he rode over to investigate. Here was a bush that burned and burned and did not go out. Moses was baffled by the sight, and when he approached it, a voice spoke to him out of the bush, saying, "Take off your shoes, for the ground on which you stand is holy ground." He said, "Yes, sir," just like you or I would have done. If a voice speaks to you out of a burning bush you do what it says. This voice said, "Moses, I am the God of your fathers Abraham, Isaac, Jacob, and Joseph, and I have taken pity on my people back in Egypt and I want you to go and bring them out."

Moses said, "Who, me?"

And the voice said, "Yes."

126

Moses said, "Whom shall I say sent me?"

And the voice said, "I am that I am." This was the unutterable name, the awful name represented by the four consonants in the Hebrew alphabet JHVH. It was an intensive reflexive form of the first person of the verb "to be". Hebrew grammar is not like Indo-European grammar. It conjugates its verbs according to a different system and this is the form of the verb "to be" which was never uttered out loud among the later Jews, except by the High Priest once a year when he went into the Holy of Holies in the Temple. When he did that, of course, they tied a rope around his waist so that if the experience killed him they could haul him out without having to go in after him. That's a fact. The notion is that when you pronounce the name of God, you invoke His presence. This is the name that the voice from the burning bush gave Moses, and furthermore, it told him to go bring His people out of slavery, out of Egypt. It wasn't personal slavery such as we had in the American South before the War Between the States; rather, it was more of a State slavery, a forced labour levy. You will remember that a number of things happened to the Egyptians before they were willing to release this free labour. There were pests. There were locusts. There were plagues, and finally the Jews got out.

Among the people who escaped with Moses were a lot of Egyptians, Ethiopians, Libyans, a mixed polyglot multitude. So the escapees were not all Jews. Even the Jews who escaped with Moses were not really Jews in the fullest sense. The Jews had been in Egypt for four hundred years, which is to say, a number of generations. They had about as much relationship to the religion which the first Jews practised in Egypt as we have to the religion of our ancestors who once upon a time were Druids. Most of these Jews had no personal memory of the desert religion that Moses was talking about.

And how did Moses accomplish all this? Well, Moses was a remarkable guy. He wore a number of hats. He was a foreman on a ranch out in Midian. He went back to Egypt and became the world's first union organizer. He went around to all the family heads and got them to agree to let him represent them to the management, in order to get a better contract. Management was stubborn and wouldn't listen, so he called a walk-out. Now, once they were out of Egypt they had problems. At this point Moses became the wagon master, the trail boss. He had to get these people through the desert. What happened was that he took this mixed bunch of Jews, Egyptians, Libyans, Ethiopians out into the desert and made them wait. Then he went up and sat on the mountain and stared up into heaven and said, "Now what do I do?" God answered and gave him a Covenant.

And this is the beginning of Judaism.

Moses came down out of the mountain with tables of organization. Back in 1849, if you had decided to go to California in a wagon train leaving out of St Louis, you would have formed part of a company with other wagon folk, and there would be a wagon master, a trail boss, and he would have articles which you would sign, rules that you would have to agree to abide by on the course of your journey across the prairies and mountains. This is the sort of thing Moses came back with. If you want to know what the Jews faced when they went out into the desert beyond the Red Sea, read in the Bible of the Amalekites, the Midianites, the Edomites, and the Hittites, and simply substitute for these names Apache, Comanche, Kiowa, and you will get something of the idea of what these Jewish people were facing. Moses's solution (or God's solution, if you will) was to say to the Jewish people, this mixed, polyglot conglomeration. "Organize yourselves as a desert tribe, adopt the lifestyle of the Comanches and Apaches. If you can't lick 'em, join 'em. Turn yourselves into a desert tribe." This is what Moses did at Mount Sinai with the Covenant Law.

Moses had lived for forty years among the Midianites and they were a desert tribe. So he was ideally suited to organize this bunch of refugee people into a desert tribe, which is what he and God did. By the time of Joshua the Jewish people were desert people, a whole generation of Jews who were raised in the desert and had no memory of the fleshpots of Egypt. There were certain values to this desert culture and in this desert religion that God apparently thought were worth conserving. Indeed, the whole of Western civilization is an outgrowth and development of the desert religion of the Arabian peninsula, fifteen to eighteen hundred years before Christ. And in all the long years in which the Jews were occupying the Holy Land they were continually fighting to preserve the purity of this ancestral religion.

Moses brought the Law down out of the mountains, though he had to make two trips to do it. Remember he broke the tablets the first time he came down when he found the tribes were worshipping the golden calf and lost his temper. When he finally went back and got the tablets all straightened out, he built an altar. He read the Law to the assembled congregation, and said, "How about it, fellows? Will you agree to this?" They all said "Yes, we will." Then he took a couple of sacrificial animals, slaughtered them and drew the blood out and divided the blood into two separate receptacles. On the altar he placed the tablets of the Law and poured the blood over the altar and over the tablets of the Law. Then he took the other bucket of blood, and probably took with him a little willow stick and whittled the end of it so that when he dipped it in the blood it would bring out some droplets. All the Jewish people got blood sprinkled on them after they had agreed to the terms of the Covenant. The altar, representing the presence of God, had blood sprinkled on it.

There were two halves to the Covenant or contract. One half was what God agreed to do, and the other half was what man agreed to do. To put it another way, the Covenant had to do with man's relation to God and with man's relation to his fellow-man, hence the summary of the Law: "Thou shalt love the Lord thy God with all thy heart and thou shalt love thy neighbour as thyself." The ritual law comes first, and that is what man is supposed to do about God. This part contains the regulations for worship. In detail, the ritual regulations that God gave Moses were not enormously different from those which Moses got from his father-in-law, the High Priest of Midian. However, there is one very significant difference: all the other religions of the world see man as seeking God and the Judeo-Christian tradition sees God as seeking man. That distinction is terribly important. All the other religions in the world are different versions of man's guessing what you ought to do to establish contact with the divinity. Here at Mount Sinai God gave Moses his unlisted telephone number with the promise that when we dial, He will always answer.

That idea is fundamental to an understanding of Judaism and fundamental to an understanding of Christianity. "When two or three are gathered in my name, there am I in their midst." Jesus knew about this Covenant agreement between God and Moses.

Now where two or three Christians are gathered in His

name does not mean that when a couple of my Christian friends and I sit down over a cup of coffee and start talking about religion and even say some prayers, it's an official gathering. "Where two or three are gathered in my name" means they are gathered together as the Church, to do what the Church does, which has always been, of course, to offer the Holy Eucharist. This is the official act of the Church when gathered together.

What Jesus said is simply, "When you do this, I will be there." When He said, "This is my blood of the New Covenant. Do this," He was remembering what Moses had said at Mount Sinai: "This is the blood of the Old Covenant. Do this, and when you do, God will be there." God's promise under the Covenant is to be present when man worships Him according to the way God has revealed that He wants to be worshipped. This is what will work. This is my unlisted telephone number. Worship me in this fashion and I will be there.

In the second part of the Covenant, God revealed how he wanted the Jews to behave toward each other. This is highly significant. This is the first time in history that anybody had ever thought that God really cared about morality. Today we have made such an identification between morality and religion because we think that religion is mostly about being good.

Being good has the same relation to religion that being sober has to playing football. If I were a football coach I would not want my team to stay out all night getting drunk and chasing women just before a big game. Now you might think that the purpose of football is to produce sober young men. No, the purpose of sobriety is to produce good football players. Similarly, the purpose of morality is to produce good religious people, and not just Christians.

Now among the Jews at this time morality extended only to your blood kin. When God said to Moses, "Thou shalt not kill," everybody understood Him to mean, "Thou shalt not kill another Jew." The more of the Amalekites you kill, the better. This is the one way of understanding the strange paradox in the Old Testament where God on one hand takes a dim view of killing, and on the other hand encourages the Jews to go out and slaughter the Amalekites. Morality is tribal morality. This assumption is what lies behind the statement Jesus made to the Pharisee who had asked, "Who is my neighbour?" His answer was revolutionary, because He said, in effect, "My neighbour is that Samaritan over there." To a Pharisee steeped in the Old Law that was really revolutionary.

The Jews agreed, having heard the terms of the Covenant, to abide by the moral law; God in His turn promised to guide them in their desert wandering, to fight with them in their battles, and to bring them at last to Canaan, to the land flowing with milk and honey. Having made this agreement, they sealed it by an adoption ceremony in which the blood of the sacrifice was sprinkled on the tablets of the Law, on the altar representing God, and on each of the individual Jews. So they now had a blood relationship that was binding.

Now there are two parts to the Covenant or contract. The party of the first part is God, and the party of the second part is collective Judaism. God at that time did not make any private deals. He said, "I am going to negotiate with the union. You have to be a member of the union to work in this factory. It's a closed shop." However, there are some consequences to this decision. If man, on his part, breaks his agreement, then God is absolved of His responsibility under the agreement. That is to say, if one

Jew breaks the Covenant agreement, all the Jews are guilty. This is the background of Jewish history without which you really can't understand Judaism. Along those lines there is a story in the Book of Joshua that's fascinating. If you will remember old man Moses, he died in the wilderness, and he handed on the command of the Israelites to Joshua, who was their general when they conquered the Holy Land.

If you'll visualize a map of the Near East, from the Arabian desert the Jews went northwest and came into what is now Jordan, and they conquered and settled down and spent several years occupying this territory east of the Jordan River. With the rich, productive land that was already theirs, the Jews had an economic base from which to launch an attack into Palestine. Now the boundary of Palestine as you come up to it from the east is, of course, the Jordan River, and if you've seen pictures of the Jordan River, you know that for a good part of the length of it, it's kind of like the Grand Canyon. There's no way you can get an army across there. Just opposite the town of Jericho there was a shallow place where the river could be forded. But this ford was defended by Jericho, a fortified city.

You know the story. The Jews crossed the river and marched around the city for seven days and they blew their trumpets and the walls fell down and zappo, the Jews conquered them a city. Part of the Jewish law is that the first fruits belong to God, which means that when a Jew took a virgin piece of land and ploughed it up and put in a crop, the first year's harvest belonged to God. After that, God received a tenth. When a heifer cow went into production and had her first calf, if it was a bull calf it belonged to God. After that, every tenth calf. The same thing was true of a vineyard, an orchard, or whatever. The

133

first fruits belonged to God. The town of Jericho was the first city the Jews captured in their conquest of the Promised Land, so as a consequence, it was dedicated to God. It was put under a "taboo"; it was declared to be holy. So in a sense the Holy City was under a curse. For that reason all the citizens except Rahab the harlot, who had harboured Jewish spies and treated them kindly, were put to death. All of the material wealth of the city was either taken by the priest to be used in religious services or else burned and destroyed. The city was levelled, razed completely, because they either had to garrison this city with some of their own troops or else they had to destroy the city. Not only was it a good religious gesture to destroy the city, it was a good military gesture as well.

However, there was another little city just a few miles up-river. It was not as big as Jericho, but nevertheless it was a city from which a military movement could have been launched and would have cut off the Jewish access to the river crossing. Joshua dispatched a regiment of troops to go do the same thing to this town that they did to Jericho. But the Jews were roundly defeated when they attacked. Now God had promised the Jews that they would win their battles, and yet they had lost one. How could they account for that?

It turned out that the children of Israel had committed a trespass in the accursed thing, that is, the spoils from the town of Jericho. For Achan the son of Charmi, of the tribe of Judah, had taken of the accursed thing; as a matter of fact, in sacking the city he had found some bars of silver and gold, and a brand new suit of clothes. He'd taken it for his own use and had hidden it in his tent.

The anger of the Lord was kindled against the children of Israel. So when Joshua sent men from Jericho to the next town, his 3,000 men turned and fled from the enemy, and they smote them in the going down wherefore the hearts of the people melted and became like water. And Joshua rent his clothes and fell to the earth and put his face before the Ark of the Lord until the eventide. He and the elders of Israel put dust on their heads and Joshua said, "Alas, O Lord God, wherefore hast thou brought all this people over Jordan to deliver us into the hands of the Amorites to destroy us? Would to God we had been content and dwelt on the other side of Jordan." And Joshua went on, "What shall I say when Israel turned its back on its enemies, for the Canaanites and all the inhabitants of the land shall hear of it and shall encompass it and shall cut us off, cut off your name from the earth. Then God, what shall you do for your reputation?"

God said to Joshua, "Get up, wherefore liest thou thus upon thy face? Israel hath sinned and they have also transgressed my Covenant which I commanded them. For they have even taken of the accursed thing and have also stolen and dissembled and put it even among their own. Therefore the children of Israel could not stand before their enemies but turned their backs before their enemies because they were accursed."

This is God talking. If you Jews can't keep your agreement, then phooey on you. "Neither will I be with you any more except you do destroy the accursed thing from among you." So what the Jews did was to search the tents and they found Achan. Joshua and all Israel with him took Achan, the son of Charmi, and the silver and the garment and the gold and his sons and his daughters and his oxen and his asses and his sheep and his tent and his guppies and his parakeets and all he had and brought them into the valley of Achor. And all Israel stoned them with

135

stones and burned them with fire after they had stoned them, and they raised over them a great heap of stones under the sky. So the Lord turned from his fierce anger. They sent an army back to the little town of Ai, and this time they were victorious.

That's one of the weirdest stories in the Bible. Can you believe that this stuff is the inspired word of God? What you get is this man who steals something; okay, that's a reprehensible crime, a crime of sacrilege as well as theft. He takes it and hides it for his own use in his own tent, and God gets mad at the whole durn tribe, because one man had sinned. The Jews then took out this poor old sinner and his wife and his children and his asses and his puppy dog and his kitty cat and stoned them all. Then God said, "All right, that's more like it. Now I'll be good to you and come back and dwell with you and help you win your battles."

That is not the God of love that we know through Jesus Christ, surely not. But wait a minute. We had spoken earlier about the corporate nature of man. Have any of you mamas and papas had the experience of Johnny's teacher keeping the whole class in after school because nobody would tell who threw the eraser and hit her in the neck? Let's see how unjust and irrational God was behaving here. Why did God get mad at all the Jews for Achan's sin? Perhaps the Jews in those days were like the Americans now, had convinced Achan that the man who dressed in fine clothes and had money in his pocket was somehow a better and more honorable man than the man who dressed poorly because he was in need. Had they in any sense participated in his guilt? You're durn right they had. I wonder how many other Jews who did not take all these spoils for their own personal use had complained about giving them to God.

So all these righteous Jews took this sinful Jew outside to the edge of town and put him to death, vigorously and violently. And when I pick up a stone and throw it at Achan and say, "Take that, you dirty rascal," I am saying to myself, "See, I'm not like that. See how much I hate that sin." This is what a lynch mob really is. It is a human sacrifice by which the community purges itself of its guilt. In other words, when an Achan does openly what I have done only in my imagination, in my fantasies, that frightens me. It scares me to death. It tells me that with adequate provocation under the right circumstances, I could do that, too. And I'm not willing to admit to myself that I'm like that. Therefore I will prove my purity and my innocence by the fierceness of my wrath against the sinner, and put him to death.

What the Jews had here was a law-abiding, righteous community with one rotten member, and they had to deal with this. The way they dealt with Achan was to get rid of him. He will cause the rottenness to spread because rottenness is contagious. At least, that's the way it looks on the surface.

The truth of the matter is that once upon a time some men brought to Jesus a woman taken in adultery and the Law of Moses said she should be stoned like Achan. The Roman law said, "No, only Romans can assess and carry out a capital sentence." And these smart-alec lawyers in Jerusalem got Jesus in a real trap. Here's a gal who is obviously guilty. They had witnesses to that. So what do you say, boss? If He says stone her, He's breaking Roman law. If He says let her go, He's breaking Mosaic Law. He's in a trap. You know what He said, of course. "Go ahead, stone her. But just for sport, let him that is without sin cast the first stone."

Nobody threw any stones. You see, there *is* no righteous community. These same people took Jesus and hauled Him outside the camp like Achan and put him to death. You'll notice that this is the reverse of the Achan story. The way the Old Testament deals with sin and the sinner is to get rid of him, exclude him, kick him out, put him to death, to protect the community from the contamination of the wicked member. As we shall see, there are two kinds of people that society will not tolerate: the very, very bad, and the very, very good. When a saint comes along there are only two things you can do: one of them is to acknowledge his moral superiority and try to imitate him, and the other is to throw rocks at him. They took Achan outside the camp, outside the city. That's important. They didn't want to contaminate the camp with the blood of this vicious man. The result is a purified community which in psychological terms is free of its nagging sense of its own guilt. See how righteous we are.

In the case of Jesus, the rotten community with one righteous member, they also took him outside the city and put him to death. Where is the Covenant? On the one hand with Achan, you have a separation between the presumed righteous community and the wicked one. On the other hand, you have a separation between the unrighteous community and the righteous one. The Covenant is with the righteous. And so when Christ was led outside the city and nailed to the tree, where is the Covenant? It happened, you see, that Good Friday night all the pious Jews went to bed, pulled the Covenant up over their heads and went sound asleep. When they woke up the next morning, the Covenant was gone. Somebody snuck in in the night and pulled all the covers off them and they were naked, shivering, and cold. Under the Old Covenant, under the

Natural Man theory, the way of dealing with Achan is the only way man can deal with sin: to separate himself from it.

I want you to feel how inevitably right the Jews were in treating Achan in that fashion. They couldn't do anything else. Not only their religion, but their military discipline would have been hopelessly compromised if they hadn't dealt with Achan in this way. There's no way you can deal with sin except the way they dealt with it, right? And yet God turns that whole programme inside out and upside down. The Covenant is now with those who will go outside the city and identify with Jesus. There is only one way into the New Covenant community, and that is through penance. Even of those who crucified Him, Jesus prayed, "Forgive them, God, the stupid dumb clucks. They haven't the foggiest notion of what they're doing."

9

THE JUDGES AND JESUS

After the conquest of Jericho we move into the period of the Judges, when the Jews moved into the Holy Land God promised that they would conquer. For a number of generations the Jews occupied the hill country of Palestine, only gradually becoming agricultural people, marrying and fusing with the other dominant culture. The result was a cultural amalgam. During the time of the Book of Judges, the Jewish tribes led a rather wild and lawless life, fighting their enemies and each other. One phrase summarizes these times: "There was no king in those days and every man did what was right in his own eyes."

But one thing the Jews retained was their notion of history, the belief that God had intervened and meddled in human affairs, that the future was not predetermined. During the time of the Judges, the Jews found what they believed was a pattern in history. After they invaded the Promised Land, settled down and prospered, then they forgot God and began to flirt around with those alien gods of the Canaanites. The result was apostasy, which is the technical term for the abandonment of one's faith. As a consequence, God would punish them through an invasion of their land by other Bedouin tribes from the desert, tribes that burned, raided, raped, and destroyed. Then there would be a national repentance, a return to Jehovah, and at that point God would raise up a deliverer. This pattern was repeated over and over again in Judges. Peace was followed by prosperity, which was followed by apostasy, followed by catastrophe, and then repentance and the deliverer.

Following the period of the Judges these tribes of Jews united first under Saul and David, and then established themselves as a kingdom. Under David's son Solomon, the Jews had built a rich and prosperous empire. But, true to form, they could not stand prosperity; the empire held together during the time of Solomon, then broke into a northern kingdom and a southern kingdom, and political fortunes began to fail. From number one, Israel became the low man on the totem pole and, as a consequence, was kicked around.

The inhabitants in the north were conquered in 597 B.C. and the army, nobility, and merchants were carried off into captivity, leaving the peasants behind. In 586 the southern kingdom was also conquered by Babylon and again the upper crust was carried off to captivity and scattered, and lost their identity as Jews. The Jews from Jerusalem who were carried into captivity into Babylon were allowed to congregate and as a result did not lose their identity. After Persia conquered Babylon, a tiny handful of Jews were allowed to return to Palestine to the capital city which was laid waste, to a land that was desolate.

Slowly the fortunes of the Jewish people improved, and Jerusalem became again an important city, both culturally and economically. In the Diaspora or dispersal the Jews spread into the Gentile world and became merchants and craftsmen. When Alexander the Great conquered the Persian empire, the Jews allied with him and were absorbed without incident. When Alexander died, this empire was divided into three parts: Africa, Europe and Asia, with Damascus in Syria as the capital. The Damascene emperor decided that all the subjects in his empire would speak Greek, would worship Greek gods, and adopt the Greek culture. The Jews rebelled and fought a war of liberation, after which they established independence briefly under the Maccabees. When peace came these Jews asked for help from Rome, and Rome was happy to furnish aid, so Palestine became a province of the Roman empire with their own rulers, and this was the situation at the time of Jesus.

Now Rome had an enlightened colonial policy. They allowed people to maintain their religion and customs, just as long as they kept the Roman peace and paid their taxes. But even this mild form of foreign dominion was too much for the Jews, who felt that this was another catastrophe. Long before this time, as you can see from their history, they really did not have an awful lot to crow about. They remembered a time when they had been top dog; they were God's chosen people, and they could not understand why God was allowing his favourites to be so unimportant. In addition, they had just emerged from hard times under the Macedonians, when it was a capital offence to own a copy of Jewish Scriptures. The Jews had had enough trouble to convince them that they had neither the power nor the wisdom to amount to much. They began to think of a deliverer who would come. Of course, it was inconceivable that their deliverer would be other than a son of David. The family of David had ruled in Jerusalem, and their king should be of that line. Because a man was made king by anointing, they began to speak of the "anointed one". So they thought it was time for God to raise up the Messiah, the Anointed One.

The Jewish conception of what that Messiah would be like was based on several dogmatic assumptions. First,

The Judges and Jesus

there was the notion of the Covenant. God had chosen the Jewish people and He was not going to go back on that choice. He had made a promise and would fulfil it. Thus the Jews had a unique position as defined by their relationship to God. We belong to the Covenant, they said, and immediately that thought called up a mental picture: the image of the sacrifice at Mount Sinai, the slaughtered animals and Moses sprinkling blood on all the people.

Another idea which dominated the thinking of the Jews was the notion that once upon a time they had been the top dogs of the known world. They remembered Solomon and were forever hoping and planning to restore his kingdom. The mental picture that went along with that idea was that of an oriental potentate, sitting in a huge palace with marble floors, fluted columns, chariots, slaves, gold and precious gems.

Finally, when the Messiah came, they told themselves, he was going to lead a successful revolution against the Roman Empire, overthrow the empire, and establish a Jewish nation, one of righteousness, replacing Rome with Jerusalem as the centre of world political power and inaugurating a universal reign of justice.

As a matter of fact, at the time Jesus was born and for years thereafter, every so often there would be a guerrilla operation in the hills started by a superpatriot who would claim himself to be the Messiah. He would attract hippies, runaway slaves, college students, and left-wing radicals. The superpatriots would gather around such a leader and begin low-level military operations. To support small-scale operations, they needed money, and these bands would finance their operations by raids on wealthy Jews who collaborated with the Romans, those who were content to be Roman subjects. A merchant caravan would be pounced on, and a band of attackers would carry away booty. They called themselves patriots, but of course the Romans called them bandits. The Romans would put up with this resistance long enough for these bandits to feel secure in their hideouts, and then Rome would say enough, and would send out legions to meet the upstarts in battle. Rome would always win. Those not killed in battle would be crucified, not as rebels but as bandits.

There had been a dozen or fifteen Messiahs, all of whom turned out not to be the Messiah, because they ended up on crosses and the Messiah was a winner, not a loser. The true Messiah, they believed, would conquer the Romans and establish a kingdom of God. And if he's not the Messiah, then the Romans would crucify him.

There were three things the Jews expected the Messiah to do: to cure poverty, to establish world empire, and to come in glory. When John the Baptist appeared urging repentance, he was speaking to Jews who were aware of the sequence of events of peace, prosperity, apostasy, repentance. John preached baptism, washing the filth and slime off the Covenant, and the place he chose, the Jordan River, was the place where the Jews had entered the Holy Land. This was calling the Jews back to their origins. The time is come and God will free His people, but it is conditional upon a national repentance.

When Jesus accepted the baptism of John, He went off into the wilderness and like Moses before Him, said, "What do I do now?" And there in the desert He planned His ministry. Satan appeared to Him and the first temptation offered Jesus was to cure poverty. Satan said, "Turn these stones into bread. You're the son of God and the people out there who are waiting for the Messiah will expect you to do that." And Jesus replied, "It is written

144

that man shall not live by bread alone, but by every word that proceedeth out of the mouth of God." The old prophecy meant something more than bread, and so Jesus rejected that concept of the Messianic office.

The next temptation was that Satan took Jesus up on a high mountain and showed Him the glory of the world, and said, "Do it this way. You are the son of God so you can't possibly lose. Fulfil this expectation and rule the nations according to God's law and justice." Satan was trying to tempt Our Lord to the sin of personal aggrandizement, to be the world conqueror, to which Jesus replied, "I can't do that." The only way the world can be conquered and brought under one rule is by making compromises that the honourable man can't make. So Jesus rejected that temptation.

The third temptation had to do with the expectation that the sky would open, there would be a clap of thunder and a blare of trumpets, and down would come the chosen one, legions of angels following him from the throne of glory. Satan took Jesus up on the pinnacle of the temple and showed Him the throng of worshippers below and said, "If you float down out of the sky, people will accept you as the Messiah." But Jesus rejected this as the cheapest trick of all, and this exhausted the possibilities of the expectations of the community at large. Jesus returned to the world to preach that the kingdom of God has already happened, is already here. All they had to do was to get on the bandwagon. And yet when they looked about, nothing much was really happening. For the Jews expected the Messiah to come as another David, but Jesus thought of Himself as another Moses. They expected Him to come to renew the kingdom, not renew the Covenant.

If you notice, gospel stories told about Jesus parallel

over and over incidents in the life of Moses. When Moses was born a wicked king was killing all of the little Hebrew boy babies. Moses came out of Egypt and Jesus went down into Egypt so He could come out. Seventy elders assisted Moses in the judgement of the Jews, and seventy were sent by Jesus, two by two, into every village. The Old Covenant had twelve patriarchs; Jesus chose twelve apostles. The Old Law was given on a mountainside and the New Law was given in the Sermon on the Mount. His one life and ministry was the prophecy accomplished by Moses. Jesus came to restore the Covenant.

This, however, was not what was in the minds of the disciples. In a small way Jesus repeated the ministry of almost any good priest today, ministering to a people who don't see the world the way He does. He baptizes people who have no idea what baptism is all about. He marries them, and they have no notion of what marriage is about. They take communion and they don't know what communion is all about. The last phase of His public ministry resulted in a demonstration, beginning at the city gate of Jerusalem. There was a triumphal procession. People broke branches, shouted, "Hosanna to the Son of David! Blessed is He who cometh in the Name of the Lord!" Now this was open rebellion and the Romans knew it. It was Passover and the city was crowded with many thousands of pilgrims who were taking part in the observance. There probably were not more than a thousand Roman soldiers facing half a million Jews. Undoubtedly word spread like wildfire, and the Roman soldiers got to their battle stations and expected the worst.

The Temple was in front of a large square. Opposite the Temple was the Citadel, the barracks-fortress of the Romans. All expected an attack on the Citadel and the subsequent overthrow of the Roman garrison. So when Jesus led a mob of superpatriotic, zealous Jews into the centre of the square, all expected Him to say, "Go get 'em." Instead, He turned His back to the Citadel, ignoring the Roman army, stormed into the Temple and overthrew the tables of money changers, scourged them, and kicked out all the cattle. In the quiet that followed, He said, "It is written my house shall be a house of prayer and yet you have turned it into a den of thieves." Then He turned and went on out of the city leaving everybody standing there with their jaws slack. People often wondered why the crowd which was so enthusiastic on Sunday could crucify Him on Friday. In all probability there were many of the same people there and He had let them down, had disappointed them. They had their appetites whetted for battle but He turned away.

He came back the next day and taught in the Temple. You can imagine the tension in town. Sometime during the week a man named Barabbas had attacked the Citadel and was thwarted. He and a couple of his lieutenants were captured. All during the week the Jewish big shots would come and say to Jesus, "Are you the Messiah, tell us!" On Thursday, Jesus was asked, "Is it lawful to give tribute to Caesar?" You know the answer. He asked for a denarius and said, "Whose image is on this?" "Caesar's," they said. "Render unto Caesar the things that are Caesar's and unto God the things that are God's." From that moment He lost the support of the mob, which was revolutionary in temperament. That night He came into town for the Last Supper by back alleys.

Let's see what happened at that supper.

Jesus knew that death was coming, the death of Achan. And He knew that death would be regarded by all as a sign of God's rejection of Him. God would repudiate Jesus on Friday, or so the Pharisees would say. But Jesus conceived of His death in terms of another Covenant sacrifice. What He was doing was repeating the sacrifice of Sinai, offering Himself as the sacrifice of a New Covenant to end all sacrifice.

How could He get that across to these people? In the early days of the Old Covenant every family head was qualified to offer sacrifice. Later on the privilege was reserved for the priesthood, with one exception – the small, intimate, domestic dinner would always retain the ideal and character of sacrifice, the table blessing at the family meal. Likewise, Jesus gathered His disciples together at the Last Supper, and returned thanks. The form was prescribed. It was the same in every family. The daddy or host at the dinner party would stand at the head of the table and say, "The Lord be with you."

The others would reply, "And with thy spirit."

Then he would say, "Lift up your hearts."

And they would answer, "We lift them up unto the Lord."

"Let us give thanks to the Lord our God."

"It is very meet and right so to do."

"It is very meet and right and our bounden duty that we should give thanks unto Thee, O Lord most holy . . . especially do we thank you for the fruits of the earth of which we are about to partake."

Then they would take one of those little hard French rolls and break it into as many pieces as there were people at the table, pass it around, and all would eat of the common loaf. Then they would go in to dinner. After dinner the daddy would stand at the head and take a cup of wine in which had been mingled a bit of water. Daddy would take the wine and say, "The Lord be with you . . . Lift up your hearts . . . and especially do we thank you for the Covenant."

When Jesus blessed the cup, this was a sacrifice, and all present knew it. At the Last Supper Jesus took the bread into His hands and said, "The Lord be with you." No Jew would have dared to alter that table blessing. They had heard it every day of their lives. It had always been exactly the same. But Jesus at the Last Supper did a crazy thing. He said the regular blessing but as He broke the bread He said, "Eat this because it is my body which is given for you. When you do this we will meet again." No explanation. After supper, Jesus took the cup of wine and said the blessing: "The Lord be with you," and so on. "Especially do we thank you for the Covenant." Now before we continue, remember that the one thing the Jews do not do is drink blood. But Jesus said, "That's my blood you're drinking." Peter goes, "Arhhhg." Yet they all drank. He said, "This is my blood of the New Covenant." What was the blood of the Old Covenant? At Mount Sinai. Jesus said, "All you drink this. Do this, and you will know me again."

Then He pulled the footwashing. This was reminiscent of the washing of the feet of the High Priest in the Temple before he takes up his duties, and also reflected the custom of the dinner party host ordering a slave to wash the feet of his guests. Jesus waited until after dinner to wash the feet of the disciples. "I am your master," He told them, "and look what I am doing." Jesus told them over and over again that he who is the big shot must be the servant. Peter said, "You're not going to wash my feet." To which Jesus replied, "If I don't wash yours, you will have no participation with me." This was a reference to the High

Priest and the Covenant, but it's not been repeated as a sacrament because the Christian is always on duty.

At the Last Supper Jesus instituted the sacrifice of the New Covenant and inaugurated priests into their duties. Then He got up and took them outside to Gethsemane and waited and prayed. Judas came with the soldiers who arrested Jesus. He was tried and put to death. Clearly, according to many Jews, God had rejected Jesus and His Messianic claim.

Three evenings later, two of the disciples left Jerusalem and were going to the suburban town of Emmaus outside of Jerusalem when a stranger came and walked with them and asked them why they were so downcast. They said, "You must be a stranger in these parts." And they proceeded to tell him about Jesus, whom they had thought to be a man of God, the Messiah himself. They admitted that they must have been mistaken because he was crucified and put to death. "We trusted that he should have been the one to redeem Israel." The stranger said that it was necessary that the Messiah should suffer, but the disciples still didn't get the message. It was near evening and they invited him to supper. No devout Jew would say grace in another man's house, but this stranger did. He began with those words, "Lift up your hearts." Suddenly their eyes were opened and He was known to them in the breaking of the bread. They jumped up and ran all the way back to Jerusalem, saying to everyone. "We figured it out!" It was the Eucharist that they saw in the crucifixion. As often as you eat this bread and drink this cup you explain the Lord's death until He returns. What Jesus had done in the Last Supper was to fix it for ever so that any Jew who knew what had happened at the Last Supper would identify and associate the sacrifice of the bread and the wine with the sacrifice of His body and blood, with a Covenant sacrifice. He had, then, exactly reversed the relationship between the community and the individual as symbolized in the Achan story. The Covenant got up and left town and moved out on the hillside and gathered itself about the cross. When He said, "As often as ye do this," what was this?

This was eating supper.

How often did He expect them to do this?

Every day.

Though they were doing good works in various parts of the country, He expected them to get together for meals. He also said when two or three are gathered in My Name, there am I. "In My Name" makes the gathering official.

What He had done was to inaugurate a New Covenant, and He was a new Moses and a new Adam. God had made a new start. He had not given up on man. The Old Testament said that God rested on the seventh day, which was therefore holy. The Christians came along and changed that day to Sunday, because after the Fall there was a new creation, a new Adam, a new humanity, and God finished this job on Sunday with the resurrection of Jesus Christ. In the mind of the early Church there was a link between the Eucharist and Good Friday which was essential and fundamental. And it was in the breaking of the bread that the early Church was primarily aware of the continuing presence of Christ in their midst. What we do in the Eucharist is to celebrate and offer the sacrifice of the New Covenant.

10

· ·

ATONEMENT I

If you drive your car down a backwoods road in Georgia or
east Tennessee or west Texas, you are liable to see a sign
tacked up on a fence post that says, "Jesus saves." No one
will quarrel with that. It is the one doctrinal statement which
everyone who remotely professes the name of Christian will
agree with. But if you want to see someone squirm and
stammer, ask him what it means, this phrase, "Jesus saves."
What are we saved from? What are we saved for?

Salvation has meant different things in different ages.
While the Church, through her tradition, through her
general councils and through the *consensus fidelium* has
carefully and explicitly defined a great many things, she has
never defined what she means by salvation. Each new wave
of Christian civilization has redefined the doctrine. After
all, Christianity has been the religion of half a dozen
civilizations; when you have a different set of dogmatic
assumptions you have a slightly different notion of how to
define the question of what's the matter with man. The
fascinating thing is that as Christianity moves into these
different civilizations – the classical, the medieval, the
Byzantine, the modern, with their different notions of what
the human problem is – people still find it true that "Jesus
saves." There is a universality about the salvific works of
Jesus Christ that makes them valid and effective no matter
how you define the problem.

In the New Testament we have the testimony of both Jews and Greeks that people here were interested in salvation. When Paul and Silas were in prison and the angel came and released their fetters, the gaoler's first question on finding them still there was, "What must I do to be saved?" The Jews were constantly saying, "What must I do to be saved?"

In the time of Christ both Jews and Greeks were part of the Roman Empire, and it was a common expectation among everyone, educated and ignorant, religious and irreligious, that the world was coming to an end fairly soon. As you will recall, there's much talk in the New Testament about the coming end of the world. Jesus talks about it and the disciples talk about it, St Paul as well, and of course, St John in the Book of Revelation. Men's optimism had turned into defeatism throughout the Roman Empire as well as among the Jewish people. There was a common notion of a coming cataclysm. On the other side of this cataclysm there would be survivors who, having lived through the purge, would enjoy a new earth and a new Heaven. Certainly that idea was involved in the notion of salvation. The question, "How can I be saved?" then meant, "How can I survive the great cataclysm?" The answer: "Believe in the Lord Jesus Christ and thou shalt survive the coming cataclysm."

With only a slight difference of emphasis, this interpretation of a cataclysm in which some survivors are renewed in fresh vitality can be identified with the survival or the resurrection of the body after death, where all is fresh, new, and vital. The first-century Christian, then, was living between two events: the crucifixion and resurrection of Christ, and the final denouement of history. As for his identification with the final end in catastrophe, it might be said without doing an injustice to the view of St Peter and St Paul that the death and resurrection of Christ was an anticipation of the first fruits of the new life that would occur after the cataclysm, and that all of us by our union with Him in His mystical body were guaranteed that survival.

That's one view, and that view has never been entirely abandoned. It's in the Creed: I believe that Christ will come again. I believe in the resurrection of the body and the life of the world to come, which is the world on the other side of the end of the world.

Apart from the coming of a great cataclysm, what did the Jew regard as his chief problem? One of the things that we need to try to recover from the New Testament is the idea that the resurrection of Christ was a victory over Satan, the demons, and the Host of Hell. That doesn't mean a great deal to us today because we don't believe in demons. And that proves that Jesus defeated them, because once people did. When I say the death and resurrection of Christ was a victory over demons you say, "That's ridiculous. The demons don't bother us anymore," and I say, "You see? It worked. The demons have gone!" They haven't, of course. But they have been largely put in their place. They don't pester us like they pestered people two thousand years ago.

The Jews of Our Lord's day lived in a world realistically inhabited by demons. It's hard to understand just what it meant to believe in the reality of a host of demons. Read in St Paul and in the gospels about "the Law". "Law" to St Paul and the rabbis meant the ritual law. These laws were what some would call taboos or superstition, but those are words we use to describe someone else's belief and not our own. When the Jew had violated a taboo, after a horrible sense of shame there was also a real dread that the goblins have seen you commit your sin and are going to get you. It's precisely because you don't know what they will do that they are objects of dread and fear. That is what the Jews and Greeks and everyone else meant by the demons.

When the Jews spoke of breaking the Law, they made no distinction between breaking the ritual law and breaking the moral law. Touching a dead body was taboo. Menstruation was spooky, since the Jews believed that the life was in the blood, so they were scared of the ladies once a month and could not even go near them. And there were other things: eating pork, working on the Sabbath, and thousands of other pesky things you couldn't do. Also cheating your neighbour in a business transaction or committing adultery or envying or coveting; these too were forbidden. They made no distinction between what we would recognize as a moral prohibition and a cultic ritual violation because in any event, the result was the same. The natural condition of man was to be exposed to the goblins. *It was keeping the Law that kept the goblins at bay.* So the Jew was careful to keep the Law.

Now if he broke the Law, he sought to rid himself of guilt in order to be able to offer sacrifices. Certain of these sins or violations were remitted by the payment of a money fine for use in the temple. Occasionally there were certain ritual washings. Normally, however, purification was achieved by the passage of time. You had to wait the prescribed amount of time, thirty days, six months, and then you went back and got a clean bill of health and offered the sacrifice. You did not offer the sacrifice to take away the guilt; you got rid of the guilt in order to offer the sacrifice. That's the Jewish way of thinking. Then they continued to offer the sacrifices because that kept the demons at bay. Think of that in terms of the all-sufficient sacrifice of Christ once offered for the sin and guilt of all mankind. Satan was solidly and finally defeated by Christ on Calvary.

The weekly Christian sacrifice assured this, the reminder of the victory of Christ over the demons. With this in the back of your mind, go back and read St Paul's epistles and the gospels, and note all of those demonic references. The Christian by his incorporation into Christ at baptism is dead and buried and risen with Christ. He has passed through and come out on the other side of that world inhabited by demons. This, in large part, is what salvation meant to the Jewish Christian of the New Testament.

Now bear in mind that what terrifies you most about demonic attack is that you don't know what they are going to do, but you know it might be ghastly and brutal. Consequently, the moment you are most exposed to demonic attack is at the moment of death, when you step out of the familiar time and space into that strange and unfamiliar spirit world from which none of us has returned. That's when the goblins are most likely to grab your soul and go shrieking off to hell with it. It is precisely this fate that the Christian had learned not to fear because Christ had gone through that for us and come back, and in our baptism we have been united to Him, on the other side of His death. So death is an experience that is already behind us, and not something we need to fear as we look foward to it.

Another view of the atonement occurs slightly later than the contemporary ideas of cataclysm and a redemption from the demons. Within a generation after the death of Christ most Christians were non-Jews. They were spoken of in the New Testament as simply Greeks, but Greek here doesn't necessarily mean Greek. Although Rome was the political master of the Mediterranean world, the victories of Alexander the Great had made Greek culture, language, philosophy, and religion the dominant influence in the Mediterranean world. In the New Testament when they speak of Jew and Greek, what they really mean is Jew and Gentile. Greek civilization had become universal in its influence.

Of course, this Greek culture became diluted as it travelled into Gaul, Italy, Spain, and Britain, and became intermixed with the elements of local culture, so that it wasn't exactly the same civilization you find in the classical world of Homer and Aristotle. It is known as Hellenic, in contrast to pure Greek. This Hellenic culture was profoundly influenced by Greek literature and drama. All over the Mediterranean world you find ruins of outdoor, open-air theatres where Greek plays were performed. And the dominant mode of Greek drama was the tragedy, a literary form that contained the Greek statement about the human problem. Almost everyone who lived in the Hellenic world and who attended the tragedies knew and understood the essential religious origin of the tragedy, the tragic theme which evolved and developed out of the Greek religious reflection upon the human situation and the human condition.

Aristotle says that the tragedy is divided into four parts, or acts. The first of these acts presents a situation, usually a social situation, in which there is a certain harmony and equilibrium of all the elements of the play. The act continues long enough for you to identify how the plot of the play is going to develop, but essentially Act I represents a relative stability. Act II introduces into this harmony an alien factor. At first this factor seems innocent and insignificant. And yet throughout the act a conflict develops and it is soon apparent that there is an irreconcilable incompatibility between opposing forces. This conflict erupts in Act III which Aristotle called the Scene of Suffering. Something goes; something is destroyed. Now let me point out here that tragedy is not the story of conflict between good and evil. That's a comedy. Tragedy is the conflict between two forces, both of which are good. This is what makes the tragedy so tragic. And in the process of the third act, one of these goods is destroyed and sometimes both of them. Someone dies or commits suicide or everybody kills each other. There is a fourth act in which it is evident that as a result of the catastrophe a new and higher harmony has been achieved.

To fix this pattern in your mind I want to give you a hypothetical tragedy, a melodrama, if you will. We first want an opening scene in which there is harmony and equilibrium. So we will select the parsonage of the Methodist church of a Midwestern nineteenth-century town in which the preacher and his two daughters are seated around a piano on a Sunday afternoon, singing hymns. Now you can hardly beat that for peace and harmony. Then in Act II the travelling salesman comes to town. He looks for room and board for a week or two and the parson says, "Why don't we let this nice man have our guest room?" And of course, this is a pious act of Christian charity. Nothing can go wrong with this except that the two daughters fall in love with the stranger who perfidiously courts both of them, so we begin to get the sense of impending disaster. And sure enough, the day arrives when the salesman leaves town and a short while later it turns out that one of the girls is pregnant and in her shame and humiliation she commits suicide. Now that completely wrecks the harmony, and the scene is of suffering. As for Act IV, the surviving daughter becomes a medical missionary to China, and in the last scene we see her serving the heathen Chinese with serene and godly contentment on her face. That's the tragic pattern.

Greek tragedy doesn't say that this is the way things are, but the way things ought to be. The conflict between good and incompatible good is built into the human condition. There is no way of avoiding the fact that there are irreconcilable goods. We have to make choices between goods, but that really isn't the essence of tragedy. Tragedy is when these two goods butt heads so that one destroys the other.

The truth was recognized at this time, not only by the Jews but by the Gentiles, that Judaism was the finest thing the world had seen up to that time. By the time of Christ there were Jews living in a Jewish colony or ghetto in every major city in the Roman Empire. Any town of ten thousand people had a synagogue. In addition to the Jews who attended, there were large numbers of non-Jews who also attended the synagogue and these were known by the term "God-fearers". As we read the New Testament account of the Roman centurion Cornelius, it is said of him, "He was a man who feared God." God-fearers were simply pious people strongly attracted to the Jewish religion who attended the synagogue every Sabbath, people who were already intimately acquainted with the Old Testament and therefore familiar with the idea of a Messiah who was to come. They recognized the ethical monotheism of Judaism as imminently respectable and were very much attracted to it.

It was largely from these Gentile "God-fearers" that the first converts came. And they were already acquainted with the Old Testament. And the Old Covenant was the finest thing the world had seen up to that time. No doubt about it. The Jewish religious leaders, the members of the Sanhedrin, were not really wicked people. On the contrary, they were earnest, sincere, devout, pious men, reverent and devoted servants of the Lord.

The Roman governor Pontius Pilate was not a wicked man. The idea of justice was important to Romans and Pilate was a conscientious administrator of Roman law. It was not a ruthless, tyrannical system. The population of the city of Jerusalem that cried, "Crucify him!" was not a bunch of fanatics setting out to burn the suburbs. They were devout. They were earnest and sincere Jewish people. Also, Roman military discipline was probably the best the world had ever seen. Roman soldiers were dignified, disciplined, and well-behaved troops. All these people believed whole-heartedly in the Old Testament Law, in Roman justice, and they regarded Christ as a threat to the established order.

It was into this scene of relative harmony and equilibrium that the tiny little baby was born. Throughout the life of Jesus, during the first of His public ministry He was received gladly and joyfully. The common people flocked around, He healed the sick and fed the hungry. He preached the optimistic doctrine that the kingdom of Heaven was at hand. But as time went on it became more difficult to reconcile the life and ministry and message of Christ with that of the authorities. Tension mounted and the community showed more and more strain. Finally there was a scene of suffering in which Christ was crucified. This is the stuff of tragedy.

Now, at first glance it would seem like the good thing that was destroyed was Christ. No so. What was destroyed by being exposed as inadequate is that initial equilibrium – the goodness of the Old Covenant religion, the justice of Roman law. When the centurion at the death of Christ says, "Surely this was a just man," he was condemning Roman justice, because you can't say that and at the same time say that justice had been done. Putting to death a just man is not justice. Therefore Roman justice and Old Testament religion were broken, shattered, utterly destroyed.

Aristotle had further said that the purpose of tragedy is to act as a spiritual and psychological purgative by which our baser emotions and expectations are cleansed, exalted, and elevated. You don't go away from a tragedy feeling sad. You go away from a tragedy saying, "Wow! I hadn't realized what potentialities for greatness lie in the ordinary human heart."

So the Gentile converts to Christianity had no problem seeing the Christ story as the fulfilment of the Hellenic understanding of the human condition. After sufficient instruction and when deemed spiritually ready, he was baptized and for the first time was allowed to participate in the communion service.

Let me describe one of these early Eucharists. When Papa and Mama and the kids left home to go to church, first they would go to the bread box and take out a roll or biscuit. Also, each member of the family would have as essential equipment a small amphora, a little bottle about the size of a perfume bottle. Each member of the family would fill up his little bottle from the family stock of red table wine. So everyone went to church with their own bottle of wine and their own biscuit, taken from their own pantry. This represented the common stuff of ordinary life. When they got to church, after some initial reading of prayers and Scripture, the communion service began. Everyone in the congregation would go to the altar and there would be a deacon with a large platter. Each person would put his biscuit on the platter. Another deacon would have a large goblet and each person would pour his amphora of wine into the goblet. Then he would go back and sit down and sing hymns while the procession brought the bread and wine to the priest. Then the priest would bless it, as Christ first took it and blessed it. A convert was told that in the act of blessing, Christ entered into the bread and wine. It was Christ's sacramental body and blood; it had undergone a transformation. What you have here is the invasion of the natural by the supernatural. The ordinary equilibrium of man's daily life is being infused with an alien element.

After the prayer of consecration, then, the priest would take the bread and break it into tiny pieces. Now it is interesting that before I place my biscuit on the platter, I can point to it and say, "That's mine, and that one over there is yours." But once we have poured my wine into the large goblet, I can't say, "That's my wine." And once the bread is broken and fragmented, what I have now is not a collection of individual biscuits, but a pile of crumbs. Mine, my own individual bread and wine, loses its identity. It is lost and merged into that larger identity of the whole. And the bread which is the body of Christ is broken, fragmented.

This is the scene of suffering. My natural self, represented by the bread and wine, is destroyed, demolished. What was "mine" is gone. Visibly and spiritually it is no longer just plain ordinary bread; it is very special bread: the bread of life, the bread of angels, the body of Christ. And then in the fourth act, we all go up and receive again what we have brought. I have brought my own individual bottle, and I receive from a common chalice. I have brought my own individual biscuit and what I receive is a handful of crumbs no longer definable as mine, a means whereby Christ returns in a kind of Easter to me and becomes a part of me, so that I now become a part of Him and His risen life, His glorified life, His post-resurrection life, which is then lived in me.

The Hellenic convert to Christianity was intimately conversant as a spectator with the tragic theme and pattern of action. When he participated in the communion service, he recognized the Christ story as the tragedy which exemplifies in itself all of the elements of the tragic story and raises them all to the cosmic plain because it is God Himself who dies on the cross and comes back to life again. And this Hellenic man has witnessed this, not as a spectator from the balcony but as an actor in the drama. That is, he himself has gone through this drama – spiritually, sacramentally, symbolically, but really – in the offering to God of the ordinary stuff of one's daily life, allowing God to enter into it and to be broken so that not only is God's body broken in the Mass but my own natural goodness is also destroyed. Then my natural goodness along with God's body is returned to me so that I participate in and share in that fourth stage of the new and elevated and more perfect equilibrium, which is the risen life of Christ communicated to me.

This was undoubtedly the way salvation was experienced by the Hellenic Christian convert of the first, second, and third centuries. And again you will notice the centrality of the communion service. Salvation, for him, then, was not just something he heard about, something a man assented to in his mind, but something which happened to him over and over, Sunday after Sunday.

By the fourth century, after Christianity was legalized, the first Christian Emperor Constantine divided the Empire into two governments, one in Rome and one in Constantinople, named after himself. From then on the Roman Empire was divided into two separate cultures. Then the western part was overrun by Germanic barbarians, and this further accelerated the cultural decline. The eastern part continued as a Greek-speaking people and it evolved after a thousand years into that characteristically Eastern European city known as Byzantium. Now this was a new civilization with a new set of dogmas. Their conception of what was wrong with man was interestingly enough not unlike that of the twentieth century. They regarded the human condition as a kind of spiritual disease. Man's nature was a visible consequence of an endemic spiritual sickness, and Christ had come to bring spiritual wholeness and health. They believed that we are united to Christ and His healthiness in baptism, and they even spoke of communion as the medicine of immortality whereby the spiritual sickness of man is cured and healed in order that he might become holy. Out of this view the Eastern Orthodox and the Byzantine Church produced a vast number of saints and a remarkable degree of Christian holiness in ordinary and sometimes illiterate people.

The other half of the Empire was the Latin West, and included everything in Europe west of the Danube: Germany, Austria, Italy, Spain, Scandinavia, France, and Britain. And these people also found that Jesus saves. But their notion of what was wrong with man was different again, and very interesting. This is the notion that man has rebelled against God, broken His Laws, and because he has sinned, he merits eternal damnation. This has been the theory of atonement in both Protestant and Catholic Christianity up until quite recent times. It's not as satisfactory today. Very few people, especially nice people like you, would believe that their sins merit eternal burning in hell for ever and ever. The God of love that I know, He wouldn't do that to me.

Yet according to this claim, man has sinned and merits eternal damnation, and yet God sent His Son Jesus Christ to pay the penalty for our sins; that is, He suffered what we had coming to us even to the extent of going to hell. If I have faith in Jesus, God will not give me the punishment I deserve. On the principle of double jeopardy, my sins have already been punished; Christ took the punishment that I deserve. He let me off the hook.

Now you don't buy that. I don't buy that. The reason we don't buy that is that we are of a different civilization, with a different set of dogmatic assumptions, particularly a different notion of what's wrong with man. But for a thousand years people bought that, and I'll tell you why.

When the Romans conquered western Europe they brought with them Roman law and an interesting concept of justice: those who enforce the law also have to obey the law. Before the Romans arrived, government had been the arbitrary personal rule of a chieftain, leader, or king, who might change his mind overnight, and you'd never know whether he had or not.

Everyone outside of the Roman world was under this kind of government, this arbitrary personal rule. But when the Romans came, they brought law that was the same for everyone, even those who enforced the law, because the law is something superior to those who enforce it. The law is my protection. I love the law. While I don't entirely approve of all the laws that we have, I'd rather have them than not have law at all. If you don't have law, what you have is tyranny. The Romans brought law to their conquered provinces.

This was the basis of the Pax Romana, the Peace of Rome. Within the framework of this peace the Roman people could buy and sell, educate their children, and own property. They could lead a normal life. The law was an umbrella for protection against barbarians on the frontier and against tyrants at home. Of course, Roman justice was not perfect; after all, the Romans were fallen people, too. There were a lot of abuses of Roman justice, but within the Roman system itself, as within our own, there were means of correcting abuses and injustices. They thought it was the task of the lawgivers to understand natural law and spell it out in what lawyers call "positive law", or statute law. This notion of law protected those who were obedient from interference by the authorities.

The Christians had no trouble in coming up with the idea that in back of the natural law was divine law. That is, even before He created the world, God knew how things were going to be. He knew the law of gravity before He made the planets. One thing is certain in natural law and that is if you break the law, you will be punished. If I overeat, I will get fat. It will shorten my breath and then it will shorten my life. If I spend all my money lavishly on wine, women, and song, I will go broke. There's no way you can violate the law and get away with it. The punishment is built in.

Now, by the Middle Ages a new element had been introduced into western Europe which was the Germanic idea of feudal loyalty and chivalry; it added to the Roman concept of law the idea that the gravity of the crime was in proportion to the worth and dignity of the victim. For example, in Saxon England, there was no death penalty for murder. The punishment was an amount of money paid first of all to the king, because murder deprived the king of the services of his subject, and then a fine to the members of the murdered man's family. The fine increased in proportion to the social worth of the individual. You had to pay a whole lot more if you killed a nobleman than if you killed a slave. The more worthy the victim, the more horrible the crime. It was an established principle.

Now sins against God are sins against the infinitely worthy victim, and therefore merit infinite punishment. The reason I deserve going to hell for ever, even for a small crime, is because that crime is against an infinitely worthy and meritorious person. This notion was characteristic of the Middle Ages. Now man owes an infinite debt, but he is a finite creature and cannot pay the debt. So in order to get us off the hook, God becomes man, and as God, His suffering had infinite merit. The suffering was offered to God by a man, and therefore man's infinite debt was paid. It wasn't that God wanted to punish us by sending us to hell for ever for a small offence against Him. He had to, because those who administer the law have to keep the law. Sending Christ into the world to redeem us was God's way of keeping the law and still getting us off the hook. It was an act of mercy.

This explanation was very pleasing to people in the Middle Ages. It satisfied them and answered the problem of man's sin and rebellion as they defined it. This explanation is known as the Juridical Theory of the Atonement, and is easily corrupted into the notion that God demands His pound of flesh, that He is a harsh, judgemental, and vengeful God who hates the sinner. This is not the way the medieval theory goes. As a matter of fact, when this theory was first spelled out by St Anselm, Archbishop of Canterbury about 1100, he thought of God as marvellously merciful to have done this entirely unnecessary thing, since, after all, no man deserved redemption. God was loving and merciful to have done this, and clever too, since He figured out a way to circumvent the law while still keeping it. And because men accepted and believed that they merited eternal damnation, they received this notion of redemption with great gladness.

Even this ties into the Eucharist. In the Middle Ages, each Eucharist was seen as a repetition or renewal of the sacrifice of Christ. When I receive communion and offer the Mass for my sins, this gives a direct and personal application of Christ's redemption to me. And if I sin again between now and next Sunday, I can go and offer that Mass again and Christ will go through the sacrifice once more whereby his infinite merits are offered to God in exchange for my infinite guilt. The Protestant Reformation rightly and properly rejected this idea of the Mass but they did not know what to put in its place, because they still had this idea of the infinite gravity of the sin against God and finite man's total inability to render his debt. So the Protestants, while they retained the theory of the atonement, simply made the application of it come as a result of man's act of faith. Up until fairly recently this was the way a Western Christian, whether Catholic or Protestant, thought about the atonement. They still thought in terms of the medicine of immortality, our incorporation into Christ, the infusion of His wholeness into our imperfectness, and the continual nourishing of our soul on the body and blood of Christ whereby we grow gradually into the likeness of Christ. This process is our salvation.

The Western folk have also thought in terms of what is rather like a transaction in bookkeeping in which the merits of Christ are applied to our account. Now this all sounds crude, barbarous, and entirely unsatisfactory, but it may satisfy some. Most people in the twentieth century don't think that way, so what we have to do now is seek in the Scripture a theory of the atonement which is consistent with twentieth century man's understanding.

11

· ·

ATONEMENT II

Man's universal impulse to offer sacrifice arises out of a feeling of overwhelming sin, which has created such a barrier that no amount of God's reassurance is going to relieve man's conscience and make him feel good about sidling into the presence of God. What can he offer God as a recompense for the damage he has done to God's universe? Even if he gave God total obedience from now on to the end of his days, that still would not satisfy the debt. There is a universal impulse to feel guilty, to acknowledge sin, and to desire to make some offering to God to balance the account. Our consciousness requires sacrifice.

For example, suppose I lend you a book, and while my book is in your custody you leave it out in the rain. You may know what happens to the ordinary clothbound book when it gets wet. The paper becomes crinkly and wavy, and the whole book swells up about three times its original size. Soon it's shaped like a gourd. It's not at all the same book you borrowed. But it is my book, and was in your custody because you borrowed it. What would you say when you finished reading it? Would you bring it back and say, "This is the book I borrowed from you?" Now, believe it or not, some people would do that. Some people don't even bother to bring books back, even if they don't get rained on. Some, however, are sufficiently conscientious that having spoiled a borrowed book, they would insist on replacing it with a copy just as good as the one borrowed and bring it and still be apologetic. "I'm sorry that the book you lent me is ruined, but here is a replacement."

Would you want to do that, even if I said, "For heaven's sake, don't worry about it"? Now, you have borrowed my book; it's a little one, worth about $5.00. You have allowed it to get rained on and ruined, and that makes you feel uncomfortable around me, particularly when I talk about people who borrow books and don't return them, and you remember that you have one of mine. There is a moral, psychological, and spiritual barrier between the two of us, and this barrier is going to remain there though the barrier is in you. I'm not mad at you for ruining my book. A book is not that important. But you are not going to forget. You are going to insist on replacing the book with another one just as good or better. There would be something morally deficient in you if you did not feel that way. That's the kind of barrier that exists between man and God.

Now let's take it a step further. Suppose that this is not just an ordinary book, but suppose it's a rare first edition and a family heirloom. How do you replace that? Or suppose my wife and I have a violent quarrel and in my fury I decide I have to get out of the house. I get in my car, back it out of the garage, and run over and kill your children's brand new cocker spaniel puppy that they got for Christmas. Now what do I do? Do I go to you and tell you that I will buy them another puppy? They cry that they want *that* puppy. Now how do I look those children, those parents, in the face? That's the kind of barrier that exists between God and man. In my carelessness I back my car out of the garage and run over one of my neighbour's children. *Now* what do I do? I haven't got any way to replace that child.

No offering or sacrifice that man has ever made, even the sacrifice of his own life, has ever satisfied man's consciousness, until Christ came along and offered Himself on our behalf to God the Father as a sacrifice that was commensurate with the gravity of man's offence and the depth of his gratitude for God's mercy.

Notice also that the essence of sacrifice is not the destruction of the victim. The important thing about the sacrifice is not that I give it up, but that God gets it. But the sacrificial animal is in my world, and God lives in the invisible world. If I give my prize-winning lamb to God I have to transfer the lamb from where I am to where God is. One way to do that is to burn the sacrifice so that it goes up in smoke and the smoke is dissipated into the upper atmosphere, and what was visible becomes invisible. Now don't think for a moment that the Old Testament folk really thought that they had accomplished the transference from the visible to the invisible. They weren't that stupid. This was just as close as they could get; it was a symbolic gesture, their willingness to make the offering was expressed.

Consequently, the sacrifice of Christ, in order to be a sacrifice, must necessarily include the Ascension. The sacrifice of Christ is not complete until He is seated at the right hand of the Father. What is given to God is not Christ's death but His life. The death is the means whereby the life is given up, is turned over. Jesus made this sacrifice. And because He was perfect man as well as divine, Christ was infinitely meritorious, so that the worthwhileness, the goodness of the sacrifice, far more than compensates for the gravity of the sins of all the men who have ever lived. Therefore, this human sacrifice does what no other can do – it relieves man's conscience so that he can go into the presence of God. It's kind of like you borrowed that $5.00 book of mine and let it get rained on, and instead of buying me a new copy, have bought me a $400.00 set of new encyclopaedias, something of far greater worth than the item that you allowed through carelessness to be destroyed. The sacrifice of Christ tips the balance the other way, so that now we can come into the presence of God without the hangdog, shamefaced, fearful guilty feeling.

Let's say that I am going to preach an evangelical sermon in church next Sunday, and I want three or four good points. So I get up and preach a sermon to the effect that man has been alienated and estranged from God, but in the divine humanity of Christ, God has crossed the barrier and reunited man to God. In the power of this union Christ has engaged our ancient enemy Satan in mortal combat and has come off victorious. He has lived a perfect sinless life, tempted in all things even as we, yet without sin. He has given us a perfect example of a model human life, of how we ought to live. He is the final word of God's revelation. And at last He has offered to God an infinitely worthwhile sacrifice. End of sermon.

Sitting in the back row, a young man stands up and says, "Mr Preacher, I want equal time. I've heard your sermon, and I confess the force of what you say. But I have a problem. You say that God and man have been separated, and that God and man were reunited in Christ. Okay, I'll buy that. The man Jesus was united to God through the Incarnation. How can I be united to God? You say that He conquered sin. I believe that. But I can't conquer sin. I'm tempted and I fall daily. How can I conquer sin? You say that He lived a perfect life for my example – that was two thousand years ago and the thousand miles away and in a totally different culture. If God were serious about having a model for me to imitate, He would be incarnate here in this city, in my own generation, and in every hamlet and town around the world. I'm not even sure that I can imagine how Jesus would react in a traffic jam, for example. There are all kinds of problems and situations which I face daily which He did not face. He gave us an example of how to live in first-century Palestine. I'm living in twentieth-century America. You say He gave us the final word of revelation, to put an end for ever to all the doubt and uncertainty about the true and false prophets. I don't deny that He did that, but for two thousand years the Christian preachers have been quarrelling about what He said. And I can go to twenty different Christian theologians and find twenty different explanations of what He meant by what He said. You didn't solve the problem at all. You said that He offered to God an adequate sacrifice. Sure He did, that's right. But what have I to offer? I'm going to stand in the presence of God one day, with my soiled and broken life, feeling shame and guilt, knowing that Jesus Christ two thousand years ago offered God an adequate sacrifice. What is *my* sacrifice, what have I to offer? You see, I don't think that your salvation touches my life at all. When I finish hearing your story I believe that one man, a Jew named Jesus Christ, was saved, But how can I be saved?"

Now that is a good question. But before I answer that let me lay some groundwork.

Jesus did not become incarnate, live a perfect human life for thirty-three years, die on the cross, ascend into Heaven, in order to save souls. That attitude has resulted from the unfortunate nominalism of Western European philosophy over the last six hundred years. Western man tends to think individualistically, forgetting that we are a community of people who are connected to one another through the accident of being together in the same place at the same time. This is not simply a Jewish idea or a Christian idea. We are a community. Jesus came to earth to renew the Covenant. His message, which was proclaimed as Good News, was a communitarian message. The message is this: the kingdom of God has begun. It is here. Jesus came to establish His Church. It is through and by means of the Church that souls are saved.

The extreme evangelical view of atonement holds that if I surrender to Jesus and make an act of faith in Jesus, then I am saved. The evangelical experience of salvation is essentially a lonely and individualistic ordeal that takes place outside of the Church. Conversion takes place and you are saved before you enter the Church by baptism. That's typical evangelical theology, and as a consequence, salvation is a result of a relationship established between me and Christ after I heard the Gospel and accepted it in faith and surrendered my life to Jesus. Zap. *Fini.* But that's not what happens.

Let's take the boy's question again. "How can I be reunited to God?" Answer: In Holy Baptism. That's what happens in baptism. God's Holy Spirit comes upon a person because he enters through baptism into the Spirit-bearing Body of Christ, which is the Church. Baptism bestows the Spirit because baptism effects your membership in the Body of Christ. In this baptism, in this spiritual event, I am united with Christ. As a result of my baptism I can say with St Paul, "I live, yet not I, but Christ liveth in me." There is an invasion of my spirit by the divine Spirit so that God and I are united. The event that unites me to Christ is that event which makes me a member of Christ's mystical body. That's strict New Testament theology. God through His Church effects or accomplishes in me and for me what He effected and accomplished in the humanity of Christ, which He took from the womb of the Blessed Virgin Mary. The divine and the human are one. The difference between my baptism and the Incarnation is that the person who is reunited to God in the Incarnation is a human person. Nevertheless Jesus' humanity and mine are taken by God and joined with God by means of the sacrament of Holy Baptism.

The boy is already on his feet in the back row.

"Wait a cotton-picking minute. I am not going to buy that. I've been baptized. If I were united to God, why do I keep on sinning?"

I say, "I'm not through." What happens in baptism? Although I am united to God in baptism, this does not override or overrule my freedom. We've said that the Holy Spirit comes upon you in baptism. It's like this: Let's think of a house and this house is my life and I am the occupant of this house. Let's say that the furnishings in this house are those traits of character and personality that I possess. I am baptized. The door opens and the Holy Spirit enters. He's a tidy little gentleman with a frock coat and a Vandyke goatee. He bows graciously and says, "How do you do. I'm the Holy Spirit and I have come to live with you."

I say, "Great, that's fine. That's what they told me would happen. Welcome."

The Holy Spirit looks around Him and says, "You'll pardon my saying so, but the furniture you have is rather shabby."

I'll say, "Yes, I know, but it's all I've got."

He says, "Don't worry. I've got a moving van parked right outside with a whole new set of furniture which is the exact model of the furniture that is in God's house. It is yours free."

I say, "Marvellous."

He says, "Shall I bring it in?"

I say, "Sure."

So he picks up a table and starts out with it. I say, "Wait, what are you doing with that table?"

He says, "If I'm going to bring in this new furniture, I will have to get rid of the old furniture."

I say, "Yes, I can see the sense of that. But if you don't mind, can I keep that table? You see, that table belonged to my mother and I am very attached to it."

The Holy Spirit is good-natured, and He puts the table down. He picks up a lamp and starts out with it.

I say, "Sorry, if you don't mind, I'd like to keep that lamp. You see, a few years ago I took a course in woodworking and made that myself. I am very attached to it."

The Holy Spirit says, "Okay, but let's get something straight. If you are going to get the new furniture, you are going to have to get rid of the old furniture. Any time you are ready to change the furniture, let me know."

And then I discover that my problem is not how I can conquer sin. My problem is that I am not sure that I want to. I am attached to my sin. It's not that I haven't tried and tried to overcome my sins, but that I have been trying half-heartedly. I am really very fond of my sin. When God confronts me with a clear choice, it's kind of like St Augustine, who wrote in his *Confessions* that he had prayed as a young man, "Oh God, make me chaste – but not yet."

How can I conquer sin? The answer to that again is in the Church. Christ has given us the means whereby we can overcome vice, grow in virtue, and become saints. But we have to use these tools and techniques. If we don't use them, nothing is going to happen. The Holy Spirit will continue to dwell in our house but the house will continue to be shabby, disorganized, rather disreputable until we make use of the movers. We must discover that Christ, through His Church, has given us a large number of instruments or tools for growing holy. There are two kinds: negative and positive. And you discover upon analysis that Christian goodness is also of two kinds: negative and positive.

For example, I am sure you have known people who were thoughtless. I have. But they "didn't smoke, they didn't chew and they didn't go with the girls that do". There are some people who are "good" and yet their goodness is so unattractive that you think, "Man, if that's the kind of people who are going to Heaven, then I want to go to the other place. At least the folk there are interesting."

Goodness is more than not committing sin. Sin is the absence of something. The concept "sinless" is really a double negative, and a rather unfortunate term. We speak of Christ as sinless and that tends to suggest that there are a number of things that He did not do. Now if that's all goodness is, not smoking, not drinking, you can have a life and character that is so lacking in anything attractive that no one would want to live that way.

On the other hand, I am sure you have known some people whose lives are filled with noble aspirations but nothing ever comes of them because they are so undisciplined. True goodness requires the denial of certain impulses and the expression of certain others. And either kind without the other is not real goodness. We have to get rid of the old furniture and move in the new furniture.

Now the young man's third question was, "If God had been serious about providing us with an example, He would have had an Incarnation right here in the twentieth century." Well, He has, not once, but many times. His mystical body the Church is here, and Christians see an Incarnation every time there is a baptism. This Incarnation serves as a model of human perfection. Now I hesitate to use the word "perfection" because it is ambiguous. At the time of the Renaissance, human perfection meant that a man was a perfect athlete, a perfect poet, a perfect lover, a perfect politician, a perfect musician, a perfect artist. In one sense that is what human perfection is. That's not what the Christian means by perfection. Christian perfection consists in doing one's duty to the best of one's ability and to the glory of God in that station of life to which it pleases God to call you. Christian perfection does not consist of some lofty or exalted state of mystical ecstasy. This is given to relatively few souls. There are saints in Heaven with very low IQs. We are given innumerable examples of Christlikeness in the lives of the saints: Sts Paul, Francis, John of the Cross, Xavier, Teresa, Thomas Aquinas, Augustine of Hippo, Hugh of Lincoln, Elizabeth, Patrick, Katherine, and many more. They have lived in faraway lands and in different times, but I had a pastoral theology professor who said that God will see to it that there is at least one saint in every congregation to keep His priest humble. The overwhelming majority of saints have gone into eternity unremembered by man.

These saints show us, in every place and time, how we can grow closer to God, and what we can become.

12

ATONEMENT III

Those of you who were not "born free" but "bought freedom at a great price" will remember the first time you ever set foot in a church. You saw a lot of weird jumping up and down and bowing and crossing. You felt that everyone else was watching you to see what you were doing, and whether or not you made mistakes. You felt exposed, like a bad dream in which you are naked on Main Street at noontime. It's a dreadful feeling to be in a situation where you don't know what to do.

Adam and Eve woke up in a garden that was strange and new. Adam said, "I wish someone would tell us what the rules are." God said, "I'll tell you. It's very simple. Just don't eat out of that tree." Adam's response was, "No one is going to tell me what I can and can't eat." That's the human situation. We are rebels. Every small child between eighteen months and two years discovers that he has a will. But he doesn't have the education or experience to use that will affirmatively, to say, "I want some of that" or "I want to go there." He uses his will to say, "No." Somehow, even at that tender age, he realizes that the most precious possession he has is his free choice.

After about three years he passes out of the negative stage and becomes very loving. Then he makes another discovery, that he can blackmail his family with love. Then he enters another rebellious stage in adolescence. He knows that

180

being an adult means directing his own life, making his own decisions, deciding for himself when to go out and when to come in and who to go with. He resents authority. Those of us who have raised children know perfectly well that children, given their own way, would destroy themselves and the rest of the human race. One small child turned loose in a house can be more destructive than a herd of buffalo. Parents have to say no to a child; they have to restrain and discipline him, and when the child looks in a mirror and sees himself begin to take the shape of an adult, he resents the restraint of parental authority.

We rebel against all kinds of authority. Most of the things that people learn, they learn by making a mistake innocently, by doing what they sincerely and honestly believe is the right thing to do, or at least a harmless thing to do, and then suffering the consequences. You can't explain to a child the pain of getting run over by a car, so you give him the lesser pain of a spanking when he plays in the street. Now he doesn't know it is a lesser pain – it's a pretty severe pain, he thinks. As I recollect, a good part of getting a spanking is not just the physical pain but also the humiliation, the indignity of it.

So we grow up with the feeling that there is all around us, in nature, society, and the home community, an authority which is designed to oppress us, to prevent us from using our free choice. We tend to think of authority as repressive and tyrannical. As long as authority comes upon me unexpectedly from without I will resent it and resist it. Man is a rebel.

At a deeper level, my most compelling urge is my own perfection, the thing which the theologians and philosophers call the tendential nature of being. It is to be observed in the fact that acorns given half a chance will grow into oak trees. Eggs tend to hatch into chickens, puppies grow up to be dogs, kittens turn into cats. A nine-year-old girl, when her mother leaves her at home when she goes to the grocery store, will sneak in and put on Mama's lipstick, earrings, and shoes. We want to be grown up. We want to actualize our potentialities, to be someone important, to be great, to be a hero. I want to make my mark, to leave the world a little better place than I found it. Incredible, conceited, vain, arrogant, and presumptuous as this attitude is, it is a very natural sort of thing. But the truth of the matter is that I really don't believe in myself, I don't even like myself, and neither do you.

As we are growing up with this burden upon us, quite early we learn to ask ourselves, "How am I doing?" and to answer that question in terms of what other people around me seem to think of me, how they react to my behaviour. If they react with approval then I must be doing pretty well. If they reject me or criticize me or make fun of me, then I am not doing too well. I read in their behaviour some indication of my true worth. As we grow older this attitude tends to produce a chameleon effect in us and we change our values, behaviour, standards, ideals, and vocabulary to the company that we are with. Quite often, this characteristic lasts into maturity, and you can spot such people a mile away. Sometimes people get frozen into this kind of phoniness, hungry, lonely, friendless people who are overly eager to please. Indeed, in acute cases it becomes a social and sociological cannibalism. The more lonely people are, the more people avoid them.

Because of my anxiety to approve of myself, I have a self-image. I know that I am a nice guy, kindly, benevolent, patient, long-suffering, generous. But I discover to my astonishment that lots of people think I have a nasty

temper. Some people are even afraid of me. How can
anyone be afraid of me, dear, kindly old Fr Rogers?
Somehow the image I have of myself and the image that
other people get of me aren't entirely in accord. I don't
really know who I am, or what I am like. I am always a
little bit surprised and considerably disappointed every
time I see my reflection in the mirror. This image is the
only me that I know. And because I am anxious to get you
to accept this image, this is what I present to you when we
are together. And if you are playing the same game, then
your unreality and my unreality are having a difficult time
communicating, because you can see through my mask,
and I can see through yours.

Now I do occasionally do things that are harmful to
others. I step on someone's toes and he says, "Ouch." That
means that I am more or less imperfect, and I don't like to
think of myself like that. So I look for some fault in him.
When I find it I can tell myself that I was simply giving him
what he had coming. The alcoholic is a good example of
self-justification. I am a drunkard and every time I get my
paycheck I go on a binge, and my poor wife with our small
children has to take in washing to pay the rent and feed the
family. I come home drunk and beat her up. Then I'm
embarrassed and she's humiliated. This goes on year after
year and she endures me with the patience of Griselda, then
finally she breaks down and bawls hell out of me for being
a drunken bum. Now that's why I drink, I've got a nagging
wife. Any of the unfortunate consequences of my drinking
that caused her any pain or inconvenience, it's her own
durn fault.

When Jesus was crucified He prayed, "Father, forgive
them, for they don't know what they are doing." Now
Jesus was certainly enough of a moral theologian to

understand that if they did not know what they were doing they were not committing mortal sin and therefore had no need of divine forgiveness. What, then, can be the meaning of this prayer? Simply this: the sin for which they needed forgiveness was not the sin of the crucifying Him, since they thought they were doing God's service by putting Him to death. Their sin was in not knowing what they were doing. They were blind, but their blindness was a wilful condition, the kind of blindness that we choose as a defence against the truth about ourselves. The people who crucified Christ were not wicked people. Each of them was serving a cause, a righteous one, but not the best cause available. Each had identified with the cause and made it his own. Pilate was a just man because he was a Roman colonial administrator and he did not have to prove his own justice. The Sanhedrin were righteous men because they were Sanhedrin. The Roman soldiers were doing what was right because they were Roman soldiers and they relied on Roman justice. They did not have to think.

There are two kinds of people that society will not tolerate. One kind is the very, very wicked, like Achan, and we react to them with lynch mobs. The other is the very, very good – and the reaction is the same. Achan comes along and he reminds me that I, too, have a little of the traitor deep down in the dungeon of my subconscious, and I don't like to think of that. And when a saint comes along, his genuine righteousness reveals my counterfeit righteousness as the tawdry thing that it really is. And I react by persecuting him. In fact, there are only two things you can do when a saint comes along: 1) admit his moral and spiritual superiority and try to imitate it, or 2) throw rocks at him. Jesus came along and these righteous people were unwilling to admit to themselves that He was so absolutely righteous because that would have meant admitting to themselves that they were not. And so they began with the supposition that the guy was a fraud, a charlatan.

These religious leaders of the Jewish people couldn't admit to themselves the remote and distant possibility that Jesus was really the Messiah. That country bumpkin from Nazareth even spoke with a hill-country accent. He wasn't even a college graduate, so He could not have been much of a prophet. But the common people thought He was a good guy, so the religious leaders, taking their own responsibility, set about to discredit Him. They sent their best debaters out to engage Him in controversy. Every time they took Him on, He had this astonishing trick of very simply, without ruffling a hair, making them all look like fools and sending them all home with their tails between their legs. They tried to trick Him with the woman taken in adultery, because if He said, "Let her go," He would be confounding Jewish Law, and if He said, "Stone her," He would be advocating a violation of Roman law. So He said, "Go ahead, stone her, but just to make it interesting, let him who is without sin among you be the first to cast a stone."

"Is it lawful to give tribute to Caesar?"

Jesus asked for a coin and said, "Whose picture is that?"

"Caesar's."

"Okay, render unto Caesar the things that are Caesar's and unto God the things that are God's."

They couldn't puncture His balloon. So they redoubled their efforts, but the harder they worked the bigger asses they appeared, even in their own eyes. It became imperative that they do one of two things: either accept the man for what He claimed to be, or else get rid of Him. And they had too much at stake to do the former.

It wasn't such a bad state of affairs in Jerusalem, except that everybody there – the Pharisees, Pilate, the Jewish population, the Roman soldiers, Judas – was concealing an enormous amount of pride. Their righteousness was real, but it was not an adequate righteousness. The righteousness of Christ made their righteousness look shabby. So they attacked Him. In addition to hanging Him on the cross, they spat upon Him. Why were they not content just to let Him die? Why did they have to stand around and taunt Him? They were hoping against desperate hope that He would curse them. If He had, they would have gone home feeling perfectly justified. "We knew all the time that He wasn't that good." "Did you hear those vile words that came out of His mouth while He was dying on the cross?" The victory of Christ on the cross is precisely His refusal to sin back. He kept His integrity. The devil wants us to be angry with those who get angry, because that makes twice as much anger in the world. We should be intolerant of those who are intolerant of us, and that way there is twice as much intolerance in the world. Sin tends to generate sin. I call you a dirty name, you call me a dirty name. And therefore I am justified in calling you more dirty names because you are the kind of person that calls people dirty names. Things build up and I hit you and the next thing you know we have a full-scale war going on involving half of the nations of the earth.

The only way sin can be dealt with effectively, God's way of dealing with sin, is to suffer the consequence of other people's sin without sinning back. Therefore He said to resist not evil but overcome evil with good. When a man strikes you on one cheek, turn the other cheek. If someone compels you to go with him a mile, go with him two miles. If a man knocks you down and takes off your coat and runs away with it, call him back and say, "Hey, you forgot my britches." The alcoholic who drinks because he has a nagging wife – if she suffers it's her own fault. But those two little babies, they also have to suffer the consequences of his drinking. It's not their fault. From the beginning of mankind until today, the only thing that has ever stopped sin is innocent suffering, people who are willing to suffer the consequences of sin and not sin back. How does that make up an atonement? Well, it's like this.

God, as we have said, has an unchanging attitude of love and an eternal attitude of forgiveness. It is represented in the story of the Prodigal Son. The Father in the story is God, who is always anxious and willing to receive us back. But it is man whose nose is out of joint. The point is that not even man can forgive the impenitent, because sin, as we have seen, is estrangement, alientation, a breach in communication, in comradeship. And therefore forgiveness is the repairing and restoring of a friendship, and it takes two to make friends. Not even God can forgive and accept back into a relationship a person who is unaware that he has ever been away. And this frightful thing blinds us to our sin. Now when Jesus died on the cross, after refusing to sin back, St Mark quotes the centurion as saying, "Surely this was a just man." The Roman centurion was concerned with justice. He had been engaged in the grim business of torturing a man to death. If I am going to do that I've got to believe that the victim is getting what he deserves. And when the Roman centurion after seeing Christ die, said, "Surely this was a just man," then the corollary is inescapable: "Surely I am not."

To be engaged in putting to death an innocent, guilt-less person meant that Roman justice had failed. The centurion's ego-supports had collapsed. He could no longer find any self-justification in his righteousness in being a Roman soldier and obeying orders. When Christ died, He put into practice what He told us to do; that is, He turned the other cheek and He went the second mile. He resisted not evil but overcame evil by absorbing it. And all of this He did at the cost of great pain to Himself, great suffering. All the people who had participated in the crucifixion were forced then to re-examine and re-evaluate their own motives and their own moral character. No longer could they go on pretending that everything was okay. What pride does is prevent us from accepting God's forgiveness because it prevents us from seeing our need of forgiveness. The only thing that will ever force me to see my need of forgiveness is when my righteousness imposes pain and suffering upon some innocent person. Now that doesn't mean that I am going to quit. But it does mean that if I don't quit, Jesus would have to change His prayer to, "Father, forgive him, because he knows damn well what he is doing." The moment that I am willing to admit that something is wrong with me, I am open to God's love and God's forgiveness and the re-establishment of a loving friendship, and that's the redemption.

One of the axiomatic dogmatic statements of the Church is that the sufferings of Christ on the cross were infinite in merit and nothing could be added to them. And yet St Paul says, "I make up in my own bodily sufferings that which was lacking in the sufferings of Christ." What could be lacking in the sufferings of Christ that St Paul or I should have to make up what was deficient? Quantitatively and qualitatively His suffering was infinitely meritorious and lacked nothing. What was specifically lacking, of course, was that it happened on one Friday, on one little hillside outside one little town in Palestine. If God were really serious about redeeming mankind through the sufferings of Christ, He would have a crucifixion right here, today. And He does – in you and me. For that is our vocation as Christians. When I come into the church wearing my mask and asking you to accept me at my mask-face value, you are not going to do that. We can't play that game. The only thing that will allow me to drop that mask is when someone knows the real me inside the mask, the real sinner that I am, and loves me anyway. You prove that to me when you allow me to abuse you and you don't become vindictive, angry, or vengeful, and don't hit back. This is the task of the Church, to act as if all the sins in the world were its fault.

It is said that Jesus died for our sins. That means simply this. If some joker spends all of his paycheck on drink and gambling and loose women, his wife and kids are not going to have any Christmas. That son of a gun ought to be made to go to work and provide his kids with Christmas toys, but he won't. So I will. I will act as if their lack of Christmas toys were my fault. I will accept the responsibility and will absorb the pain and the punishment and the consequences of all the hurt and all the suffering. I can't do all of that, of course. But seven of us can accept seven times more of it than any one of us can by ourselves. And there are 270 in this parish and 30,000 Episcopalians in this diocese. There are millions in the country, and we could make a start at it. That's our business.

You see, God isn't finished with me. I don't know what

I am going to be like, but I know I am called to be something astonishing, something ridiculous that the world has never seen before. I am called to be St Homer. That hasn't happened yet. I have no notion of what that would be like if it did happen. Inside me there is another Homer Rogers whom God has been making all along, and I don't even know he's there. The mask is dropped and shattered as my pride and my defences are broken. What emerges from the wreckage is the real me, and that is always something attractive.

It is a psychological experience and is exactly what the preachers have been talking about for 2,000 years and calling the conversion experience, the born-again experience of popular evangelical Christianity. It's a paradoxical kind of transformation. When my pride is shattered and broken and I admit that I am a son-of-a-bitch, all of a sudden I discover that I am not. I am a real nice guy. But since I don't know what I am going to be like when I am finished, I adopt as my goal some model, some hero to emulate. And the only model I can choose to imitate is Jesus. He took my humanity. And therefore I can take His. The saints, interestingly enough, are amazingly different. You can take as many as you can find and not find two that even remotely resemble each other, yet all of them resemble Jesus.

Every sin that has ever been committed from Eve eating the persimmon to the lie told five minutes ago has been committed in defence of this false self-image. You can name any sin in the catalogue and if you dig deep enough into the motivations behind it, you'll find that what people are trying to do when they commit that sin is to protect and defend this false image of themselves. It may be a distorted image, and they may be trying to impress an insignificant little gang of fellow criminals, but it is the defence of the phoney mask that causes sin.

The only way that you and I can enter into a real, loving, honest communal relationship with each other or with God is not by trying to impress people, but simply by loving them. I know that you can't be worth loving, and how do I know that? Because you are like me. Okay. Now having said that, we can forget it and get on with the much more important business of loving and enjoying each other's company. And when we do that, we discover that there is no need for sin. Nothing is to be gained by sinning. The Church is such a community, and that is why she has always insisted in theory from the very beginning that the way you enter this community is on your knees, by confessing your sins. If I got what was coming to me, I'd hang on that cross before Christ. You and I are called to follow Christ in accepting the consequences of the sin of the world without sinning back, because we love the sinner and we know that we are sinners, too.

Look at how Alcoholics Anonymous works. I know that once a man has ruined his liver, alcoholism is a psychological disease. If I don't like myself, then I go out and get drunk because when drunk. I like myself just fine. I don't even remember what damn fool things I did while I was drunk, and all you folk who saw me when I was drunk, oh, what a fool I was. What must you be thinking of me? So I go get drunk again so I won't have to think about it. Then I go to an AA meeting and someone gets up to talk. He says, "My name is John Doe, and I am an alcoholic and I want to tell you what damn fool things I have done while I was drunk. My wife divorced me and my children wouldn't speak to me and I lost my job, and I lost my home, my car, my self-respect, and control of my bowels and bladder. I wound up in the gutter, then in jail."

In the course of the conversation the guy mentions that he hasn't had a drink in twelve years, seven months, and four days. You listen and say to yourself, "If he can do it, maybe I can do it."

In that particular community everybody is a drunkard. No one can scorn you or ridicule you or condemn you or judge you, because they are all drunks, too. So for the first time since you can remember, you don't need to hide.

If I, as the priest of this congregation, am going to minister to you, a sinner, it is absolutely essential that I communicate to you the fact that I, too, am a sinner. My name is Fr Rogers and I am a sinner. I am not ashamed to let you know it. I know that you are a sinner, and I love you anyway, and if I can prove it, maybe you can believe that God loves you. If that ever gets across, you can go out of here and quit feeling ashamed. There's no need to wear the mask. When you drop that mask you will discover that inside there is a beautiful you that God has been making all the time. You have the potentiality to be a saint, with a heroism, a nobility and moral grandeur and sublimity and incredible wisdom and an awesome holiness.

13

BAPTISM

Before we talk about baptism, let me say a word about grace. Grace is a supernatural power given by God to man in order to supplement man's natural capacities to enable him to live on a supernatural level.

The inclination of the natural man is to think of himself, and if you don't believe it, just watch any small child. It never happens that the baby who wakes from his afternoon nap cold, wet, and hungry, reasons with himself, "I would love a dry diaper and a warm bottle, but after all, Daddy is taking a nap and Mother has a headache, so I will wait a while before I cry." It is natural for the child to act in terms of his own comfort and pleasure, and quite supernatural to put someone else's comfort and pleasure before his own. Even the act of standing back to let someone go before you through a door indicates that the natural impulses have been curbed and disciplined, and to a considerable extent, overcome by the forces of civilization. What grace does is to elevate and perfect nature.

As God created us, our nature was intended to be governed by a spiritual faculty which would actually rule and direct the intellect, which in turn would rule and direct the will, the appetites and passions, and finally the bodily nature and the organic life that keeps man being a body. The only truly natural man in the full sense is the supernatural man. Actually, if you take fallen man as natural, then what

God does is to raise his natural level to a supernatural one. Grace is the divine assistance which is given to man to enable him to grow up into the fulfilment of his true nature.

Grace is God Himself living and active in the human soul. You can't feel grace. A lot of so-called mystical experiences that accompany the reception of grace are not grace itself, but the effect of grace, the feeling which is the consequence in the bodily organism of the action of grace. The only way you can know for sure that you have had grace outside of the sacraments is that it produces a moral improvement. Lots of people have visions and hear voices and are visited by St Anthony or the Blessed Virgin; experiences can be duplicated from the literature of abnormal psychology, and there is no way you really can tell a true vision of God from the effects of eating too much Mexican food. The only verification of visions which the Church has ever accepted is a significant moral improvement in the life of the recipient.

The normal way for God to communicate with us is spiritually, since God is a spirit and a spirit doesn't have a local presence. The only difficulty with God working mystically in the soul is that, outside of the sacraments, there is no way that we can be sure that it is God. On the morning of 16 April 1934, I had a real "call to preach". I was a Baptist at the time. If God is going to speak to a Baptist, He's going to have to speak Baptist, and the only way a Baptist can recognize a call to preach is by a mystical experience. And boy, I had one. I gave up a good job and went off to Baylor University to study for the Baptist ministry. After several years, I was an atheist. I never doubted that I had had the experience, I only doubted what it meant.

194

Eight years later I knelt in front of the bishop in St Barnabas Church, Denton, Texas, and he put his hands on my head and said, "Receive the Holy Spirit for the office and work of priest in the Church of God . . ." I did not feel a thing except his hands on my hand, but there were witnesses, and I've got a certificate to prove it. This is an objective experience, one which can be apprehended by the bodily senses. I frequently wonder why God called me into the ministry, but never whether. It was an absolute, certain, undeniable fact. It was a mystery and a puzzle, but it happened, and in the realm of objectivity. There was an outward and visible sign.

The sacraments do not make God enter us. The sacraments give us the assurance and certainty that it is happening, or has happened. Whatever God can do in and through the sacraments, He can also do outside the sacraments, and He does. God is not bound by the sacraments, we are. In the sacraments, we are not doing anything. God is doing something. He uses a human instrument who is the minister of the sacrament, but the active agent in the sacrament is God Himself.

The effect of the sacrament is conditioned by our subjective attitude; that is, if you receive the sacrament without faith or penitence or charity, you have still received the sacrament. The grace is given, but it is latent and inoperative in the soul until the proper subjective conditions occur in which the grace can be fruitful in your life. For example, an infant who is baptized has received grace, but many of the fruits of baptism are not effective in the life of the child and only become so as he grows, matures, and becomes rational and volitional.

Because the sacrament is not only a means of grace but also a pledge to assure us of that grace, the Church is concerned with what is known as the validity of the sacraments. Since one of the purposes of the sacraments is to give us the certainty that we have received grace, then necessarily we are concerned with whether or not the sacrament is valid. For the sacrament to be valid, four things are necessary: form, matter, minister, and intention. Something must be done, and something must be said. If you offer God a gift, you have to express the fact that you are offering a gift, and not just killing a sheep or putting an egg on a flat rock.

In a sacrament, the something said is the form of the sacrament, and the something done is the matter of the sacrament. There is also the need to have the proper minister, since the minister is the one who has been authorized by the Church to act for the Church to perform this sacrament. The form, matter, and minister vary with each of the sacraments, but the intention is the same throughout.

What makes a sacrament valid in terms of intention is that the minister of the sacrament intends what the Church intends. If a person watching him would from all evidence of his performance be given the impression that he is acting for the Church, then he is acting for the Church. It has nothing to do with the subjective piety or orthodoxy of the minister.

When I celebrate Mass or baptize a child or hear confessions and give absolution, I am acting as the agent of the Church, to do what the Church does. When I was teaching pastoral theology at the seminary, one of my jobs was to teach young men how to say Mass and baptize babies. We would borrow a baby and go into the church.

I would stand up in front of the class and say, "Now I am going to demonstrate the proper way of baptizing a baby." I would say all the words and pour the water and do everything I would normally do at a baptism. The baby would not be baptized because ostensibly I was not baptizing, rather, I was demonstrating how to baptize.

Once you have the proper minister and he performs the sacraments, giving every outward evidence of doing it sincerely, then the sacrament is valid. The intention then is the sincere intention to do whatever the Church does in this sacrament. What governs the meaning of the sacrament is not my faith or your faith, but the faith of the Church.

Let me describe for you baptism as it took place in the second century. People opting for Christianity in the second century were placed in the catechumenate for two to five years, during which time they received careful scrutiny and instruction, and the catechist made certain that they had in fact renounced the flesh and the world and the devil, and were ready for baptism.

These folks are brought to the church on Easter Eve in the evening. They have been instructed to wear some old clothes. They are met at the door by an officer of the congregation, a priest or a deacon, and are asked if they renounce the flesh, the world, and the devil. They say that they do. Then they are exorcised, which is a formal, official notification to Satan that these folk no longer belong to you, they belong to us. Then they are stripped absolutely buff, birthday naked. The clothes that they wore are taken out and burned. When they renounced the world, what they were renouncing was Roman citizenship, because Christians had no civil rights in those days. As a matter of fact, they were facing the real possibility that they might be thrown to the lions or crucified.

Originally, the baptistry was a cistern, in the atrium of the house. There were sloping roofs that drained the water into the cistern. The Romans went in for nude bathing in the impluvium, or cistern. Although the Jews were a little bit leery of it, nudity wasn't all that shocking to the Gentile world, rather like Japan today. The congregation stood around on the patio, and the candidates for baptism were brought stark naked into the midst of the congregation. The first candidate walked down into the bath tub or pool, and a deacon went with him. A priest stood at the edge, and addressed him. "Do you believe in God the Father, the maker of Heaven and earth?" He said, "I do believe." The priest said to the deacon, "Baptize him." The deacon either dunked him or more likely, because many of these pools which archaeologists have ascertained to be Christian baptistries are only about eighteen inches deep, he took a dipper. (The word "baptize" in the original Greek means to take a bath.) The deacon takes this dipper of water and dumps it over the head of the candidate and the water cascades over him. This was being baptized in the name of the Father, after having professed faith in the Father.

Then the priest said, "Do you believe in God the Son, in Jesus Christ Our Lord, who was conceived by the Holy Spirit, born of the Virgin Mary, suffered under Pontius Pilate, was crucified, died, and buried, descended into hell, and on the third day rose again and ascended into Heaven, and sitteth on the right hand of the Father, and from thence He is coming in glory to judge the living and the dead?" The candidate said, "I do believe." And the priest said, "Baptize him again." This was being baptized in the name of the Son, after professing faith in the Son.

Then the priest said, "Do you believe in the Holy Spirit, the Lord and giver of life?" The candidate said, "I do believe." And he was baptized for the third time in the name of the Holy Spirit, after professing belief in the Holy Spirit.

Having then been baptized, the priest gave him another name. He had come there that night as Charlie, but from then on he would be George. Then he was led out of the water on the opposite side from which he entered, and still naked, was dried off with a towel and greased from head to foot; that is, he was anointed with oil. Aaron, Saul, and David were anointed. The word "anointed" in Greek is *Christos*, equivalent to the Hebrew in which anointed one was *Messiah*. Christ is the anointed one. Christians are so called not only because they are followers of Christ but also because they, too, have been anointed.

The candidate was then dressed in a new suit of clothes, all glowing white, very much like the alb that the priest wears when he goes to the altar. The candidate was given milk mingled with honey to drink. The priest led this freshly baptized candidate up to the bishop, who had been sitting at the head of the room, and introduced him. "Right reverend father in God, may I present unto you this person, now named George." The candidate kneels, and the bishop puts his hands on his head and prays that the Holy Spirit would come upon him. He then stands aside, and the next candidate is brought in naked.

By the way, if you are embarrassed by this naked baptism and the greasing down of freshly washed candidates, bear in mind that when the Romans had a bath, they realized that the body oils were being washed away; it was perfectly normal when finished with a bath to anoint the whole body. Lady candidates were anointed and rubbed down by lady deacons, and gentlemen candidates were anointed and rubbed down by gentlemen deacons.

When all the candidates had been baptized and been presented to the bishop and had hands laid on them with the prayer that the Holy Spirit would come upon them, the bishop then turned and celebrated the Holy Communion. The newly baptized people were the first in the congregation to receive their communion. It was the first time they had ever seen a communion. Then, and only then, were they Christians.

According to Hippolytus, the entrance rite of becoming a Christian in the second century consisted of this entire procedure, the changing of clothes, the changing of name, the public baptism, the anointing, the vesting in a clean new garment, the drink of milk and honey, the laying on of hands and the prayer by the bishop, and the communion. That was what made you a Christian.

It should be apparent now that in the primitive Church there were not two separate sacraments of baptism and confirmation, but only one sacrament which was called baptism and which contained in one initiatory rite both of these experiences which today we call baptism, confirmation, and first communion. It is interesting to trace how in the course of history these two sacraments have become separated.

The first Christian churches were organized on the order of the Jewish synagogues, that is, they had a government consisting of a committee called the Sanhedrin, or elders, under the principal rule of a president of the Sanhedrin. The whole committee of elders under the president of elders exercised the oversight of the congregation. Since

Greek was the predominant language of the Roman Empire, the Greek word for oversight is *episcopos*. The *episcopos* was the bishop, a member of the ruling committee of elders, all of whom shared the episcopal oversight. By usage in the course of time, the term *episcopos* came to be restricted to the one man who was the head of the committee. The *episcopos* was the one who said Mass and preached, and the others, the elders, although they were apparently adjudged authorized to say Mass, never did so when the *episcopos* was present. If he were absent or died or was arrested by the Roman authorities, one of the elders would step up and say Mass for the congregation. They worshipped normally in the home of the bishop, which limited the size of the congregation.

When the congregation grew so large that the bishop's house was not able to accommodate everybody, they simply divided the congregation, and everybody who lived east of Main Street would meet at elder Smith's house. The bishop would take turn about, one Sunday in one place and the next Sunday in the other place. When he was in the first place, a priest would say Mass for the other congregation. After a while, the congregation would grow so large that two houses were not enough, and they had four, and six, and twenty. The bishop was only coming around every twenty weeks. Nevertheless, Christians in any one town thought of themselves as members of one congregation under one pastor, meeting in a number of different places. When they had a baptism, they all went back to the bishop's house.

When the Church moved northward into the tribal lands of Gaul, Spain, Germany, and Britain, the territory under the administration of a single bishop came to be much larger. If you look at the ancient dioceses in the

Mediterranean world, there was a bishop in every town of any size. But in Gaul, what is now France, and the other northern lands, the diocese would extend 150 miles. The bishops could only get around every year or two. The practice arose of doing that part of baptism which the priest and deacon customarily do, and then when the bishop came, he could do his part.

As a consequence, these two parts of the same service became separated. Today at a solemn High Mass, the sub-deacon reads the Epistle and the deacon the Gospel and the priest at the altar says Mass. If you had the sub-deacon reading the Epistle on Tuesday and the deacon reading the Gospel on Thursday, you would have a situation comparable to this, where the one service was divided up, not only in terms of ministers, but also in terms of time. What is being confirmed, contrary to recent theory, is not the layman confirming his baptismal vows, but the bishop confirming what the priest has done. Confirming means strengthening.

It should be noted here that if a community is going to have any viability and value, it must guard its ethos, its spirit, against contamination and against the conflict of alien loyalties. If a community is going to function at maximum efficiency, it must have the undivided loyalty of its members. This is accomplished by diminishing a person's dependence upon the former community and enhancing his sense of dependence upon the new community, so that the identity that is given him will be that of the new community.

Coming into a community, by birth or by initiation, means acquiring the ethos or spirit of that community. There are initiation ceremonies in primitive societies which have been exhaustively studied by sociologists and anthropologists. A little boy is initiated into manhood at puberty, a little girl into womanhood. There are rites and ceremonies whereby a member of one tribe becomes a member of another tribe. There are initiation ceremonies whereby a man becomes a member of a college fraternity, or a woman a member of a sorority. There are initiation ceremonies when you join the Masons. But there is a certain basic structural similarity in all initiation ceremonies, and they have a very similar rationale.

When a child is initiated into manhood in the African tribal village, the adults want to make certain that none of those childish habits and attitudes are carried forward into his status as a man and a responsible citizen of the tribe. So an effort is made in all initiations to embarrass, to humiliate, and to destroy the previous identity, to instil in the candidate a sense of the worthlessness of his previous identity, precisely so he can receive a new identity as a gift of this new community.

There is often a period of sequestration in which the candidate is instructed in the ethos of the new community. There is frequently a ritual putting to death or ritual killing in some of the tribal initiations. A person is swallowed up alive in the earth or goes down into a cave and then is brought back up again. He may be subjected to wounding, scarification, or physical injury, to impress upon him the essential vulnerability of his identity. He is often forced to empty his digestive tract by fasting. There is frequently nudity, because nobody is as vulnerable and as totally aware of inadequacy and helplessness as when you take all of his clothes away from him. In baptism each of these negative things is balanced by a positive thing: his clothes are taken away from him, and he is given new clothes. He is asked to fast so that he can be fed. He is humiliated so that he can be honoured. In being brought into the new community, he is given the uniform of the community, given the name, given a reception, given a banquet.

The spirit of a community is, first of all, a knowledge and an acute awareness of our belonging to a certain community, plus gratitude toward it and the desire to promote its welfare. The early Church was convinced that the spirit which enabled the Christian community to live differently from the crazy world out there was, in fact, the Holy Spirit of Christ Himself dwelling in the community. Nowadays we are much more inclined to think of the giving of the Holy Spirit or the receiving of the Holy Spirit as something that comes to us individually. In the account of Pentecost, the Bible says that they were all together with one accord in one place, and then the Holy Spirit came upon them. The Wisdom literature of the Apocrypha makes the Holy Spirit say, "My dwelling place is in the full assembly of the saints."

Of course, the individual receives the spirit; that is the point of the bishop's prayer. The spirit which God bestows upon me in baptism-confirmation is the spirit of the community, the Spirit of the Church, which is God's Spirit. It belongs in the body. Coming into this community and leaving aside the world, we acquire a new identity, a new personality, a new set of priorities, new ways of looking at reality. This spirit which becomes ours as we participate in this community is the Spirit of Jesus Christ. It is His Spirit, His priorities, and His values.

This is not something that happens all at once. It is something in which, as the New Testament says, you grow. You grow in the spirit; that is, you grow more and more absorbed and immersed into identification with the spirit of this community.

By the time a person has been in the Church for fifteen years, it is not at all uncommon for him to say that he doesn't have any close friends who are not in the Church. This is not a conscious thing that a person deliberately plans, it just happens. Changes have taken place gradually, and we seek associations and friendships with people who largely agree with us about all the important things. Changes occur, although the most radical change that can occur is that initial transference of one's primal loyalties from out there to in here. The Sacrament of Holy Baptism provides a concrete experience that you can see, taste, hear, and smell, rather than a purely mystical, invisible experience.

As a consequence, there is not a lick of sense in baptizing someone unless he intends and has the opportunity to continue to have a close and intimate association with the community of which he is becoming a member. It is the life of the community, not the baptism ceremony, which changes who he is. Active membership in the Church is the opportunity for the Church to mould and fashion one's life and character. What baptism does is to start something.

In order for a child to realize the fruits of his baptism, it is essential that he experience the love of the congregation, that he be nurtured and taught and trained in the Christian moral and spiritual life. Clearly, this obligation is first of all upon the parents. It is Mama and Papa's job to see that he gets a Christian upbringing. He also needs to know that there are others besides Father and Mother who love him. This is actually the job of the entire congregation, but since everybody's business is nobody's business, the Church designated certain individuals, usually of the generation of the parents, to act as kind of spiritual aunts and uncles, to be the liaison between the child and the larger congregation, the bridge over which the child passes into membership into the larger community. These people are godparents.

The origin of godparents goes all the way back to primitive times when the candidate for baptism needed someone to vouch for him. When the Church was under persecution and government spies were standing around with little notebooks taking down the names of Christians to be turned over to the magistrate, every candidate for baptism had to have somebody who would certify to the congregation that this guy was not a government spy, and that he probably wouldn't break under torture and give the names of the rest.

What these godparents are supposed to do, first of all, is to aid and assist Mama and Papa in the religious education and nurture of the child. There are concrete and specific things they can do, like sit with the child at Mass. Godparents should seek the association of the child, should remember birthdays and anniversaries in the same way that parents do, not necessarily with gifts, but with a telephone call or a card. Godparents should spend some time with the child, in order to cultivate a relationship with that child so that he will have confidence in another adult besides his parents.

Now a godparent has a further duty, a rather subtle one that is seldom mentioned. You recall the story in the Old Testament about Achan and the Old Covenant: if one Jew broke the Covenant, it was broken for the whole community. Well, that is also true of the Christian Church. For several hundred years after the time of Christ, if there were 267 listed communicants in this parish, there would be 267 people at Mass on Sunday. If there were 265, we would know that two were sick in bed. There is a very real correlation between the spiritual vitality of the entire Christian community and the percentage of its membership who are active. In the year 220 A.D., in any Christian church in Christendom, anybody who missed Mass on Sunday without an excuse just did not bother to show up the following Sunday. He would not have been let in. To miss Mass voluntarily was regarded as the repudiation and denial of one's Christian profession. Not only did everyone go to church, nearly everyone maintained a very high and lofty standard of morality. If a person committed what we call a mortal sin, he was excluded from the community. They wanted a 100 per cent effort from 100 per cent of the community.

Now here we have a little baby. We know it is our duty, as the Prayer Book says, to worship God every Sunday in His church, to follow Christ, and to work, pray, and give for the spread of His kingdom. Obviously the baby can't do that, so someone does it for him. The church is entitled to his prayers; he is a member of the church and every member of the church is supposed to be praying daily. If we are not, the church is weakened. But a little baby can't pray, so someone says his prayers for him. A godparent should not only say his or her own prayers, but should say the baby's prayers until the child is old enough to say his own. The church is entitled to the financial contribution of anyone in the congregation who has a dime in his pocket. A godparent should take two sets of offering envelopes, one in his name and one in the name of his godchild, and put a nickel in the collection plate for his godchild. A godparent could sing in the choir as his own contribution to the life of the church, and serve as an acolyte or on the altar guild in the name of his godchild. Not only is it the godparent's job to let the child know that the congregation cares about him, but in the name of the child, he lets the congregation know that the child is pulling his share of the load.

If this seems strange, remember that we do this ordinarily in every other aspect of the child's life. We select his clothing for him, we plan his diet for him, and when the child is eight months old and can't talk and Aunt Susie gives the child a $10 bond, we say thank you because the child can't. No one sees anything particularly odd or strange about this.

In Christ's humanity, He and I are one. In my humanity, the godchild and I are one, one with each other in Christ's humanity. There is a spiritual link, a spiritual unity, between me and my godchild, based upon the fact that there is a spiritual unity between both of us and Christ.

Ideally, the godparent ought to be a member of the local congregation. There is, unfortunately, the custom of having godparents who are not. The father's employer would be deeply wounded if he were not asked to be godfather, although he is an apostate Jew and never goes to church himself. The godmother is the mother's best friend who lives in Cincinnati, who would also be deeply wounded if not asked. That's okay. Just go ahead and select three more people from the local congregation in which the child is going to be raised. If, when the child is four years old, you move to Memphis, after you've been there a while, select members of that congregation and ask them to serve as godparents to the child. A godparent needs to have access to the child, and he certainly ought to be someone who is himself devout and well-instructed in the faith in which he is going to be influencing the child's growth and development.

Baptism

Baptism is spoken of in Scriptures and in the popular theology of evangelical Christianity as death unto sin and resurrection unto God. The dying to the old self, or "being born again", is actually a spiritual experience which is the interior, subjective side of baptism. It need not accompany the baptism in time, because baptism is principally the beginning of the corporate life in the Christian Church which the baptized person experiences by being set in the midst of the congregation.

We grow in grace.

14

EUCHARIST

This sacrament is the only one which is combined and united with the service of corporate public worship on Sunday. From the days of the Apostles until the sixteenth century, no Christian, orthodox, heretical, of whatever stripe, ever went to church on Sunday for any other purpose than to participate in the Holy Communion. The idea that you could have a Sunday worship service for a congregation of Christian people that was not focused on the bread and wine on the altar was an absolutely novel and original idea with the Reformers of the sixteenth century. People went to church to go to Mass, and the suggestion that they could do anything else in church on Sunday morning would have met with blank incomprehension. The absolutely central, focal Christian act is the celebration of the Eucharist.

It says in the Acts of the Apostles that "The Church continued daily in the apostles' teaching and fellowship and in the breaking of bread with prayer." What that says plainly is that in the infant Church in the city of Jerusalem before any missionaries ever went out to spread the Gospel to the rest of Judea and Antioch, and even before Paul began his missionary journeys to the Gentile world, in the days and weeks and months immediately following the resurrection of Christ, they had a daily Mass. The Church continued *daily* in the apostles' teaching and fellowship, and in the breaking of bread with prayer. It is hard to see how anybody can claim today to have a modern, twentieth-century Church which is modelled on the New Testament Church without celebrating the Eucharist daily.

The earliest name for this particular service, the one that is perhaps the most common in the New Testament, is simply the Breaking of Bread. This service has been known to history by many different names, but perhaps the most common, of course, and the one that has gained currency in the last few generations, is the Eucharist. This is a Greek word which means simply "the thanksgiving". Now as we said before, the text, the ritual part of the communion service, is based upon the Jewish table blessing, the returning of thanks at the Jewish family meal. It was out of this table blessing at the Last Supper that our Christian communion service developed and evolved.

Liturgy is another word which again goes back to the earliest times. It is also a Greek word which means "the work of the people", or the public work. It was originally a secular term which applied to something of a spectacular nature performed in the community on behalf of the town by some benefactor or millionaire patron who wanted a big spectacle, for the sake of the people. One is tempted, of course, to read into the etymology of the word "liturgy", "the people's work", but that's not really what it meant. This is not something that we're doing for ourselves. It's something we are doing in the Body of Christ as representative humanity in the same way that Christ died on the cross for all men; so the Church offers day by day the memorial of His death and resurrection on behalf of all men. The liturgy, whether it be the Holy Communion, the morning and evening offices, the Litany, baptism, confirmation, a wedding, a burial, or any other public liturgical service of the Church, is never something that the Church does merely for its own benefit or for the sake of the members. It always looks beyond itself to the whole of humanity.

It has been called the Lord's Supper; perhaps this is the term most common in Evangelical and Protestant churches. You might think it's something that the Baptists thought up, but you find the term as early as the second century, and perhaps it has an earlier history than that. The notion here is that it's Jesus Himself who is the host at this dinner.

It has frequently been identified with the nuptial banquet, and although there is no particular name to suggest this aspect of it, Jesus in several of His parables said that the kingdom of Heaven is like a man who gives a wedding feast for his son. There are nuptial and even sexual images that run all the way through the liturgy, such as in the Holy Saturday liturgy. In the form we have it, it is the oldest and most ancient of the liturgies of the Church, because it goes back to a time in which the only Bible the Church had was the Old Testament. There are no New Testament lessons in the Holy Saturday liturgy. It has come down to us from at least as early as the first century, and yet in the solemn blessing of the baptismal font there is something that is almost pornographic. The priest takes the Paschal candle, clearly a penis symbol, and prays that this font will be fertile in the coming year in the production of new life for Christ. There are layers and layers of meaning here, and while it is not explicit, if all the old ladies could read that into it they would run screaming out of the church.

Nevertheless, what this leads to and is directed toward, is that moment in which the Church as the Bride of Christ goes to the altar and receives into her body the body of the bridegroom, in a fertilizing and fecundating union, so that the Christian and Christ become one flesh, and we are His mystical body, in the same way that a man and a woman in marriage become one flesh.

Another term in common use among scholars is the *anaphora*, the lifting-up, the offering. It's called the Holy Communion, the Blessed Sacrament, and the name by which it has been known most widely throughout most of Christian history, the Mass.

It's commonly said that the word "mass" derives from the dismissal, the "*Ita missa est*" at the end of the medieval Latin Mass. It doesn't, however; the English form of this word is "mess", as in mess hall, the officers' mess, or as my old Alabama grandmother used to say, "Go out in the garden and gather a mess of turnip greens." The word means a meal, dinner, supper. It's related to the Spanish word *mesa*, meaning table, in much the same way as the English word "board" as in "room and board" relates to the table the meal was served on. In Latin you have the word *mensa*. The word "mass" simply means "the supper", "the feast", "the dinner".

Now let's look at the structure. When I teach small children, I compare the Mass to a hamburger. What does it take to make a hamburger? Well, you need bread and meat. Some people use mustard, some people use ketchup, some people use mayonnaise. That's optional. But the bread and the meat are not optional. Some people put on pickles and some people put on onions, and some people leave the onions off. The essential ingredients of the hamburger are the bread and the meat, and everything else is up to you.

There are essential structural parts of the Mass, and then

there are the pickles and onions. The Mass actually consists of two services. You know that the early Church was Jewish, and all the apostles were Jewish. The Church spent several years in Jerusalem before it began to spread out into other parts of Palestine, and even when it was planted in Antioch, it was in a Jewish community in Antioch. These new Christian churches were full of people who had been raised in the synagogue, and when they organized a new Christian church they had a synangogue service. And when the synagogue service was over, they added the distinctive Christian thing, the breaking of bread with prayer, doing what Jesus had done at the Last Supper with His disciples. So there are really two services that have been conflated and are normally thought of as one service. The first is the synagogue service, the *proanaphora*, or the *missa catechumenorum*, the feast of the learners; because of its principal emphasis, it is also called the Liturgy of the Word, since it centres around the reading of Scripture.

There are four principal parts to the Liturgy of the Word: the Collect, the Epistle, the Gospel, and the Creed. Everything else is pickles and onions. Those are the structural parts. That concludes the synagogue service. It is then followed by the other service which also has four parts, in which we do what Jesus did at the Last Supper. He took bread, He blessed it, He broke it, and He gave it. Then He took wine and blessed it and gave it. The parts were combined so that you take the bread and wine, which is called the Offertory; you bless the bread and wine, which is called the Consecration; you break the bread, which is called the Fracture; and you distribute the elements, which is called the Communion.

The Jewish table blessing, which becomes the *anaphora*,

Eucharist

or the *missa fidelium,* the feast of the faithful, was a recollection, a remembering of the Passover, so that the Christian communion service continues this very Jewish thing almost all the way back to the Exodus in Egypt. Now Jesus said to His disciples, "Do this in remembrance of me." What Jesus had done was to take the ordinary everyday Jewish table blessing and give it a new significance, a new meaning, and every time the disciples got together to eat, they would return thanks and do what Jesus had done. Clearly, obviously, they did it *every day.*

When Jesus said, "Do this in remembrance of me," the word He used was *anamnesis.* This is a Greek word which shows up in the English word "amnesia". The Greek root is *-mnesis,* which means "knowing". Amnesia is a not-knowing, since the Greek *a-* is a negative prefix. But the Greek prefix *ana-* means "again". An *anamnesis* is a "knowing again". It's a much stronger word than just remembering. To remember something in English means to call to mind something that exists in the past and exists in the present only as a memory. The Greek word *anamnesis* is more like doing it over again. This is related, of course, to Our Lord's statement, "Wherever two or three are gathered together in my name, there am I in the midst of them." *In my name* means in official capacity, when the Church gathers together as the Church, and what the Church did when she gathered together for sixteen centuries was to celebrate the Eucharist. When two or three are gathered together in my name, officially, there am I in their midst. It's interesting to note how many of the post-Resurrection appearances recorded in the gospels have to do with eating. Jesus appeared to His disciples again and again when they were eating. St Paul talks about Jesus coming back and eating and drinking with the disciples. There's a strong Eucharistic implication in the post-Resurrection appearances of Christ.

What is the meaning of this thing that we do? There is a quotation from Rabbinical literature from the Intertestamentary period, in which some rabbi makes the statement, "In the days of King Messiah, all sacrifices shall be done away with except the thank-offering." Except the Eucharist. There were a number of different kinds of sacrifices in the Old Testament religion, but the critical thing to notice is that the early Christian Church understood its Eucharist as the continuation of, the completion of, the fulfilment of, the Jewish temple sacrifices. John the Baptist, when he was introducing Christ to his disciples, said, "Behold the Lamb of God, behold Him who taketh away the sin of the world." Christ was put to death on Good Friday, which was if not the actual Passover day, close enough for the connection to be obvious; it was clearly the Passover season. So that the death of Christ on the cross is the replacement of the Passover lamb that was slain to avert the destroying angel in Egypt, and was slain again annually on the anniversary of the Passover. It was the major feast of the Jewish religion.

Look at the sacrificial implications in the Eucharist. God the Son from all eternity was giving Himself to the Father. It's a sacrifice. When He was born of the Virgin Mary and entered human history, what did He do? He continued doing on earth what He had always been doing in eternity, giving Himself to God the Father by an act of total, perfect loving obedience. He didn't hold back even life itself. When Jesus rose from the dead on Easter, and forty days later ascended into Heaven and now sits at the right hand of the Father, He is giving Himself wholly and totally to the Father. It's a way of life with the Son, and we shouldn't obscure the fact that it's also a way of life for the Father.

And this total donation of the Father to the Son, and the Son to the Father, is what God wants to share with us His creatures. The way He does it is by uniting us to His incarnate Son through the Holy Spirit at baptism, making us to be the Body of Christ.

What happens at Mass is that the mystical body of Christ offers the sacramental body of Christ to God the Father; the same Christ, the same offering, not a new offering, not another offering, not a different offering, because the offering of Christ to the Father is an ongoing thing, eternal in its nature, in order for us to enter into and become a part of that eternal offering; which was made visible pre-eminently on Calvary's hill on that first Good Friday outside the city walls of Jerusalem. We become a part of it so that we offer Jesus and He offers us when He offers Himself, because He has identified Himself with us by His Spirit which He has given us. What we do at Mass is what Jesus is doing in Heaven. It's not that we're doing something like He's doing in Heaven, it is the same identical offering which we are privileged to participate in, to become part of. This is the sacrifice of the Mass.

One of the characteristics of sacrifice is the offering for sin, and so part of the Eucharist is a General Confession, but let it be pointed out that what we are doing in the General Confession in the Eucharist is not confessing my sinfulness, but the sinfulness of humanity, the sinfulness of every sin since Cain killed Abel. The sinfulness of all terrorist activities, all kidnappings, all embezzlements, all lying and stealing, all wife beating and child abuse, all false advertising; all the sins of the world are being offered along with Jesus in this sacrificial sin offering.

Another very primitive notion that goes along with and is closely associated with this is the totem sacrifice. The American Indian tribes each had a totem animal, as did the African tribes and the Australian aborigines; the early tribal people in Europe also had totem animals. This is the notion that some particular form of animal life, like a bear or a wolf or a badger, is the present embodiment of the original tribal ancestral deity. This is a sacred animal. On solemn religious occasions you eat the body of the totem animal and this is like eating of the deity. The idea here is very simple. When I get hungry, I get weak, and when I put food in my mouth after I've been weakened by hunger, my strength revives. Now if I get spiritually weak, there must be some kind of spiritual food to compensate for and offset my spiritual weakness. This is the function of the totem animal.

This totem idea is very widespread, and I want to try to get some idea across to you of why this is so. Americans think, you know, that chickens come wrapped in cellophane, but they don't. They come with feathers on them. In order to eat a chicken somebody's got to kill it. And it's only our highly urban, civilized society today that insulates us from the fact that, if I'm going to go on living, something else is going to have to die. Life depends on death. If I had bacon and eggs this morning, a pig gave up its life for me, and the two eggs I had were two little chickens that never saw the light of day. And I should give thanks to that little pig and to those little chickens. They gave up their lives for me. Notice further that if I eat bacon or chicken, they were dead when they got to the table, but the protoplasm that made the chickens and pig is now busily at work inside me turning into Fr Rogers. So that in a very real sense, chickens live on in my life and become a part of me and are taken into me. This is the underlying idea behind that passage from St John's gospel: "Except a man eat my flesh and drink of my blood there is no life in him. He that eats of my flesh and drinks of my blood, dwelleth in me and I in him." Remember, there's that mutual indwelling that takes place between the Father and the Son, and it also takes place between us and Christ. There is a passage of the being of Christ into you and me, so that He becomes us and we become Him.

This is a sacrament. It is the sign of an inward and spiritual grace. What is happening outside externally is also happening inwardly spiritually. And that brings us to the question of what we mean when we say that Christ is really present in the Blessed Sacrament. In what sense does that bread and wine become the body and blood of Christ?

Let me say right here and now that never, in the long two thousand years of Christian history, has any orthodox Christian theologian ever for a moment suppposed that the bread and wine undergo any sort of physical or chemical change. Obviously, it does not. And I'm quite sure that when Jesus broke the bread at the Last Supper and said, "This is my body" and handed it around, Peter tasted it and muttered, "Tastes like bread to me." The change of the bread and wine into the body and blood of Christ is not a physical or chemical change. The Church teaches that the bread does not symbolize the body of Christ, it *is* the body of Christ. Remember that a body is any material thing which the spirit uses to make its presence known. And the bread and the wine is what Christ uses to let us know He's here, and we have His word for it. Certainly we are not to suppose that Jesus comes down and squeezes Himself into a little thin wafer. But Jesus is there in the bread placed on the altar and used for Holy Communion. In the Middle Ages they were wrestling with this problem, and came up with a theory they called transubstantiation, which has been badly misunderstood because of the change in the meaning of words over the centuries.

Though this theory doesn't for a moment explain the Real Presence, it will at least give us a handle on a way of thinking about it. It rests on the distinction going all the way back to Aristotle between substance and accident. The word "substance" is a Latin word meaning a "standing under." To Aristotle and the medieval theologians, substance is in the thing. For example, a table doesn't need a specific number of legs to be a table, nor does it need a specific shape. The number of legs and the shape we would say are incidental. In the Middle Ages they called it accidental, but it meant the same thing. All the material properties of a table are incidental, and are not essential to its being a table. Where we use the word "essential", in the Middle Ages they used the word "substantial". The essence of the table is not material at all. The essence of the table is what it does. It's the way we treat it, the use to which we put it. And that's separate from any of its material or physical properties. So the substance is something non-material and yet you couldn't really deny the substance is somehow in the table. It isn't anywhere else. How can you change the substance without changing the accidents?

Over there about 300 yards away is a deep, narrow ravine, about five feet wide. The kids coming from this neighbourhood going to that school over there have to walk five or six blocks out of their way, so I go out and take a door off the hinges and put it across that ravine and it becomes a bridge. And it really is a bridge. It's no longer a door, although incidentally, accidentally, nothing has changed. And yet we stop talking about it as if it were a door and start talking about it as if it were a bridge; we start using it as a bridge and it functions as a bridge. We've changed a door into a bridge without changing any of its material properties. What we've changed is what it does, the way we treat it, and what we do with it.

The doctrine of transubstantiation says that when the bread and wine is consecrated, materially it is unchanged. What is changed is the inner reality, what it accomplishes, the way we regard it, and what we do with it, and its inner reality becomes the means whereby our souls are nourished on the divine life of Christ Himself. A spiritual reality changes, a real change takes place in the thing itself, just as a real change takes place in the nature of that door when I turn it into a bridge. It ceases to do what a door does and now it does what a bridge does. And the bread and the wine of the Holy Communion become the means whereby Christ conveys Himself to me in a spiritual fashion, uniting Himself to me again and bestowing His grace upon me and drawing me to Himself.

Now, one other thing. St Paul says, "As oft as ye eat this bread and drink this cup ye do show the Lord's death till He come." All the sacraments are a participation in the death and resurrection of Christ. What happens at the Eucharist is an aspiration, a rising up of this world to be united with Heaven, and a descent of Heaven to be united with this world. There is a coming together of time and eternity, of Heaven and earth, of God and man. And this, of course, is what happens when you die. You go to be with God. In the Eucharist you go to be with God.

Here is what I believe to be the most cogent, the most emphatic, the most complete statement of Eucharistic theology that has ever been phrased:

Here we offer and present unto Thee, O Lord, ourselves, our souls and bodies, to be a reasonable holy and living sacrifice unto Thee, humbly beseeching Thee that we, and all others that shall be partakers of this Holy Communion, may worthily receive the most precious body and blood of Thy son Jesus Christ, be filled with His grace and heavenly benediction, and made one Body with Him, that He may dwell in us, and we in Him.

Here is that theology of mutual indwelling, of the mutual giving and receiving, and the sacrament is an outward and visible sign of an inward and spiritual grace. The outward and visible sign is that we give something to God and God gives it back to us transformed, changed. And the giving of our bread and wine is a token by which we give ourselves to God and He is giving Himself to us. This is what's going on in Heaven – the donation of the Father to the Son is the procession of the Spirit from the Father to the Son. God looks down from Heaven and sees the Church, the mystical body of Christ, and He loves Christ in us and the Holy Spirit comes. This is the epiclesis. The Son offers Himself to the Father and the Holy Spirit returns to Heaven, carrying our love, our prayers, our devotions, our self-offering. So we are entering into and sharing in and participating in the divine mutual self-offering of the Father and the Son.

I want to conclude with a passage from Dom Gregory

Dix's *The Shape of the Liturgy*. He's talking about the Mass:

The whole has a new meaning fixed for all time in the Upper Room. But the form of the rite is still centred upon the Book on the lectern and the Bread and Cup on the table as it always was, though by the new meaning they have become the Liturgy of the Spirit and the Liturgy of the Body, centring upon the Word of God enounced and the Word of God made flesh.

He had told His friends to do this henceforward with the new meaning "for the *anamnesis*" of Him, and they have done it always since.

Was ever a command so obeyed? For century after century, spreading slowly to every continent and country and among every race on earth, this action has been done, in every conceivable human circumstance, for every conceivable human need from infancy and before it to extreme old age and after it, from the pinnacles of earthly greatness to the refuge of fugitives in the caves and dens of the earth. Men have found no better thing than this to do for kings at their crowning and for criminals going to the scaffold; for armies in triumph or for a bride and bridegroom in a little country church; for the proclamation of a dogma or for a good crop of wheat; for the wisdom of the Parliament of a mighty nation or for a sick old woman afraid to die; for a schoolboy sitting an examination or for Columbus setting out to discover America; for the famine of a whole province or for the soul of a dead lover; in thankfulness because my father did not die of pneumonia; for a village headman much tempted to return to fetish because the yams failed; because the

Turk was at the gates of Vienna; for the repentance of Margaret; for the settlement of a strike; for a son for a barren woman; for Captain so-and-so, wounded and prisoner of war; while the lions roared in the nearby amphitheatre; on the beach at Dunkirk; while the hiss of scythes in the thick June grass came faintly through the windows of the church; tremulously, by an old monk on the fiftieth anniversary of his vows; furtively, by an exiled bishop who had hewn timber all day in a prison camp near Murmansk; gorgeously, for the canonization of St Joan of Arc – one could fill many pages with the reasons why men have done this, and not tell a hundredth part of them. And best of all, week by week and month by month, on a hundred thousand successive Sundays, faithfully, unfailingly, across all the parishes of Christendom, the pastors have done this just to *make* the *plebs sancta Dei* – the holy common people of God.

To those who know a little of Christian history probably the most moving of all the reflections it brings is not the thought of the great events and the well-remembered saints, but of those innumerable millions of entirely obscure faithful men and women, every one with his or her own individual hopes and fears and joys and sorrows and loves – sins and temptations and prayers – once every whit as vivid and alive as mine are now. They have left not the slightest trace in this world, not even a name, but have passed to God utterly forgotten by men. Yet each of them once believed and prayed as I believe and pray, and found it hard and grew slack and sinned and repented and fell again. Each of them worshipped at the Eucharist, and found their thoughts wandering and tried again, and felt heavy and unresponsive and yet knew – just as really and pathetically as I do these things. There is a little ill-spelled ill-carved rustic epitaph of the fourth century from Asia Minor: "Here sleeps the blessed Chione, who has found Jerusalem for she prayed much." Not another word is known of Chione, some peasant woman who lived in that vanished world of Christian Anatolia. But how lovely if all that should survive after sixteen centuries were that one had prayed much, so that the neighbours who saw all one's life were sure one must have found Jerusalem! What did the Sunday Eucharist in her village church every week for a lifetime mean to the blessed Chione – and to the millions like her then, and every year since? The sheer, stupendous *quantity* of the love of God which this ever-repeated action has drawn from the obscure Christian multitudes through the centuries is in itself an overwhelming thought. (And all that going with one to the altar every morning!)

It is because it became embedded deep down in the life of the Christian peoples, colouring all the *via vitae* of the ordinary man and woman, marking its personal turning-points, marriage, sickness, death and the rest, running through it year by year with the feasts and fasts and the rhythm of the Sundays, that the eucharistic action became inextricably woven into the public history of the Western world. The thought of it is inseparable from its great turning-points also. Pope Leo doing this in the morning before he went out to daunt Atilla, on the day that saw the continuity of Europe saved; and another Leo doing this three and a half centuries later when he crowned Charlemagne Roman Emperor, on the day that saw that continuity fulfilled. Or again, Alfred wandering defeated by the Danes staying his soul on this, while medieval England struggled to be born; and Charles I also, on that morning of his execution when medieval England came to its final end. Such things strike the mind with their suggestions of a certain timelessness about the eucharistic action and an independence of its setting, in keeping with the stability in an ever-changing world of the forms of the liturgy themselves. At Constantinople they "do this" yet with the identical words and gestures that they used while the silver trumpets of the Basileus still called across the Bosphorus, in what seems to us now the strange fairy-tale land of the Byzantine Empire. In this twentieth century Charles de Foucauld in his hermitage in the Saraha "did this" with the same rite as Cuthbert twelve centuries before in his hermitage on Lindisfarne in the northern seas. This very morning I did this with a set of texts which has not changed by more than a few syllables since Augustine used those very words at Canterbury on the third Sunday of Easter in the summer after he landed. Yet "this" can still take hold of a man's life and work with it.

Dom Gregory Dix, *The Shape of the Liturgy*, Westminster: Dacra Press, 1945, 743–45.

15

MARRIAGE

Everyone who was ever born knows in his bones by the age of fifteen that he was made for rapture. No one has to tell us this, we simply know it by listening to our hearts. The Christian wants total rapture and bliss, but knows he's going to have to wait until he dies and goes to Heaven to get it. Everything that the Christian loves and enjoys has the tinge of sadness to it because of its impermanence and finiteness. The pagan, like the Christian, wants total bliss and happiness, but he expects to find it on this earth, and in this life. The pagan is on a quest for the Holy Grail, the Golden Fleece, the Bluebird of Happiness, or whatever will grant him bliss.

The average Christian is doctrinally a Christian and dogmatically a pagan. You see, if I was created for bliss, for perfect beauty, for romance, and I've got to find it on this earth, there's one thing for sure. It's not where I am, doing what I'm doing. I love my job, but my job was romantic for about a month. I'm married to the most wonderful woman in the world and she stayed that way for about six weeks. This is what's behind our sense of restlessness. We are a questing people, looking for rapture. As you get older, this aggressive questing turns into a wistful, backward-looking "if only". If only I had taken the other job, if only I had married the other girl. At fifteen you want rapture, at twenty-five you'll settle for happiness, at thirty-five peace, at forty-five security. This is the dogmatic religion of most of us, with its own mythology and hymns (popular songs). When I stop and think, I'll behave as a Christian, but when I feel, most likely I'll behave as a romantic. I'm a product of this culture and it's been deeply implanted in my bones.

In ages of faith, people could afford to follow their impulses and act as Christians. They weren't any better than we, not more saintly, but the unconscious dogmatic assumptions of society then were Christian. Not today. If I don't like my job, I'll change it. If I don't like my wife, I'll change that, too. If someone offers the romantic a job at twice the money in Maine or Alaska, he says, "I can't turn it down." The Christian says, "Well, I'm not happy on what I'm making here with friends, why would I be happy with twice as much somewhere else?"

Because we are looking for rapture and bliss in this life, and because the closest we will ever get to experiencing it sensibly, in a bodily fashion, is sexual orgasm, romanticism always homes in on sex. I was once asked to deliver a lecture at a college campus on the underlying assumptions of the relationships of the male and female students on campus. In trying to figure out how you could go about getting at the underlying assumptions in the minds of boys and girls who go courting, the thought occurred to me to check out the lyrics of the popular songs of the day. We all grow up listening to and hearing love songs. So I analyzed popular songs. I went to the drug store and got a magazine with lyrics, got a columnar pad and summarized the themes, ending up with eight or nine. As I worked through more than a hundred songs, something began to sound familiar. I remembered I had once run across lyrics of religious hymns which had been sung in the temple of

Aphrodite in about the sixth or seventh century B.C. I had read them with interest and forgotten them. Now I dashed back to the library and opened up the lyrics of the Aphrodite songs, and as God is my witness, you could have published the sixth-century stuff and no one would have noticed the difference.

What are these themes? First of all, the popular love song will be sad. These songs are sorrowful, and they're singing about a love affair that didn't pan out, about a broken heart. "Love makes the world go round." "Love is the greatest thing." "I can't live without you." "It's that old black magic." There is a strong element of fatalism. You *fall* in love; you can't control it. You must follow where your love leads.

Also note that the language of love is also the language of religion. "I adore you." "You are an angel." "Heaven is in your arms." "She is a goddess." Since love is the *summum bonum*, if you fail in everything else and succeed in love, you're a success.

The final tip-off is that sex and death are interchangeable in these songs. "I love you so much I could die" really means "I love you so much I want to go to bed with you." This is explicitly stated in the metaphysical poetry of John Donne, George Herbert, and others in the seventeenth century. This is an old idea; in none of the great classical romances do they get happily married in this life. They get married in the grave, like Tristan and Isolde.

This romanticism evolved from the ancient mystery religions which went underground with the advent of Christianity. Paganism was still there in the culture, and it took the Church about a thousand years to build up a synthesis of the Christian religion with every other aspect of human life. One of the reasons the Church calls itself catholic is that not only does it contain the whole of Christ's teaching, but also that the whole of Christ's teaching has some relevance to the whole of human life. There is a Christian way of educating children, there is a Christian way of carrying on politics, a Christian way of doing business, and certainly a Christian way of conducting one's life and family. The legalization of Christianity meant that the Church found herself in partnership with the State, and then had to construct a Christian way of life for all people. She worked out, painfully, laboriously, a Christian implication for all the different aspects of human life, building all of this up into a harmonic and unified synthesis, which began to unravel in the fourteenth century.

Social organization is basically a way of conducting one's relationships with other people. If you have a system of inter-relationships which is beginning to break down, failing to function harmoniously and smoothly, it is likely to show up first in the place where interpersonal relationships are most constant and most intimate, that is, in the family. I don't have to see the bishop much, so there is less adjustment of his sinfulness to my sinfulness. I see my curate more, and therefore there is more opportunity for friction to be generated between us. But I see my wife most of all. I see her every day, and under conditions of intimacy where stress is most likely to become apparent. So it is in the family that the breakup of the Christian social synthesis is most evident.

Marriage today is not really in a very happy state. For all of the couples who get divorced, there are almost that many more who go to marriage counsellors or who contemplate a divorce and tough it out because they consider that the alternative is perhaps even worse. When half the marriages fail, this is more than just a human failure. If half the students in an English class fail, it is probably the fault of the teacher. If half the businesses this year go bankrupt, the nation is in a major economic depression. In other words, individuals frequently fall victim to causes which are social in nature and are larger than the individual component. There's an enormous amount of conflict and friction that goes on behind the surface in marriage, but the real reason for the failure of so many marriages is not the human failure, but rather the institution of marriage which is a failure.

When a large number of people in any human society have a similar problem and somebody solves the problem, and the solution is a good and successful one, other people will imitate that solution. And that solution becomes the characteristic way that society deals with that problem. We have business and economic institutions for the production, processing, and distribution of consumer goods. We have a legal insitution which is designed to prevent me and my neighbour from having to fight it out if we have a disagreement. We have policemen, judges, law courts, the right of counsel, trial by jury, rules of evidence, and all that. We have public entertainment institutions such as television, radio, movies, the theatre, professional athletics. We have recreational institutions: golf clubs, country clubs, national parks. The Church is an institution designed to deal with the problem of man's hunger for the transcendent, his sense of contingency in the midst of mystery. Marriage is also an institution, whereby people can deal with sex, babies, parental responsibilities, the inheritance of property, and that whole complex of relationships built upon and developing out of our sexual and reproductive proclivities.

The kind of marriage that we have inherited in the West is one that was invented by the Christian Church to achieve specifically Christian goals and objectives. We tend to take our institutions for granted, and not only that, but if the problem is a serious one and the institution is at all successful, we will defend the institution with an enormous weight of public opinion because we are vaguely aware that without the institution we would be in a situation of chaos. But as the situations change, the institution becomes less adaptive and less efficient, and there begins to arise public pressure aimed at changing the institution. You have a lot of people who want to keep the institution unchanged and a lot of people who want to change it. Sometimes this dichotomy exists within one person. I have an image of what a marriage and family should be like. I want a vine-covered cottage in the suburbs, with shutters and roses growing up the trellis over the door. I want children rushing out to meet me when I come home from work, and a lovely wife to meet me at the door with a kiss who escorts me into the house where I sit down at the table in front of a hot supper which she has just prepared. In the evening, of course, Father and Mother and the children play together until the children's bedtime. This image is somewhere in the back of the mind of everyone who thinks about getting married. It's a pervasive image that comes to us out of the past, an idealized image of marriage and family. That's what I want.

But I also want apartment life, somebody else to mow the lawn, a free swimming pool, tennis courts, and a swinging lifestyle, and I want to be able to take off and travel to Acapulco and Bermuda. But someone has to stay home and feed the dogs and cats while my wife and I are on our six weeks' vacation. So inside of us there is a conflict about a lot of our institutions, but particularly about marriage. We want the values produced by contradictory sets of images, and the result is frustration.

A great many people, young, innocent, starry-eyed, and virtuous, get married and to their immense astonishment wind up within six months hating the sight of each other and wondering what happened. "We were in love with each other a year ago, and now I can't stand her. She can't stand me. We're constantly bickering, constantly at odds, quarrelling with one another. What has gone wrong?" When you go into a situation expecting to realize one set of values and you come up with another, you are frustrated and disappointed. Though the other values may be good, they're not what you expected. This unresolved hostility is largely because the excuse for most marriages is that two folk are "in love". What most people mean by that in the context of marriage is romantic love.

There is an awkwardness in the English language concerning our word "love". We use one word to mean a number of different relationships. A man can say to a woman, "I love you," and she can respond, "I love you, too," and they can mean exactly opposite things. The Greeks had several words for love: *eros*, *agape*, and *philia*. Eros, from which we get the word "erotic", does not mean sexual love, but rather a love directed toward self-realization. It is a way a person loves naturally anything which does him good: "I love apple pie." When I say I love apple pie, any apple pie within earshot better look out. I have designs on its existence. I fully intend that the apple pie should get littler so that I can get bigger. I want to take its being and use it for the benefit of my being. This is a perfectly good, legitimate use of the English word "love". The synonyms are "like" and "enjoy". The hungrier I am, the more I love apple pie. But when I have just finished a big dinner, I don't love apple pie. My love for apple pie becomes at that point an entirely theoretical thing. I put it in abeyance until I get hungry, because this kind of love is strictly from hunger. It grows out of need and emptiness. In the lyrics of romantic love songs, the synonyms for love are "need", "want", "desire".

Essentially, this is the way we love something that we feel is going to make us happy. It is not a sinful type of love; it is perfectly natural. It is good that we should love apple pie in this way. But when it is applied to the relationship of human beings, it won't work. You can have romance or marriage, but not both. They will absolutely cancel each other out.

The most important decision for a young couple facing marriage is what thing they both agree is more important than their happiness. The family is a community, and any community which exists for the happiness of its members will self-destruct. If we get married to be happy, what will we do when the days come – and they will come – when we make each other unhappy? At such times we hold together because there is something which together we value more than happiness.

The first purpose of marriage, then, is to create a human cultural community in which the lives and characters of its members are shaped and fashioned according to the truths of the Gospel. This is far more important than our passing pleasure and happiness.

The second purpose of marriage is to create a moral environment in which, in order to hold the marriage together, we must grow holy. The Bible says that it is not good for man to live alone, because when he lives alone, he can do as he pleases. A person in community cannot do that. The worst thing that can happen to a person is to be allowed to grow up having his own way, doing his own thing. Such children we call spoiled brats; for such adults we have uglier names. The Church asks us to take a vow of lifelong, permanent fidelity, because she knows that it is going to get rough and we will be tempted to run away. But if we refuse to quit, we'll have to change and grow more patient, more forgiving, more understanding, more self-effacing, more humble, more loving.

Marriage is a device for turning boys and girls into men and women; only very mature people have any business getting married, but most people do not mature until they've been married twenty years. As a sacrament and a means of grace, the purpose of marriage is our sanctification. Nobody ever married and lived happily ever after. Marriage is a sacrament of moral growth. It is not supposed to be easy.

The third purpose of marriage might be called the mystical or spiritual purpose. Every aspect of the marital relationship, from adolescent courtship to grandparenthood, will reveal to us something about the nature of God's relationship to man. God's problem was this: how to reveal Himself to us while concealing Himself from us, so as not to deprive us of our freedom. The solution is in creation, in time and space, in which each creature, however diverse or insignificant, is a partial revelation of the divine nature; each creature exists by participating in some degree in the divine Being, and no two creatures are alike. Whatever it is of good in the creature which attracts us is actually what the creature reveals to us about the Creator.

Marriage is a holy thing, wonderfully rich and rewarding. Expect from it any kind of natural fulfilment, and we feel frustration and disillusion. God did not give me my wife to satisfy my need to love. She cannot, in the nature of things. Only God can do that. God gave me my wife to whet my appetite for love, and to give me someone on whom to practise loving, so that by loving her, poorly at first, and better with practice, I can become a lover and be in some degree prepared to face in eternity Him whose very name and nature is love. God has called me to live in intimacy for two-thirds of my life with a marvellous, mysterious stranger whom I shall never understand, because I am destined to spend eternity in the intimate love of a God whom I shall never understand.

When a one-to-one relationship becomes exclusive, it becomes destructive. Most marriages are saved from this by the advent of children. Love is supposed to expand and reach out and include ever more and more others. It should overflow into the parish and from that into the community, and finally to all mankind. The love of the individual is not diminished by being shared, but is rather enriched and enlarged, just as the coming of a child into a marriage gives the husband and wife additional reasons for enjoying and appreciating each other.

Sexuality at the animal, genital level, is but the reflection within biological creation of something which exists more perfectly as it ascends into the world of spirit. Nevertheless, without for a moment denying the essential goodness of genital sex, surely we can see sexuality as something which points beyond itself to a fuller and more perfect expression in the relationship of man and woman to one another in Christ, and beyond that, as the saints testify, to the most perfect expression of all in the ravishment of the soul by God in mystical rapture.

In dealing with sex, we are coming rather close to the ultimate mysteries of life and death and man's relation to the cosmos. There are two fallacies which all of us have inherited, and they influence both our feelings about sex and our sexual behaviour. The first is the impression that sex is nasty. This is essentially a Manichaean strain. It's the notion that spirit is nice and clean and that matter is contaminated, which is not what the Church teaches. You will find in all kinds of sociology textbooks the slander that the notion that sex is unclean was foisted on the world by the Christian Church. Not so. That notion has been widespread in Christianity, but is the result not of Christian teaching, but the failure to teach the Christian religion, and the corruption of Christianity by romanticism. It is the romantic who ultimately says that sex is nasty.

Remember the town of Jericho which was dedicated to God and so became accursed to man? It is precisely because the romantic has made sex holy that it is nasty to man. Whenever you have a resurgence of Puritanism, you always have a return of sexual license. We don't tell sexy jokes, we tell dirty jokes. We don't commit sins of unchastity, we commit sins of impurity. You can raise your child as emancipated as you please, but if you send him to a state school he'll come home after one term with the idea that sex is dirty and nasty. Not a person in this country has escaped this tradition. Largely in reaction to that, in the eighteenth and nineteenth centuries there grew up the idea that sex was just a natural bodily appetite. We will find today a large number of well-trained doctors who regard sex as the same type of biological need as the need to eat, to evacuate one's bowels, and so on. If that is true, then sex is necessary to one's biological health. Viscerally, most people feel that there is something evil about sex. Intellectually, most people think that sex is a natural biological appetite. As an unexpected consequence, sex becomes a necessary evil. One of the most difficult tasks in modern society is to emancipate oneself from both of these fallacious notions which influence thinking about sex. Sex is neither nasty, nor is it a necessary biological function.

Take them one at a time. Considering sex as sex, it is neither morally good nor bad. Sex is a natural good, like the ability to walk. It acquires moral significance in its attendant circumstances. Any sexual activity will always have moral consequences for the parties, not because of the sex, but because of the circumstances. Sex would be good with someone other than my wife in a motel room, but it wouldn't be morally good because it would be breaking my promise to my wife and to the community.

And neither is sex necessary. There have been no studies that demonstrated that sex has any effect whatsoever on our physical health. There are quite a few human beings who have lived their entire lives without sex and suffered no ill effects. The control of the sexual appetite is, by and large, the control of the imagination. A person who is happily engaged in some pursuit which interests him is not going to be thinking about sex. Let us say that someone is an ardent trout fisherman and he is standing knee deep in a cold Colorado stream angling for a trout and along comes a beautiful woman, stark naked, and he will say, "Shh!" It is when images enter the imagination that we become sexually aroused.

Sex is a sacrament, a holy thing. Of all the sacraments, given a basic belief in God, it is the most obvious one of all, being a space in time when a human being is brought into contact with God. You take a child to church early and teach him to genuflect at the Holy Sacrament and teach him what holy means from experience, and when he is old enough to ask questions, you tell him that his organs are the holy matter, just as the Blessed Sacrament at the altar. We don't need the caution born of fear, but the respect born of reverence.

Good sex is achieved by the simple expedient of being more concerned with giving than getting. If I use my wife simply as an instrument of my pleasure, then that is exactly what I'll eventually think of her, and I will despise her for it and also feel guilty for doing so. If I do it on Sunday, by Thursday I'll be criticizing her cooking, because I've got to transfer and project all that guilt. God is so clever that He has designed this whole creation so that anyone who wants to can cheat. But you can't cheat and win. St Paul said that a man's sex belongs to the wife and hers to her husband; each must enjoy it in order for the other to give pleasure. To treat anyone as the object of my sexual pleasure is to destroy the ultimate pleasure of sex.

On the question of birth control, basically people have no business being husbands and wives until they're also ready to be fathers and mothers. All of the pro-abortion arguments never once hint at the fact that maybe people don't have the right to as much sex as they want, when they want it. There is only one absolutely 100 per cent effective guaranteed safe-every-time contraceptive, and that's abstinence. The question is not whether or not contraceptives are good or bad. There are situations in which contraceptives ought to be used, but we shouldn't pretend they're not harmful.

Contraceptives are harmful morally because they involve having your cake and eating it at the same time. It means having the privileges of marriage without the responsibilities of parenthood. I realize that for the average American today, that is a weak argument, but I'm not at all sure that it is weak in the eyes of God, because, whether it be sex and marriage, or some slick trick whereby I can get tickets for the Super Bowl for free, mankind ought not be allowed to enjoy things that he doesn't pay for. It is dangerous to his soul. I'm not saying contraception should never be used, but we should be aware of the danger. It is said these days that there are two purposes for sex in marriage: to have babies and to express the love of one party for the other. There are also two purposes for eating: one is nourishment and the other is conviviality. When you meet an old friend, you probably suggest a cup of coffee. Every bite of food that you eat for companionship also nourishes your body. You achieve both purposes in the same act. Sex also has both purposes in the same act. Using contraceptives is like sneaking under the tent to avoid paying to see the circus.

Another objection is the reduction in the aesthetic value of the sex act, though that doesn't apply to the pill. I can conceive of circumstances in which contraceptives are indicated. But anything which absolutely contraindicates parenthood contraindicates intercourse. Any time we have sex we ought to be ready to accept any child that may be forthcoming. We ought to accept it as God's gift and to love it and be grateful for it and to take delight and joy in it. Otherwise we have no business being parents, and therefore we have no business being married.

You are ready for marriage when you are grown-up. It's not kid stuff. When you are married, you are ready to settle down and be grown-up. You have no emotional and psychological needs that you demand that the other person fulfil. You are ready to become old stodgy settled married people, people who are old enough to be parents and to have children. We shouldn't just automatically assume that we ought to sit down and plan the spacing of our children, as though we were dead certain that we are smarter than God. In the early months of marriage the man and woman have a face-to-face relationship which is deadly dangerous; no community can exist which is turned inward on itself. What a baby does is turn them shoulder-to-shoulder. If a baby comes fairly early in a marriage, that's healthy. Then there could be a second one fairly quickly. After that, the problem will not be nearly as acute because by that time the likelihood of pregnancy will have diminished just as the frequency of intercourse is diminished.

If the sexual union is the most intimate of all relationships between man and woman, it is an equally intimate relationship between the couple and God. Man by his body reaches down toward unity with all the lower orders of creation; by his spirit he unites himself with the angels in the adoration of God. It is the unique function of man to be thus a mediator of God for all the orders of creation. And he does this nowhere more completely than in sex, in which the animal and spiritual are conjoined in nuptial union, imaging the very heart of the Trinity itself and the mystery of redemption. Thus the family, which is the product of the union of man and woman, is a holy thing, a miniature church.

Marriage as a sacrament confers grace, like the other sacraments. Marriage is a vocation; people should marry in response to a call from God and for the purpose of growing holy. The heart of the sacrament is the sexual union. As in all the sacraments, the grace, the power of God, is conferred infallibly, but the effect of grace in the soul is

241

conditioned by the dispostion, the subjective state of the recipients.

The wedding is an ordination service, by which two members of the congregation are set apart just as the priest is set apart. The couple are commissioned to perform a specialized function in the life of the congregation. People whose marriages have been solemnized in the church are officers of the congregation as much as the vestrymen, the choir director, or the Sunday School teachers. They are charged with a specific job in the church and for the church. Marriage is a career in religion, a full time, lifetime responsibility which people undertake in response to God's call.

The church has the right to say who shall be married in the church. That does not mean inside the building, it means within the context of the church's life. Certainly the church has the right to say who shall be ordained to the priesthood. You don't just appoint yourself a vestryman, or a choir director, or a Sunday School teacher. And you don't just decide to get married in the church and expect the church to go along with it willy-nilly. People tell me they are very religious but don't believe in going to church, but they want a church wedding because they think that marriage has a "spiritual" side, or because they want the church's blessing but don't want the church's sacramental life, or because a church wedding is nicer, or because it is customary, or because they would be embarrassed by a civil ceremony. Too many people, even church people, regard the church as a public service institution to be patronized when you need its services, as if it were a grocery store or a petrol station. For far too long, the Church has catered to people and pampered them and degraded herself and her sacraments in the process.

Before people can be married in the church, I must first ascertain their right under the canons to be married. I must first make sure that no impediment exists. I must instruct them in their duties in the married state. They are required to sign a document stating their acceptance of the Christian religion and the Christian conception of marriage. In the ceremony they take solemn religious vows, just as a priest does at his ordination. When I am satisfied that the parties intend a true Christian marriage and are qualified to perform the religious duties they will undertake, I arrange for a solemn religious service to initiate that relationship. That's called the wedding. All this is done in the name of the congregation. You, the people of God, are authorizing these folks to undertake a Christian marriage. It is your affair. You stand at the service like at a baptism and signify your assent. Before the marriage is performed you are asked if you know any reason why the ceremony should not proceed. If you think the parties unfit or insincere or if you know any impediment, you are morally obliged to speak up.

This is exactly what happens at an ordination service. A person who takes his own religious obligation seriously will make it a point to be present at every wedding performed in the church, whether he knows the parties or not. You are not invited to be there, you are expected to be there. It is your Christian duty.

Weddings are terrifying things. Normally everyone is smiling and drinking champagne and toasting the bride as if we were celebrating a victory for our side, sublimely indifferent to the fact that half the marriages today end in divorce. But there is a reason for celebrating a Christian wedding, because this man and this woman have chosen with their eyes wide open, a life of heroism and sacrifice.

Only Christians would see anything in that to celebrate. Non-Christians ought to be scared to death. Ahead of them lie temptations, quarrels, misunderstandings, hardships, doubts, sleepless nights, dirty diapers, worry, anxiety, privation, and a host of other difficulties. These are also present in a Christian marriage, but the Christian knows they are the raw material of his sanctification. He knows that his share in the suffering of Christ is the measure of his share in Christ's glory.

What we celebrate at a wedding is the raw courage, the foolhardy gallantry of the groom and the bride. They are volunteers for this spiritual combat in which there are many casualties but in which the victory is glorious. It is a combat not with each other, though it may often seem like that, but with Satan and a host of demons. Satan is a rebellious spirit and does not approve of the Incarnation. He hates biology and sex and is shocked by the marriage-bed. As the spirit of division and disharmony, he hates love and oneness. A good Christian marriage is a victory over Satan and the hosts of evil. The Church knows this, and prays God's blessing and defence on this holy thing which two people are undertaking. As the Prayer Book says, "It is not by any to be entered into unadvisedly, or lightly, but reverently, discreetly, advisedly, soberly, in the fear of God."

Marriage is for life. I'm sorry, but that's what Jesus said. And the Church is sort of hung up on going along with the boss. Admittedly, this is a real problem. I don't know any problem in the life of the Church which is quite as hairy as dealing with the problem of divorce and remarriage. Folk don't know what marriage is all about, so young people go into marriage for no better reason than that they have "fallen in love", and that is the poorest excuse I can think of for getting married. That is an excellent reason for not getting married, at least not until the romantic ardour has cooled somewhat and you can take a reasonable look at one another. It makes for a real problem in moral conscience when you get a young man and a young woman who have been divorced and want to marry again, and you realize the first time they were married they didn't have the foggiest notion what they were doing.

The basic thing that is wrong with divorce and remarriage is that it means giving up on a human soul. Now sometimes that may be all you can do, and each case has to be dealt with on its own merits. The Church knows that marriage is going to be hard. It's a school, the building of moral character, and if it's the sort of thing that you can run out on when the going gets rough, then that's kind of like dropping the course just before the mid-term exam because you haven't studied for it. The Church says hang in there and grow holy.

Marriage, then, is a vocation, and a practice for Heaven. It is of all the sacraments the most sacramental. The sexual union of a man and a woman is a natural sacrament, a sacrament of the created order, for it reflects the union of the Holy Trinity, the union by means of a total self-donating love which produces a third. In the union of man and woman we see the supernatural reality of the wedding of God and creation. For the kingdom of Heaven is like a man who gave a wedding feast for his son.

16

. . . .

CONFESSION

The Christian religion is meaningless apart from the supposition that there is a realm of reality which we cannot see, taste, touch, or smell, and that God is that realm of reality. We are immersed in and surrounded by it all the time. Prayer is opening ourselves to that constant presence, so that God may come into our souls, so that we may be filled with God as a sponge is filled with water.

Sin, in essence, is that spiritual condition of being crusted over and locked inside ourselves so that God cannot enter. The fundamental root of all sins is pride, that condition of the soul in which all of the reality that we know or are aware of is inside our own consciousness, and everything outside ourselves is an impersonal adjunct. Sin is isolation, separation, estrangement, and blocked relationships. Pride makes us think of ourselves as special, different, and unique. It produces fear and resentment of others, a critical attitude when they don't act to suit us. It is a judgement and condemnation of others for faults which we have, but which we rationalize and excuse in ourselves and scorn in others. Pride produces a curious kind of blindness in that we are unable to see what we are really like.

The fact that Jesus took our sins upon Him means many, many things, but it means at least this; the situation between God and man is that God and man are estranged, and it is all our fault. God is totally blameless. He has never ceased loving us and desiring our friendship. The sinner, in his pride and blindness, feels that he is the victim of circumstances and that life has mistreated him. He has a grudge against the world, and this is against God. He stoutly maintains his own innocence and his own righteousness.

John the Baptist said, "Repent ye, for the kingdom of God is within you, among you, right in your midst, and you don't see it." What can this mean but that the kingdom of God, God's Sabbath rest, this peace that passeth understanding, is only a breath away, waiting only upon our simple, "I'm sorry." Every time I put someone down to boost my own self-esteem, every time I impose on another for my own comfort or convenience, or because of laziness, every time I insist on having my own way to the annoyance or inconvenience of others, I crucify Christ, for He said, "Inasmuch as you have done it unto the least of these my brothers, you have done it unto Me."

By God's intent, the Church is a community of people who are committed to loving and accepting others before they are worthy. All that Jesus asks is that we be honest and admit that we are not worthy. The person coming to that community honestly knows that he is not despised. This discovery is the death and resurrection experience that the Church has been talking about since the days of the Apostles, because she has experienced it again and again for nearly two thousand years. And the new identity is literally bestowed upon me by the Church, by Christ, by His Body, and in this we experience what it is to be loved and forgiven. God's attitude toward us is a relentless forgiving that needs only to be accepted.

Jesus gave the Church the power to forgive sin, and this power is exercised first in baptism. If the Church is being the Church, if it is truly reflecting God's attitude toward the sinner, and if the repentance is genuine, the baptized person feels himself enveloped in a love that is overwhelming. All that is required is a broken and contrite heart, and the willingness to love and to forgive back, and to pass on that love and forgiveness to others. No one will ever experience that who thinks he deserves it. As long as I pretend to myself that the love that I receive from you is due to my sterling character, my noble personality, my brilliant wit, my handsome face, and all of my other good qualities, I will never know what it means to be really loved, and obviously, I will never know what it really means to be forgiven.

There are those who fault the Church because it is always insisting that we humble ourselves. They claim it puts too much stress upon penitence and not enough upon joy. But the experience of two thousand years is that real joy is known only after penitence. The Church does not require moral rectitude as a condition for being loved, for God has taught her by every genuinely valid Christian experience that we must be loved first before we can become lovable. If, after we have known that love and joy, we sin against it, reject it, repudiate it by a wilful violation of that love, then we have put ourselves outside the community of love and forgiveness. We have abandoned the comradeship of love, and hence, that of God Himself.

The whole basis of our belonging in Christ, in His Church, to one another, is that we know that each other is a sinner, but love each other anyway. That's what makes this community so special, so supernatural. God knows that I am a no-good son-of-a-gun *all* the time. He never stops loving me because the love which we have for one

248

another is the reflection of God's love for us, and it is by the love which we receive from one another that we come to believe that God loves us and forgives us, and therefore we can forgive ourselves. That is what brings interior peace. If it should happen that we sin against the community and want back in, we must return to the original condition of penitence and admission of guilt. You don't just come back and rejoin the party as if nothing had happened. This would be forcing everyone else to participate in the pretence and hypocrisy. God loves us, but durn it, He will not lie for us. The condition of the acceptance God's love is that we stop lying to ourselves.

Sacramental confession is designed to cover this situation. We can put ourselves outside the community of love by a single act of spite or an act of rejection of our neighbour, or a deliberate act which hurts another. Inasmuch as we have done it to our neighbour, we have done it to God, who loves our neighbour and is one with him. We can also drift away by a series of little acts of not caring, by neglecting to love, or by growing indifferent and sinking back into ourselves. In either case, when we wake up and find ourselves outside in the cold, the way back in is through confession and absolution.

Jesus said to the Church, "Whosesoever sins you forgive, they are forgiven, and whosesoever sins you retain, they are retained." "What you bind or loose on earth is bound or loosed in Heaven." This is not an autocratic or arbitrary power given to the priest to dispense the Sacrament of Confession. This is just a spiritual law. You cannot forgive the person who has sinned and will not admit it. And God cannot forgive him. God is willing, but forgiveness has to be accepted, and until then, it remains inactive and inoperative.

The condition of being outside the community of love, of

having lost the love of God and of our neighbour from our hearts, is called mortal sin. The soul in mortal sin is once again in that crusted-over condition of self-justification which chokes the life of God in us and leaves us barren, dry, and on our own. For such souls, confession is morally obligatory. There is no law in the Episcopal Church that says anyone has to go to confession. There is a law of logic that says, "As you sow, so shall you reap." We may attempt to spare our pride and take refuge in the idea that we can repent and confess to God privately, but this is cheating. There is also our neighbour, and there is the community of love that we have betrayed and abandoned. Confession and apology to our Christian brothers and sisters, at least in the person of our spiritual father, is required, not by rubric or canon law, but by common honesty.

There are also venial sins that do not put us outside the life of God. These are the little unintentional things we do or leave undone, that bring inconvenience and hurt upon others. These are not so much deliberate denials of love as the result of flaws in character, weakness, forgetfulness, and unintentional failures of consideration or helpfulness, ignorance or stupidity, which all of us have in adequate supply. Confession is morally obligatory in the case of mortal sin, but not in the case of venial sin. However, one may also confess and receive the comfort of absolution for venial sins. If I have hurt you, even unintentinally, and I am a gentleman, I will apologize. Not to do so would be an additional fault.

The Church gives the sacrament of Confession as an efficacious sign of our being received back into the love of God after we have abandoned it, and also for being forgiven, even for our venial sins. If we have the decency to apologize to the family of God, we have the right to expect some acknowledgement of our apology. It is a delicate and sensitive thing, tuned to the relationship of people who love one another, but it only works if we repent, and open the door to the entrance of God's Spirit to flood the soul with the joy of companionship with the Holy Spirit in the communion of the saints.

That, in a nutshell, is the theology of confession. Before examining the actual practice of confession, I would like to look at some of the common objections to it. We will find them instructive.

It is often said, "No man can forgive sins; only God can forgive sins." Strangely enough, this is exactly what the Pharisees said when Jesus forgave the sins of the paralytic let down through the tiles of the roof. They brought a man to be healed of a physical disease, and Jesus gave him forgiveness.

Now Jesus specifically gave to His Church the authority and the power to forgive sins. We don't make Jesus out to be a liar. We have already quoted Him. This passage, and other similar passages, are the scriptural basis for the idea that baptism removes both original and actual sin; it is also the basis for the Sacrament of Confession and Absolution. If Jesus said it, it must be so. We have already noted that being received and accepted into the loving and forgiving community is how we experience forgiveness. But there is more to it than that. Surely it must be that given the unceasing love of God and His compassion for His lost sheep, the same sin that separates us from God separates us from our neighbour. Pride excludes both God and our neighbour from our heart. The change of heart which opens us to love makes it possible for us to receive both God's love and our neighbour's love.

"I don't have to confess to a priest. I can confess to God alone." This would be all right if one could possibly sin against God alone. If I have grievously harmed you, caused you loss of reputation by gossip or slander, or perhaps stolen from you, or caused you grave bodily harm, then afterwards I am sorry, it is not enough that I confess to God alone. I must confess to you, too. I must also make reparation, if at all possible, for the damage done.

When we carefully examine sin, we discover that every sin is not only against God, but also against my neighbour. Every sin against my neighbour is against our common Father who loves us both. If we accept the proposition that those against whom we have sinned deserve an apology, then surely we must confess not only to God, but also to our neighbour.

When we have sinned, we must offer an apology both to God and to the Church, as well as to people yet unborn who will grow up in the moral climate that we have helped to create. We have betrayed the saints who suffered to bring us the Gospel. Every sin ever committed is a sin against every person who has ever lived or will ever live.

You may take comfort in the fact that the priest has been authorized by God through the Church to hear our apology on behalf of God and also on behalf of our fellow man, to assure us of both God's and man's forgiveness. So when in the confessional I give absolution, what I am saying, in effect, is that "God forgives you, I forgive you, the senior warden forgives you, the ladies of the women's auxiliary forgive you, the altar guild forgives you, the choir members and the Sunday School teachers, they forgive you, the whole congregation forgives you."

And you never know when I might have told somebody that in the last hour, so you durn well better act like you forgive each other. This is a community of love, acceptance, and forgiveness. We will run into sinners every time we set foot on these premises. But if you and they are acting like Christians, you will remember that Fr Rogers may have told them in the last hour that everybody in this parish still loves them. That's what absolution is.

The objection is often made, "Well, doesn't that make confession too easy and forgiveness too cheap? Isn't it an encouragement to sin?" It is usually expressed like this: "Those Catholics think they can commit any sin they want and all they have to do is go tell the priest and be forgiven." Of course, you can turn it around and say, "Those Protestants think they can commit any sin they want to and all they have to do is confess to God and be forgiven." This is not a way of making forgiveness cheap. On the contrary. And yet God went to a great deal of trouble like the crucifixion, to make it easy to be forgiven. And surely neither the Catholic nor the Protestant has ever believed that we can be forgiven without genuine repentance. The Catholic knows that he can be forgiven without going to confession. He goes to confession for another reason.

We previously mentioned the corporate nature of both sin and forgiveness. There is a further reason for confession. Far from being something that makes forgiveness cheap and sin easy, the practice of confession is a positive deterrent to sin and an aid to virtue. In the first place, if I am tempted to sin, am I likely to say, "Oh, goody, I can do this and all I have to do is tell Father about it," or will I say, "Oh, dear, if I do this I will have to tell Father about it." Nobody likes to go to confession. I've been doing it for forty years and haven't learned to like it. No matter how it feels afterwards, coming up to it in advance is always a bit traumatic. The knowledge that I must include any sin I commit in my next confession sometimes stops me from doing it. Just the regular practice of confession attaches a bit of unpleasantness to each sin and diminishes its appeal, like mustard on ice cream. It is not a cheap forgiveness, for it involves the wholesome humiliation of the self.

But more, it is a positive aid to virtue. On the purely human level, if I have told one thousand lies, the addition of one more does not appreciably increase the burden of guilt. The difference between one thousand, and one thousand and one is minimal. The difference between none and one is infinite. Going to confession is a sacrament of starting over again with a clean slate. It gives us a concrete sensible event in time and space by which we can reckon our cleansing, and it renews the incentive to keep the soul unspoiled for a little longer. There is a real, tremendous, perfectly natural human impulse that is given in knowing that we can start over from scratch, because God has promised through Jesus Christ to His Church, "Whose sins you forgive, by George, I forgive them, too."

The final objection, which is the real one that most people have, is, "I don't want the priest to know what a stinker I am." But you see, if that is the case, you are not really penitent. That is pride speaking, and pride involves the effort to pretend to be nice when I am not. I don't want the priest to dislike me when I tell him all those horrible things I have done.

This is utterly fallacious and ineffective reasoning anyway, because the priest knows that you are a stinker whether you tell him or not, because we all are, and he is, too. Your sins are not all that different from those in your age group and station in life. For that matter, your sins are not all that different from mine. When you don't go to confession, you are not really concealing something from the priest except the fact that you are sorry. What you add to his knowledge when you do go to confession is that you are humble and penitent. His reaction will be one of admiration and joy and respect. I promise you that hearing confessions is a very humbling experience. After I have heard three or four confessions, I want to get up and go make mine.

There is also something called the seal of the confessional. The priest is bound by the most solemn vow of his profession never to reveal by word or action anything that he learns in the confessional. If I am privy to a plan to assassinate the President, I cannot warn the President, although I may require you to do so as a condition of absolution. But I can't tell you and can't force you to do so. The priest can't even discuss your confession with you unless you come to him outside the confessional and tell it to him all over again.

For after all, if God has put away your sins, they are put away. They are gone; they are no more. The sins you have committed and confessed don't really matter. Nothing could be less important than a forgiven sin.

How do you go about making a confession? First, find a place where you can be undisturbed for half an hour or so. After you have made your confession a dozen times or more, you can shorten the amount of time spent in preparation. Get a pencil and paper. Get comfortable, perhaps at a table or a desk. Then pray. Ask God to enlighten you, to show you your soul as He sees it, and to help you remember your sins. Then write down your sins, one at a time, stating in as few words as possible what the sin is, how often committed, and only those details necessary to make the nature and gravity of the sin clear.

For example, do not say, "I have forgotten to say my prayers," for that doesn't state if you forgot them once, or every day for a year. It is a confusing, vague statement. But don't go into such detail that you are telling your life story. It's not supposed to be autobiography. It is not enough just to say, "I stole." There is a difference between stealing an orange from a grocer and stealing a thousand dollars from some poor widow with orphan children who have nothing else to live on. You should tell just enough of the details to make clear the nature of the sin and its gravity. Do not mention any names, not even that of an accomplice. Do not make excuses; it doesn't matter how heroically you resisted temptation before you yielded or how many times you said no to the devil before you finally said yes. This is a very humiliating thing. There may be mitigating circumstances, you may have performed heroically, but you finally sinned.

Some sins are complex. For example, we do not lie just to be lying, but because of cowardice or avarice or pride. Some sins have other sins in back of them. If you know what those sins are, mention those, too. You try to be as thorough and above all, as honest, as you can. If you don't know how many times this sin has been committed, you say such words as "often" or "occasionally" or "habitually" or "a few times". Do not intentionally omit anything. We are forgiven sin by sin, but you cannot be forgiven for some sins and not for others. The reason we mention all of the sins we can remember is to make sure we are truly repentant of all of them. If later on, afterward, you remember a sin that you did not include, don't worry about it. That was covered in the absolution.

After you have written down all the sins you can remember, it is helpful for most folk to turn to one of the primers like the St Augustine Prayer Book and use the check list to help you recall the sins that you might otherwise have forgotten. Do this in the interest of thoroughness. Later on you will dispense with the check list as your self-knowledge and your knowledge of spirituality grows.

Most adults making a first confession are overwhelmed at confessing all the sins of a lifetime. It is really not that difficult. You may have committed many sins, but you have not committed that many different kinds of sins.

For the first confession of an adult, rather than starting with childhood, you start with the last thirty days. You examine your life over the last thirty days and when you find a sin, you ask yourself, "Is this an isolated, lonely instance of this sin, or is it a sin of habit?" If it is a sin of habit, you ask yourself how long it has been going on and how regularly or frequently, and you confess it in some such fashion as this: "For as long as I can remember I have often taken the Lord's name in vain." "Since I have been married I have occasionally been unfaithful to my wife in thought." You try to discover when the habit got started and how often it has been done. You will discover by examining your conscience over the last thirty days and projecting it backwards, that you will cover most of the sins you have ever committed in no more time than it takes to examine your conscience over the last thirty days.

Then, to take care of the sins you have committed in the past that haven't occurred in the last thirty days, you divide your life into convenient segments of time, usually when your circumstances change, like before school, primary school, secondary school, college, your first job, after marriage, after moving to Minneapolis, and so on. There are sins you only commit in certain circumstances; for example, since I left school I have not once cheated in an examination. To catch that sin, I would have to run my mind briefly over my school years. Before I married, I never beat my wife. Don't worry overmuch about the long-forgotten sins. You are only confessing the sins that you can remember. If you make an honest effort to remember and you don't remember, that's okay.

Writing down your sins helps to objectify them. It also saves time, when you actually begin to make your confession. The average person with a little practice can make a reasonably thorough self-examination in twenty minutes. If you spend more than that at it, that gets to be a sin itself, which is called scrupulosity, which is the sin of not forgiving yourself, of lacking faith and doubting God's ability to forgive you. The way to avoid it is simply to be objective, as if you were confessing somebody else's sins. In other words, if there is something in your memory and you don't know whether or not to include it, then suppose somebody else were to ask you that question, how would you answer it? The principal way to overcome scrupulosity is to recognize that you are having to pray hard for God to take it away.

Having prepared your sin list, you are now ready to make your confession. Confessions are heard in most churches at posted times, normally on Saturday afternoon. But any priest will be glad to hear your confession at any time, and it is not necessary that it take place in church, though this is preferable. It may be in a hospital room, or it may be in your home. It could be on the front seat of a parked car on a country lane. If it is inconvenient to get to a church and you still need absolution, the priest can hear your confession anywhere, at any time.

Some churches have confessional booths or boxes, like little closets. In others, the priest is seated inside the sanctuary at the altar rail, facing the altar. When you kneel down at the altar rail beside the priest, you can carry with you a form for confession, or use the one in the Prayer Book. You have your list in your hand and you begin. When you get to your list of sins, try to be as unemotional and objective as you can. The first confession is apt to be a bit nerve-wracking, but don't worry about it. The priest has been there before.

I have heard every sin confessed except two: piracy on the high seas and holding up a stagecoach. There is nothing you can tell me that I haven't heard before, or probably haven't done myself. There is no reason to feel embarrassed or shamed or ill at ease. What counts for penitence is not how upset you are emotionally or how many tears you shed, but how firmly your will is fixed on not sinning again. So simply read off the list of your sins and when you have finished, you say, "For these and all my other sins which I cannot now remember . . ." You are sorry for all the sins you don't remember, because the motive for your sorrow is the love of God whom you have sinned against.

There are three things you ask of the priest. The first is counsel, which is simply advice. You may not get any. I find myself giving counsel less and less, the older and wiser I get. When I was a young priest fresh out of seminary, I felt obliged to give counsel. When I found myself struggling to think up something to say by way of counsel, I quit. If God the Holy Spirit doesn't put it into my mind what counsel He wishes you to have, don't feel cheated. All it means is that you have made a good confession, that in the judgement of the priest you have a grasp of the state of your soul, and that you are genuinely penitent, and that you are doing all right.

If you do get counsel, and if the priest knows his business, it will be brief, explicit, and to the point. You will not get a sermonette or an exhortation. You will not get, "Oh, dear." Often times you will receive counsel when the priest discerns in your confession that you are confessing things that are not sins. He will tell you so as a means of comforting you, so that in the future, if you do it again, you have the priest's opinion that it is not sinful, and not a matter for confession. Quite often people will confess to having been tempted when really the whole situation is a great moral victory rather than a moral failure. They feel slimy and dirty inside because they have been tempted to a sin which they have successfully resisted in the will. However, you are virtuous and righteous only in the will, not in the imagination and not in the emotions.

Don't worry if you don't get counsel. For that matter, if the priest gives you bad counsel, which sometimes happens, and you know better, then forget it. All counsel is advice. Confession is not the place for a spiritual dialogue about the state of your soul. It should be directed specifically and only to concrete sins you have mentioned in your confession. Now, if something comes up in the confession which the priest thinks indicates a confusion in your mind about some moral situation and he thinks that you need a longer discussion on this than the confession would allow, especially if there are others waiting, he may suggest to you by way of counsel that you come to him or to some other priest outside the confessional and open the matter for further counsel. You don't have to do that; that is advice.

You will always get penance. When you have sinned, you have four things to make right which your sin made wrong: contrition, confession, restitution, and purpose of amendment. For some sins, restitution is obvious: if you have stolen something you need to return it. But for most of your sins no direct restitution is possible, and therefore the priest assigns a penance which is a token, a symbolic restitution for those sins for which we cannot otherwise make restitution. This will normally be an assignment of certain prayers to say in the church before you leave, like the Collect for the Second Sunday in Lent, or the 51st Psalm.

Then the priest will give absolution. Remember that every sacrament has form and matter, minister and intention. The form is the words, "I absolve you of all your sins in the name of the Father . . ." Then go back to your pew and do your penance. When you leave the church, either tear up and flush down the toilet, or burn, or otherwise destroy your list. Don't leave it lying around, and whatever you do, don't put your name on it. Then resist the temptation to turn cartwheels on the church lawn. It really does feel great.

How often should one go to confession? Well, it's sort of like taking a bath on Saturday night whether you are dirty or not. It is good to have a regular time for confession. Otherwise we find ourselves postponing it until we can't make a thorough self-examination. I would say anywhere between once a month and three or four times a year would be normal, and certainly one ought not to go longer than a year without making one's confession. In the Episcopal Church, no one *has* to go to confession. If we had to do it, it would not be voluntary, and therefore would not be for real.

The priest sees you outside the confessional and he sees the bright clean face of a child of God. God has forgiven your sins, so don't look back. Don't refuse to forgive yourself. You will probably sin again, but what counts is that as we grow in virtue, our sins become less frequent and less grave. The closer we get to God, the more clearly we see God, and the more clearly we see our own faults. Ten years from now, you will be confessing sins that now you are committing and don't even notice or regard as sins at all. But remember that sins have only negative importance, and they keep us from enjoying God. Put them behind you and go forward hopefully. That is what confession is for.

17

PRIESTHOOD

All of the religions of the world have some kind of holy man or holy woman as priest or priestess. They are known by various names: the guru, the shaman, medicine man, or preacher. What we want to look at is the basic meaning of this term, whether you call it priest, or anything else.

The priests in the Jewish religion occupied a hereditary position. The Jewish temple was an abattoir, a slaughter-house. The central activity that went on was the killing of animals, the formal and ceremonial taking of animal life, though there were also other ceremonies. They had a great many more priests than they had jobs for in the temple, so they served on a rotating basis by lot, a week at a time.

The High Priest had a little room attached to the side of the temple like a barnacle on a ship, and there was a passageway from this room into the big temple. There was a pan of water in the door between the room where the priests assembled to go on duty and the temple. The Jewish priests served in the temple barefooted. (The Lord spoke to Moses from the burning bush and said, "Take off thy shoes, for the ground on which thou standest is holy ground.")

The crew that was going on duty assembled towards sundown on Saturday in this little room adjacent to the temple and took off their shoes and lined them up in lockers.

One by one they came, and the High Priest was kneeling by this pan of water. The first in line stuck a foot in the water and the High Priest would dry that foot off, and he would step over into the temple and put the other foot in the water, and he would dry that foot off. When both freshly washed, bare feet touched ground on the inside of the temple, he was officially on duty. His priesthood until that moment was latent, inoperative. He was a priest, but he had no function or duty as a priest, until the High Priest washed his feet and he stood barefoot in the temple.

At the Last Supper, after Jesus said the first Mass and offered the first sacrifice of the New Covenant, He girded Himself with a towel and took a basin of water and washed the feet of the disciples. When Jesus came to Peter, dumb, stupid Peter who was never getting the point, and offered to wash his feet, Peter said, "You are not going to wash my feet, boss, no siree." Jesus replied, "If I wash thee not, thou hast no part in me." The Christian priesthood is a participation in the priesthood of Christ, a sharing of His priesthood. I have no priesthood of my own. Any time I function as a priest, it is Christ who is functioning, not me. When I baptize, when I say Mass, when I pronounce absolution, it is Jesus Christ using my vocal cords to pronounce absolution and confect the sacrament. Priesthood is a sharing or a participation in Christ. It began at the Last Supper.

The New Testament uses the terms "bishop" and "elder" interchangeably, and therefore it is rather difficult to ascertain just exactly what the New Testament ministry was. The chief elder, the head of the governing body of the congregation, would take turn about going from one congregation to another, while the ordinary elders would simply remain as the normal minister of the congregation in the absence of the head elder. In the course of time, these terms of overseer and elder were separated out, and the term overseer, or *episcopos,* came to be applied exclusively to the head man. The term "elder" or *presbyteros,* came to be applied to the man who remained behind in the congregation when the overseer was on his perambulations. The word *presbyteros* was shortened to "prester", and finally to "priest".

Now there was a third minister in the Christian congregation that was not in the Jewish synagogue, and that was the *diakonos,* or deacon, who was the assistant minister in the sanctuary. He also had a function in the local congregation of being the social service officer. He was the almoner who distributed the alms of the congregation, he visited the sick, taught the young, conducted instruction classes, and was the trouble-shooter. In the early Church for several centuries the office of deacon was more important than that of the priest. The deacon was attached directly to the office of the bishop. For several centuries it was much more likely, when there was a vacancy created in the office of bishop, he would be replaced from among the deacons rather than from among the priests. The deacons were really administrative assistants to the bishop, whereas the priest was the pastor in residence for the local congregation.

Subsequent history has tried to see the offices of deacon, priest, and bishop as a kind of gradation of honour, prestige, and dignity in the ministry, as if when one graduates from seminary he is ordained a deacon, and then, if he behaves himself, he is ordained a priest, and then, if he is elected, he is finally consecrated a bishop. In the early Church the office of deacon was an independent terminal ministry. You were ordained to the diaconate and you functioned in the diaconate for life. You would not usually be removed from the diaconate and placed in the presbyterate, or priesthood. In the modern Church it is still theoretically true that the deacon is the Church's social service minister, although practically it does not happen. Most priests spend most of their time doing diaconal things anyway.

The office of bishop is roughly equivalent in the modern Church to the office of the apostles in the New Testament; that is, he is the man who goes around, as St Paul did, from congregation to congregation, exercising the general oversight. The reason you obey the bishop is not because he is wiser or smarter than you or I, but because he is the one who is in contact with all the congregations in the diocese. Our obedience to him is really obedience to the whole diocese.

There is a principle here that is very important. Any part of the family, community, congregation, parish, and diocese, derives its material, spiritual, and psychological health, its identity, and its cultural heritage from the larger community. The bishop is really our only contact with the Church in Wichita Falls, Texarkana, Brownwood, Waco, Sherman, Denison, Oak Cliff, and Weatherford (formerly all part of the diocese of Dallas). He is the only one who is in a position to see the whole picture, the oversight. Not only that, he is also the one who is in contact with other bishops in Georgia, Minnesota, Colorado, and Louisiana, so that our obedience to the bishop is really an obedience to the whole Church. It goes even farther than that. Our bishops are the ones who go to Britain every ten years for the Lambeth Conference to get their heads together with bishops from Uganda, South Africa, Australia, New Zealand, Taiwan, Japan, New Guinea, and India. The bishop is the pipeline between this congregation and the larger Church. His function is to govern the local diocese. He is also responsible for teaching the faith in this diocese; that is, he is the one who has the ultimate responsibility of deciding whether or not Fr Rogers is giving you the right stuff. If you question my authority and teaching, the person to whom you appeal is the bishop. He is the responsible teaching officer of the local congregation in this diocese. He is also the ultimate liturgical authority. He is the person who confirms and ordains. He is the one to whom the ministry is transmitted. This brings us to the whole notion of apostolic succession.

Our Lord gave an authority to the apostles to represent Him. He said to them, "He who hears you, hears Me." He said to them, "As my Father has sent me, even so send I you." He said, "Whatsoever you bind or loose on earth is bound or loosed in Heaven." The apostles were those to whom Christ gave the explicit authority to represent Him, to carry on His teaching and His presence and power into the Church of succeeding generations. As we read in the New Testament, these apostles selected other men after the death of Christ, to whom they in turn transmitted their own authority in order to exercise that authority in geographic locations where the apostles could not be. With twelve apostles, in no time you had thirteen congregations, then still more. It was not an unreasonable notion among the people of the Church that they wanted some assurance that the teaching they were receiving was the genuine, authentic teaching of Christ.

Bear in mind that there was no New Testament at that time. The Church did not put together and finally accept the books which constituted the New Testament for some 300 years after Christ. So for this length of time, there was no way that the Christian could take his Bible and go off in a corner by himself and read it and develop his relationship with God. He had to go through the Church. That is still the case. A Christian in social isolation is a Christian in spiritual difficulty. Since salvation means, among other things, the fulfilment and perfection of our humanity, and if man is indeed a social being, there is no way I can fulfil and perfect my humanity outside of some sort of community. The loner does not stand a chance. Any individual, including you and me and the bishop, who tries to develop his own individual, personal relationship with God will inevitably become eccentric and nutty. Even two people together are probably not going to have a big enough insight to see the thing whole and entire, to avoid coming up with some kind of crazy religion. Only as I find my identity in the wholeness of the Church, do I escape from and avoid the kind of eccentricity in religion that will thwart and frustrate the development of my humanity. This is why the bishop, the apostle to the modern Church, has the authority to represent the whole.

For example, what I am desiring and hoping is to teach a version of the Christian religion which would be recognized as authentic in any part of the world and in any generation since the time of the apostles. I would not want to teach anything which you could set down in medieval France or fourth-century North Africa and people would say, "I never heard of *that* before." I want it to be a presentation of the faith which would ring true and familiar, the old-time religion, a religion that was taught and believed in the third century, and in the fifteenth century. The authority to do that, to represent the larger Church in the local congregation, is passed down. Not only is this an authoritative teaching office, it is also the authority to perform certain sacramental and mystical acts in the life of the Church to which Christ has attached certain promises. Only the Church can do the sacraments of Baptism and Holy Communion, and the Church does it through those members of the congregation who have been authorized to do that. This authorization has been handed down from generation to generation since the time of the apostles.

When I first heard of that forty years ago, I wanted to laugh. I had been fed all kinds of notions about the Dark Ages and how obviously there was no way in the world you could prove apostolic succession. The way it works is that a bishop authorizes me as a priest to function in this congregation. Who authorizes the bishop? Other bishops. And who authorized them? Other bishops. All the way back to the apostles. While it may be difficult to trace the lineage of any particular bishop unbroken back to the days of the apostles, it can be done generally with astonishing certitude, and if we only accept documentary evidence as proof, there are many instances going back to the fourth and fifth centuries. Obviously, through deterioration of documents, through fires and mice, and the depredations of the Viking raiders, certain records will have been lost. Nevertheless, this much can be demonstrated: from the days of the New Testament, there has never been any other method of authorizing ministers than through the laying on of hands by the bishop. There is no gap in that and no exceptions until the time of the Reformation. This is the apostolic succession. It is not only a kind of relay race in which the baton of authority is handed on from person to person, it is also a continuity of identity, and a continuity of teaching.

This is not too hard to take. When I preach to you, it is

with the confidence that the bishop in apostolic succession has laid hands on my head and ordered me to this office. I speak with the authority of Christ. More importantly, when I stand at the altar tomorrow morning and take bread and wine and repeat the words of Our Lord, "This is my body and this is my blood," I have been authorized to do that by the bishop in apostolic succession. I am the spokesman for Christ because you are His Body, because His spirit dwells in us. We are His mystical body.

Whatever I say about the priesthood, bear in mind that it not only applies to me, but to you also. The fundamental, underlying idea of priesthood is mediation. We are all priests because Jesus is a priest and we are His Body. The character and activity of the priestly function of Jesus Christ is carried on through history by His mystical body the Church.

When people were kicking out priests in the northern European countries in the sixteenth century, a slogan was coined which said, "No man shall stand between my soul and God," as if the purpose of the mediatorial priesthood was to keep me and God apart. As a matter of fact, the purpose of the mediatorial priesthood was to bring me and God together. The underlying notion behind priesthood is that the natural, unredeemed man, the man apart from the grace of God and the saving action of God in his soul, is alienated or separated from God and cannot find his way back. There is nothing that man can do by his own unaided natural powers that can bring him into intimate contact with God. Only God can effect this union; the union between God and man can only be achieved on God's initiative and on God's side. Therefore, He sent His Son Jesus Christ, who is the effective mediator, precisely because in His manhood, He is one with us, and in His divinity, He is one with God the Father. In His own life and person, He united God and man, so that being drawn into union with Christ, we are drawn into union with God the Father.

Mediation can easily be understood in terms of a situation that every priest has experienced, when a man and his wife have had a falling out and are not speaking to each other. Any time they attempt to talk, they wind up in a shouting match. They have learned not to discuss anything with each other, but the marriage is obviously breaking up, and somebody suggests they go see a priest. They come into my office and the man will say to me, "Well, she did so and so," not speaking to her, but to me.

So I say to her, "Did you hear what he said?"

"Yeah, but he did so and so."

I say to him, "Did you hear what she said?"

They are communicating with each other by communicating with me. Sometimes I say, "Now wait a minute, I don't think that is what she meant." By reinterpreting and getting the wife to say, "Yes, that is what I meant," and the husband to say, "Oh, I didn't understand it like that," you can bring two people together. I've seen some come into my office not speaking to each other and leave four hours later with their arms around each other in an embrace. That is mediation – bringing together two people who belong together. The priest takes two folk who are not talking and talks to both of them. He takes two folk who are not touching and he reaches out and touches both of them. This is the priesthood of Christ. You might say that confirmation is the ordination to the priesthood of the laity. The bishop places his hands on your head and prays for the Holy Spirit to come upon you for the office and work of a lay minister of Christ's Gospel, in a way quite similar to what he does in the ordination of a priest. Your priesthood is to the world; mine is to you. It is not in my job description to go out on the street corner and contact potential converts to Christianity. That is every baptized person's ministry, to bear Christ into the world and be a witness for Christ.

We find in the Old Testament that there are three different kinds of holy men: prophets, priests, and kings. Recall that Adam was a priest, and that means that all men are priests, even apart from Christ and the Church. Our very constitution as humans means we were originally intended by God to be priests, and in a very real sense the Fall of man, the original sin of mankind, is our refusal of our priesthood. Man is by his very nature an animal with a spirit, living on a frontier with a life that is in both worlds. This is a paradigm of priesthood.

When God first called Abraham, he was performing all three functions as prophet, priest, and king. Abraham was the chieftain of a Bedouin tribe, he offered sacrifices, and he was God's spokesman. It is only with the Exodus that God begins to break out and distinguish between prophets, priests, and kings. Moses is the ideal figure of the prophet, Aaron is the ideal figure of the priest, and David is the ideal figure of the king. It is interesting that when Christ comes along, one gets the impression from reading the New Testament that Christ was a layman. He is not an official of the Jewish religion at all. In other words, He is a return to the Adamic condition. He is the new Adam in which the prophet, priest, and king are recombined in one person. He represents a going back to the beginning to start over.

First of all, God revealed Himself to us as Father and

Lawgiver. Secondly, He revealed Himself as Son and Redeemer; His earthly ministry is fulfilled and perfected in His sacrifice of Himself on Calvary. Then God revealed Himself as Holy Spirit who was fully present in the Church only on the day of Pentecost. With certain mental reservations which would be important only to professional theologians, I will say that God the Father represents the intellect, God the Son the divine will, and God the Holy Spirit the divine affectivity, or in more common language, the emotions. It's not really what the affections are, but that will do for the time being.

The function of a prophet is to reveal the divine intellect to man and to guide and direct the human intellect into conformity with the divine intellect, so as a result, man can think God's thoughts, and know God. The principal virtue which is the end goal of the prophetic ministry is faith. In plain English, the two functions of the prophet are to go to the people and talk about God, and to go to God and talk about people. One may also say these functions are preaching and intercessory prayer. We see this pre-eminently revealed in Moses, the great lawgiver and great intercessor. Again and again in the book of Exodus, God gets really put out with the Jewish people and decides to clobber them. "I am losing my patience with these folk." Moses would go to God and say, "Now, wait a minute, God. Think it over." He appeals to God for the people, and he appeals to the people for God, revealing to them the divine will in terms of the Law, and exhorting and guiding. This is the prophetic ministry on the side of God-to-man.

Preaching is a prophetic ministry. Counselling is a prophetic ministry. School teachers, whether they know it or not, are engaged in the prophetic ministry and are answerable to God at the Day of Judgement as to how they do it. In teaching a child not to eat peas with his knife, the parent is exercising the prophetic ministry. Any sort of guiding and directing which has as its purpose somebody else learning the truth is the prophetic ministry. The corollary and complement of that is intercessory prayer. Intercession is the prophetic ministry on the side of man-to-God. I do this when I teach what the Church's lore and wisdom has culled out of the Scriptures about the nature of priesthood. I am sharing with you the Church's insights and teaching, divinely revealed and guided by the Holy Spirit.

In teaching the child, the parent is speaking for God. Of course, if he is going to undertake that, he has to do the other half, too; he has to pray for the person he is speaking to. Only if you talk about people to God, as well as talking to God about people, are you fully exercising the prophetic ministry. It's not just my job, it's your job, and the job of every baptized Christian to be able to give a reason for the faith that is in him. You need to know why you are a Christian.

This is not just a one-shot deal. It may go on for years, for a lifetime. You will be learning about God on the day of your death. What we are doing here is conforming the intellect to the mind of God and perfecting thereby the supernatural virtue of faith. Faith is an intellectual virtue. What it means in the course of time is that you begin to see reality from God's point of view. The prophetic ministry belongs to all of us.

The priestly ministry is the mediation of the Son who is God enfleshed in matter, the transcedent eternal God entering time and space. The function of the priestly

274

mediation is to conform the will of man to the will of God in the perfection of the theological virtue of hope. On the man-to-God side, it is offering a sacrifice, declaring that something belongs to God. In other words, it is recognizing God's proprietary rights in His creation. In the words of St Paul, all of you are saints, or holy people, because you belong to God. A sacrifice is taking some thing which is characteristic of a class of things and saying that through this one thing which we declare belongs to God, all other things in that class are recognized as belonging to God. The offering of sacrifice is the characteristic ministry in terms of man-to-God.

Now, curiously, the God-to-man aspect of the priestly ministry is regulating, ordering, and ruling. This doesn't mean ruling in the sense of ordering people around, but ruling in the sense of carrying a yardstick in your pocket. Since the priest is the one who declares creation to belong to God, and presumably is fully alerted to the true purpose of things, he is the person, then, in his God-to-man ministry, who counsels, orders, and regulates; it is this particular ministry that conforms human life and society to the Word of God. He declares a moral dimension to this ministry. I exercise the priestly part of my ministry when I go to the altar and offer the sacrifice of bread and wine. When I baptize a child, I declare God's name upon it and anoint it, saying, "This child now belongs to God." This is the sacrificial ministry.

The other complementary aspect of that is what I do as the rector of this parish. I have authority and oversight. For example, suppose by some rearrangement of the schedule of activities in the church, a room becomes vacant. The choir comes to me and says, "Father, we need that room for a place to hang our vestments and put our music."

The Sunday School superintendent comes to me and says, "Father, we need that room for an extra Sunday School class. We are awfully crowded."

The women of the church come to me and say, "Father, we need that room because we need a place to store our needlework stuff when we work on the new kneelers."

Every organization in the church wants that room. Obviously, it is appropriate that the Sunday School and the women and the acolytes and the choir should be promoting the interest and well-being of their oganizations. I am the rector of the parish, and I am supposed to be concerned equally with the welfare of the choir, the women, the Sunday School, and the acolytes. Somebody has to make the decision. It is because I have the oversight of this community that I am the rector, and I order, direct, and arrange it in the same way that the bishop has the oversight of the larger diocese as he orders and directs and arranges.

It is also my function as rector of the parish and pastor of the congregation to be the moral guide. Moses was being priestly when he arbitrated disputes between the members of the congregation. He would say, "You do this, and you do that." But only if you ask my advice. All authority is directed toward the common good. Not even God Himself has any effective authority over the free will of another individual. My authority is directed toward keeping the public order, not to make anybody do anything, except in so far as to exclude certain activities which are disruptive of the public order. Thus, for example, as a father I can't make a child study his lessons, but I do have the right to keep him from playing his radio too loud while his sister wants to study.

All authority is directed toward the public order. The

end of this is to bring human life in its social dimension into conformity to the mind and will of God. It is the bringing about of the kingdom of God through human incorporation of the divine will. I come to will what God wills for me.

Now the royal ministry is kind of tricky. Many people don't understand kings, thinking of them as a kind of president with a right of succession, or as a ruler. Kings are not rulers, priests are rulers. Kings have a different function, which is to incorporate the national character in his or her own personal self.

This particular ministry is the ministry of the Holy Spirit. It is the function of the minister to set the pattern, to become the norm and the ideal. Notice, also, that there is not a double standard of Christian morality, one for the priest and one for the lay person. There is only one standard of Christian righteousness and goodness for all of us. Nevertheless, it is my function as a priest to lead the way, not to be better than you are, but to be good first. It is an awesome and terrifying responsibility that by my life, my moral character, and my devotion, you will get some notion of what Christian life and Christian devotion is, so that you can imitate it and follow it. However, that does not get you off the hook. Just as I am supposed to set an example for you to imitate, you are supposed to set an example for somebody else to imitate. This is the royal ministry, to be a saint. We are all called to manifest in our lives the kind of God that God is, so that a person, having spent some time with us, should go away sort of shaking his head and saying, "You know, that is the kind of person Jesus must surely have been like."

Do you remember the story in the Old Testament about King Ahab who was shot and later on died? The moment that the word got about to the troops that the king had been killed, they all gave up, not because their commanding officer was no longer there, but because when the king was killed, they were killed. There was a mystical identity between the king and his people, so that the life, the dynamic interior identity, of the nation is somehow encapsulated in the person of the king himself. There is a close affinity, a oneness, an identity between the king and his people. There is that same identity between Christ the King and His people. It is His character, His personality, His identity which one finds expressed in His mystical body the Church.

The man-to-God aspect of this particular ministry is worship. It is giving glory to God in praise and adoration. It is exercised by the official priest in his conduct of public worship, in which he performs something of the role of cheerleader. But every baptized Christian also has this same ministry. The technically correct term for going to Mass is not to attend Mass, as if you listened to it, but to assist at Mass, because you are an assistant minister. You are as essential as the priest. If you go to Mass tomorrow and the priest oversleeps and doesn't show up, you can't have Mass without him. If he turns up and everyone in the congregation oversleeps, he can't have Mass without you. The offering of worship to God, not only in the formal worship of the Church, but also in the praise and adoration which is carried about with us in our hearts, is the expression of this royal ministry.

These three ministries carry with them a separate and different authority. The authority of the prophet is called the *magisterium*, from the Latin word which means "teacher". This is the authority of the dictionary, of the man who knows. When I go to the dictionary to learn how to spell a word, the dictionary is not going to force me to spell it that way. The teaching authority of the priest is not the authority to override your judgement or force you to believe anything, but simply to answer questions. It is my job to teach you how to get to Heaven, not to make you go there. Therefore, the priest in this sense is the custodian of the Church's lore, the Church's traditions. It's his job to know what the Church has been believing for 2,000 years, and to make this available to anybody who wants to know. This is the authority which is known as *magisterium*.

The ruling authority of the priest is called *imperium*, the authority of command. It is only directed toward the inner life of the Church. It is the authority to keep public order and peace, to arrange things, to make decisions, like who is going to get the use of that room.

The third authority is called *charism*. This is the sort of authority that attaches to movie stars; it is the way boys feel about the Super Bowl champions. The authority is because of what they are and what they can do, the authority that by its own intrinsic worth commands, elicits, and evokes the response of imitation. I would like to be like whoever my hero is.

Christ has these three authorities pre-eminently. Since He is God incarnate, He has the perfect *magisterium*. What He says is true, and what He says comes to pass. He is the ultimate *imperium*, which is why on the last day He will judge the world. In this sense He is the yardstick, the standard. You either measure up to that or you are out of measure. He is the norm, the ideal. In the last analysis He has the *charism*, because it is this charismatic authority that draws us to Him. You can know all there is to know about the Christian religion and stay away from it like it was poison. You don't have to like it. You can know all there is to know about Christ's moral teaching and say, "Aw, phooey on it." The thing that draws you to Christ is the Holy Spirit, that is, His charisma, the intrinsic beauty of His person, the attractiveness of Christ himself.

And similarly in our own evangelical and missionary activities, I can teach, and not do a cotton-picking thing about eliciting any response of devotion or dedication. I can give you all kinds of moral guidance, and that doesn't do anything at all. The only thing about you or me that is ever going to attract anyone to Christ is Christ Himself living in us. The royal minister has the charisma of the presence of Christ. When somebody says, "I would like to be the kind of person that Carolyn York is," and then they discover that Carolyn York is that kind of person because she is trying to be like Jesus, that draws people. Nobody ever got converted by preaching alone.

Now the man-to-God has to come first. It is only in having been touched by God that we are enabled to perform the God-to-man aspect of this ministry. Don't bother to go out and talk to people before you have prayed. Once you have prayed, then talk. Don't bother trying to regulate and order anything until you have made sacrifice, until you have offered it to God. Don't try to pose as a witness for Christ until you have worshipped.

The prophetic ministry is Faith, the priestly ministry is Hope, and the royal ministry is Charity. All of it is the priesthood.

18

. . . .

UNCTION

The sacrament of Unction is the Church's ministry to the sick and dying. When you call a priest in sickness, you need to know what he can do about it.

The first thing a priest can do for the sick is an order for the visitation of the sick. It's not used much these days, primarily because with modern medicine, very few people are in hospital very long, and very few people are sick in bed very long. You either die or get well. About the only people for whom this would be an appropriate service nowadays would be someone in a nursing home. We might also call this the service of corporate prayer. It presupposes a congregation in addition to the priest and the sick person.

When this service was included in the first English Prayer Book, about 400 years ago. England was a country made up largely of small villages. Probably 80 or 90 per cent of the entire country lived in small villages in which there was normally no more than one parish church, with maybe a total population in the village of 150 to 300 people. They all knew one another, and possibly were related to one another. When somebody got sick, it was the concern of the whole community. There were no movies, no television, no radio. The only two things to do for your socializing were to go to church or to the local tavern. The person who was sick was made keenly aware of his social isolation from the community. This particular service of the sick presupposed that if he couldn't come to church, the church would go to his sick room. When the priest would go to call on the sick person, a number of community, certainly his wife, his children, aunts, uncles, cousins, and neighbours would be there too, and would take part in the office which consisted of versicles, responses, collects, and short verses of Scripture and Psalms in alternation.

The second ministry for the sick set forth in the Prayer Book is the ministry of counsel, "as occasion demands . . . for spiritual profit," which means specifically when the person is sick or troubled by some problem, and sickness, of course, is a time in which we are often troubled. When you get sick, you are suddenly made aware of the fact that you are not going to live for ever. Also, often when you are sick you are in pain, and pain, particularly when it is dragged out at great length, places a great strain on your soul. Also, your helplessness is an affront to your independence and sense of pride. People in illness frequently become irritable. Insofar as the patient finds his sickness a matter which raises doubts about his faith or problems about his moral behaviour, he may request of the minister counsel.

The third ministry is that of confession and absolution. Certainly, if at all seriously sick, I am going to want to make my confession.

There is also the ministry of intercessory prayer. If you are sick in bed or in the hospital, the priest may pray with you at your bedside. There are, however, people who are offended by being prayed over. As a consequence of that, I will always ask the permission of the sick person before I pray. You, too, may pray for the sick. You may pray for the sick in their presence out loud at the bedside. If you feel awkward about composing prayers in your own words, you may use the prayers in the Prayer Book concerning visitation of the sick.

Then there is the ministry of laying on of hands, which is something that a lay person may administer, though he may not administer the sacrament of Holy Unction. Normally, unction is given only once per illness, unless the person makes a recovery and then has a relapse, and then he may receive unction again. If I have previously anointed a person and am visiting him for the second or the tenth time, I will use the ministry of the laying on of hands. You may use prayer with the laying on of hands for members of your family or your friends who are sick. You may do this whether or not there is a priest available. Between the priest's visits you may use it, and you may use it more than once.

Finally, there is the ministry of anointing, which is the specific sacrament. In James 5:14: "Is there any sick among you? Let him call for the elders of the church [that is, the presbyters or priests] and let them pray over him, anointing him with oil in the name of the Lord and the prayer of faith shall save the sick and the Lord shall raise him up." I carry with me a small cylinder called an oil stock. In it is absorbent cotton, the kind that comes in a vitamin bottle. You put the cotton in the oil stock and on that you drop three or four drops of olive oil which has been blessed by the bishop on Maundy Thursday. This oil is called *oleum infirmum*, the oil of the sick. It is administered by pressing the thumb down on this absorbent cotton so that a film of the blessed oil is transferred to the thumb, and the thumb traces the sign of the cross on the forehead, at which time the priest says, "I anoint you with oil in the name of the Father, and the Son, and the Holy Spirit, beseeching the mercy of Our Lord

Jesus Christ that all your pain and sickness of body, mind, and spirit being put to flight, the blessing of health may be restored to you. Amen." In the priest's manual there is a much more elaborate ritual which you may examine if you wish.

From the ancient rubrics for this sacrament is it clear that this had been done ever since James wrote his epistle, which was probably the earliest book of the New Testament. From the earliest days from the time of Christ and the Apostles, the Church has been anointing the sick with oil. Now bear in mind the exorcism aspect of the pre-baptismal rite, the renunciation of the world, the flesh, and the devil, the recognition that the world is under the dominion of Satan. What is being done in unction is a renewal of the chrismation of baptism and confirmation. It is obviously not another baptism, because you can't be baptized twice. But it is the chrismation which has been since the days of Moses and Aaron, the anointing with oil. It has been the outward and visible sign of the advent of the Holy Spirit. You can't have holy spirits and evil spirits occupying the same place. The Holy Spirit will drive out the evil spirit. The anointing is an outward and visible sign of the invocation of the Holy Spirit.

Because it is a sacrament and works *ex opere operato*, there is an effect. That effect is obviously not always a physical healing. As a matter of fact, in my experience with this sacrament, I would say physical healing is rather more the exception than the rule. We are, however, constrained to believe by the faith of the Church that some kind of spiritual healing takes place, a strengthening or comforting. If it is the will of God that this person recover, then this sacrament will often simply work a miracle. I don't know what else to call it. If it is the will of God that the person continue in the illness for a while or actually die, then the sacrament will be the gift of the Holy Spirit for this particular purpose. The sacrament will strengthen the soul to endure whatever is in the will of God for him.

I would be the last person in the world to hint or suggest or imply that I can work a miracle of healing. No legitimate Christian healer would ever say that. It is God that does it, and He does it according to His own obscure and marvellous will. However, I think the first time I ever used this sacrament was the most dramatic. I was a young priest, fresh out of seminary, and I had been in the parish about three months. The phone rang and a member of the congregation said that Dr so-and-so had had a stroke. I asked, "Is he a member of the congregation?" and was told yes, but his name was not on the rolls. It turned out that he was known among the student body as a campus atheist. His wife did come to church occasionally; after this, she came somewhat more regularly. I took my oil stock and went down to the local Denton hospital. I walked into the sick room and the man was lying there totally unconscious as he had been since four that afternoon. He barely had a pulse and respiration. I walked in and anointed him. The moment my thumb touched his forehead his knee came up under the sheet; it scared me to death. In twenty minutes he was sitting up in bed asking for something to eat. They released him that night and he was back on the campus in his classes the next day. I would like to tell you that he came to church every Sunday from then on, but I never laid eyes on him again.

Basically, the ministry of the priest to the sick is visitation. If you are sick long enough, you tend to revert back to infancy; you begin to think like a child and become very dependent. One of the awful things about being sick is that you are out of touch with things. The reason for visiting the sick is to let them know that they are not isolated.

There are a few rules for visiting the sick. First of all, don't stay long. If it takes you forty-five minutes to get there and forty-five minutes to drive home, spend an hour and a half on the road and no more than ten minutes in the sick room. Get in and get out. The important thing is that the sick person knows that you are there and that you love him and care for him. The exception to that is if the person is convalescing and feeling well and is simply bored and lonely. Then you might take a chess board and spend the afternoon with him. Ordinarily, if he is sick, and particularly if he is in pain, don't stay very long. If he is debilitated or weak, don't stay long. Don't sit on the bed, and don't tell him about your aunt who had the same thing and died in agony. Don't worry about making conversation. Just tell them that you care about them, that you are praying for them; with their permission say a prayer with them and then leave.

The final ministry to the sick is the ministry of the communion of the sick. There are some rules about that. In our church there is a tabernacle on the altar and a sanctuary light which hangs from the crossing to indicate that the Blessed Sacrament is reserved. It is there primarily for the sick. When I take communion, I go to the tabernacle, open the door, take a host out and put it into my pyx (a little thing that looks like an old-fashioned watch case like Granddaddy used to carry that opens up but there are no works in it) and put the consecrated host inside. I have a case for the pyx with a chain that hangs around my neck and I stuff it in the inside coat pocket and put on a stole.

Ordinarily a priest does not engage in conversation while carrying the Blessed Sacrament, any more than he would engage in conversation while administering Holy Communion at the altar rail on Sunday. You used to have an acolyte with a candle and a little bell who would walk in front of the priest, but if there is an acolyte shortage, the priest will normally be wearing a white stole outside his coat in plain sight which indicates he is carrying the Sacrament.

When you call the priest and ask him to bring you communion, be sure to agree on a time. If I have said that I will be there at 10:30, I want to ring the door bell at 10:30. Some member of the family will open the door without conversation – you don't even say hello – and genuflect to the Sacrament and turn and lead the priest into the sick room. This is so he will not have to ask which room it is. It should have been understood in advance of the call whether or not the sick person wishes to receive Holy Unction as well or wishes to make a confession. If he is going to make a confession, the other members of the family will retire from the room and the priest will hear his confession, give absolution, and provide an opportunity for him to say his prayers. Then he will go to the door and invite the other members of the family back into the sick room. It is appropriate that other members of the family be there. It is convenient though not necessary, to have by the bedside a small end table on which is placed a linen napkin or handkerchief, and if you have one, a standing crucifix and lighted candle. The priest will give communion to the sick from the reserved Sacrament, normally in the kind of bread only; the wine is not usually carried to the sick. If there are other members of the family who wish to receive communion, it is appropriate that they should have notified the priest of this when they called. "Will you bring Sally her communion, and her father and I would like to receive with her." This might be appropriate if a member of the family has been staying home to care for the sick person and could not himself go to church.

The priest will read the General Confession and the Absolution and the Prayer of Humble Access, and will administer communion with the words of administration followed by the General Thanksgiving and the Blessing. Having given communion, he will normally retire from the room or remain silent until you have made whatever subjective devotions you are moved to do in response to God's coming to you in the Sacrament. The priest will usually allow you to open the conversation. If he doesn't speak first, he is simply being respectful. You may receive communion at home as often as you like for the duration of the illness.

So, the things a priest can do for you when you are sick are the ministry of public worship, the ministry of counsel, confession and absolution, intercessory prayer, the laying on of hands, unction, and communion.

Now, about dying. You are going to die as surely as God made little green apples. When God created you, it was with the intention that you could spend eternity with Him in Heaven. This life, as we have said, is a trial run, a learning experience. Life goes by very, very rapidly, and the older you get, the faster it goes. One should not be distressed about this. We believe in the life of the world to come, the resurrection of the body, and all of that stuff. Death is not so much the penalty for sin as it is the remedy. We are all going to die.

The first thing you should do, if you haven't already done so, is to make a will. Even if you think you haven't got anything at all of any value, nevertheless make a will. It will save an enormous amount of trouble, but this is minor.

Dying is the most important thing you will do in this life. The state of the soul at the moment before death is the state of the soul the moment after death. The martyr is the normative Christian, the ideal Christian, the model Christian. What he does that makes him a martyr is that he freely, willingly, and voluntarily gives up his life into the hands of God for the love of God. You can do that, too. One of these days you are going to give up your life. You will either do it willingly and gladly for the love of God, or you will do it resentfully and fearfully and angrily. Don't let it be like that. You never know when you are going to die. I could be killed crossing the street going home tonight, or I could die in my bed. But one of these days I am going to die. I am absolutely certain of that, and so are you.

Whatever happens to us, it's a matter of faith that we shall see Jesus after our death in what is known as the particular judgement. "I go to prepare a place for you that there ye may be also." "In my Father's house there are many mansions; if it were not so I would have told you." I said, you can't practise dying, yet in a way you can. This is exactly what I am about to recommend to you.

When you were little, you had a phrase in your vocabulary that was "Let's play like". You played grown-up or you played cops and robbers. What you do to practise dying is play "Let's pretend". Let's pretend that a week from tonight we know, somehow or other, that we are going to die in our sleep. We have one week to get ready. What do you do? Well, the first thing I would do is call my lawyer and make a will right quick. Then I would want to make my confession and certainly would want to go to Mass every day that week. I would want to get my soul in shape. I'd probably make a life's confession and go back over my whole career as well as I could remember and confess my sins and make sure I was genuinely contrite.

This action shows you how you arrange your priorities. It makes your values come under scrutiny. What is really important to me if I know I have only a week to live?

After confessing my sins and arranging to receive communion as often as possible during the week, I would spend some time meditating on death. By way of leaving this life and entering another one, I would remind myself that after I am dead and gone, it wouldn't be very long before I am forgotten. If I were to drop dead tonight, it would create a bit of confusion in the life of the church for a few months. Then you would call another rector and there would be a readjustment period of a year or two and after that I would not be mentioned very often. For a while people would say, "But Fr Rogers did it like that," or "Fr Rogers said . . ." But that would recede into the background fairly quickly. I must remind myself of that. The world can get along without me very beautifully. I remember when my father-in-law died and my mother-in-law moved in with us, she acted for two or three months as if she were inconsolable. She was never going to get over losing Casey. For two or three months she talked a lot about Casey sort of wistfully, with a sweet melancholy, as you do when you remember loved ones who have gone on. He was sort of a punching bag for the old lady and I suppose she missed him for that reason. Anyway, after about six months she stopped talking about him and after a year, she hardly mentioned him.

Life will go on. This is the first thing that I would want to remind myself. When a person dies, it is sort of like taking your finger out of a bucket of water; there is a hole there very briefly, then it closes up, and the world goes on. My wife and my kids might be inconvenienced for a while, but they can manage without me. If I have any particular fondness for the shape of my body, I might remember that the worms will take care of that.

Then I would spend some time looking forward to being in Heaven. I would remember all the lovely things I had been told about it, particularly the fact that Heaven is being with Jesus. I would want to talk to Him about it. I would spend some time praying, I would, I would. While I was doing that, I would put my affairs in order. When I die, somebody has to go through all my papers, my bureau drawers, my files. I am a magpie, I save every piece of paper I have ever had my hands on for thirty-five years. Certainly if I have typed anything on it, I haven't thrown it away. I have kept tons of stuff, and I am sure that somebody is going to have the agonizing job of looking at every piece of paper I have filed to see whether or not it is important enough to keep. Most of it isn't. But if I have saved any old love letters or anything else of that sort that might embarrass my wife in cleaning up my effects after me, I would get rid of them. I would take all of my important papers like the deed to the house, insurance policies, and anything of that sort, and put them in a neat brown envelope and label it and tell somebody where it is. There is no point in writing a will if you hide it and people can't find it. You also ought to file all your income tax returns for the last five years in case you get audited. These things ought to be put where your survivors can go through them with a minimum of difficulty.

Then all your business affairs should be put in order. Make arrangements to pay all your debts. Be sure that if anyone owes you and you want to collect or have any hope of collecting, that there is some record of that on file. Make sure that all of your affairs are as current as you can possible make them.

Now, about three days have passed, and I have three days to go. I would sit down and think of all my dear friends that I have been meaning to write for the last three or four years and haven't, and then I would write to them. I wouldn't tell them why, just tell them, "I've been thinking about you and am sorry I haven't kept in touch with you, but remember that I love you. Everybody here is well and happy. Come to see us when you can. Love, Joe."

Then if there is anybody in the world that you hold a grudge against, forgive them from the bottom of your heart. It's kind of silly to go into eternity holding a grudge about something that happened last year. Forget it and forgive them. And if there is anybody who has a grudge against you, whether or not it is legitimate, make peace with them. Call them on the phone or write and say, "I know that you are soreheaded with me about something, and I don't know what it is, and I want to apologize and say that I'm sorry and I want to be friends." They may tell you to go to hell, but that's all right, you have done your part. You have already made peace with God, so make peace with everybody you can think of that you need.

Then comes the last night – Tuesday night. I am going to die in my sleep. I would make it a point to be the last one to bed. I'd make some excuse. I'd tell my wife. "Go on and go to bed. I'll see you in a little while." Then I would say

Unction

goodbye to all of my material possessions, those little intimate personal keepsakes that I have been hoarding like my favourite pipes or my diploma, or my books. I would tell them goodbye. Their only purpose was to excite in me the love of and gratitude to God, and if they have done that, they have served their purpose and I am through with them now. I would hate to leave my first edition Chesterton, but after all, I am going to see Chesterton himself. I don't need his books. Forget them. Turn them loose, say goodbye. Then I would go around to all the bedrooms of my children and my wife while they are sound asleep and remind myself that God loves them far better than I do, and that He will take care of them. I turn them over to Him. Blow them a kiss goodbye. "I am leaving. I will see you when you get there. Take care, I'll be praying for you from the other side." Then you go to bed and go to sleep. You wake up on Wednesday morning and it is like being born all over again. The sky is bluer and the grass is greener and besides that, all your affairs are in order and your bills paid, and it's wonderful. You have a new lease on life and you really do appreciate being alive. It's a marvellous experience.

You do this once or twice a year for a couple of years, then you do it about four times a year. The more often you do it, the less your affairs are in a mess and the less straightening up you have to do. See, you already have a box labelled with your insurance policies. You won't have to do that again. A good part of the work has already been done. Then you do it about once a month, and about twenty-four hours is all it takes to get ready that way. Everything is all straightened up. You go to confession, go to communion, and look forward to meeting God face to face in eternity. Then you do it once a week, and finally you to it every day.

293

It is the way Our Lord told us to live – one day at a time. This may possibly be the last day on earth for any one of us. You don't expect it, and neither do I. We pray in the Litany, "From battle, murder, and sudden death, good Lord deliver us." I want to know that I am going to die. Life is a fatal disease. You start dying the day you are born. It's nothing to be scared of or shamed of, if you play the game right. Now what this little exercise that I have described does is to prepare you. If you do it realistically and often enough, you will discover that when your time comes to die, it is old hat.

First of all, it gives you a sense of detachment from and independence of things. I have said that I am a magpie; I collect everything in the world. But I have learned that if I love that pipe and I drop it on the pavement and it breaks, it wouldn't upset me greatly. I think I can turn loose of things.

I think I have come to the point where I have no particular desire to be remembered. It's not important. I know that I am going to die if I live long enough. I want to be able to do it gracefully, and particularly, I want my death to be the kind of death that will be a witness, a good holy Christian death. To go into eternity confidently, serenely, and happily, looking forward and not backward, is one of the most powerful sermons that can be preached. The best way I know to achieve this is by practising it, and doing all the things you would do if you knew you only had a week to live. Play the game, do it realistically, and man, waking up can be so much fun.

Now, a word about funerals. They ought to be from the church for Christian people, and not from the funeral home. There ought to be a requiem Mass in connection with the funeral. It is also a good idea to plan your own funeral. Write out on paper what it is you want: choir, hymns, clergy to officiate, all that sort of thing. If you want fifty hot and cold dancing girls, specify it. There's no guarantee you'll get it, but most people want to honour the request. Don't be afraid to plan your own funeral. Write it out and give it to your priest to file. It's real handy. Funerals don't have to be particularly expensive. What I would like for my funeral is to be wrapped up in a tow sack and put in a hole in the ground. I want my body to return to earth as rapidly as possible. All this embalming business, trying to pretend that you are an Egyptian Pharaoh and that your mummy will survive for 5,000 years – if you've ever seen any of those mummies, you wouldn't want to look like that anyway.

There's nothing particularly wrong with cremation. The reason that the Church was so long opposed to cremation is that she was opposed to the reason people gave for wanting to be cremated. They could not think of lying out there in that cold damp ground and letting worms eat the body. Well, they aren't out there in the damp ground. The body is. You want to do something with this precious keepsake the body, but you can't keep it. So you bury it with some solemnity. Fundamentally, the purpose of the funeral is to convince the survivors that the person is really dead. It is the way of establishing a ceremonial, a ritual termination of the relationship. It should not be a time of weeping and crying or sorrow and sadness. The casket should not be opened. If you must look at the cosmetic effects of the undertakers, do that at the funeral home. Close the casket and at the funeral and the burial, leave it closed. Preferably, there should be no flowers. It is a sombre occasion, a solemn one, but not a sad one.

It is particularly fitting that the members of the family receive communion at the time of the funeral because, you see, the Christian Church believes that the dead are not dead. They are with Christ. Because I am in Christ, a member of His Body, and because the dead are also in Christ and are members of His Body, my closeness, my union with the deceased is closer now than during their lifetime.

When I was a wee one, they taught me to say

> Now I lay me down to sleep,
> I pray the Lord my soul to keep.
> If I should die before I wake,
> I pray the Lord my soul to take.

When I was little I sort of liked that, I guess because it rhymed and I didn't think very much about what it meant. By the time I was twenty-one years old, even though I was seriously thinking about the priesthood, I thought how dreadful to think of teaching a small child about dying in his sleep. Then I read something when I was in seminary that brought me up short. It seems that in the Middle Ages there was a monastery somewhere in Switzerland, probably one of those Benedictine ones that kept some of those big St Bernard dogs. When a young man entered the monastery as a novice, his first assigned task was to build his coffin. That became his bed and he slept in it every night for the rest of his life. My first reaction was, "How dreadful, how morbid," but then, all of a sudden, it dawned on me, how wonderful to wake up every morning and step out of your coffin. Besides that, in Switzerland it's cold in the winter time, and the sides of the coffin would keep the draughts off you, probably making for good sleeping. Finally I thought about that little prayer. It's a pretty good prayer to teach children, and a pretty good one for grown-ups, too. Can you say, with an absolutely clear conscience, "Now I lay me down to sleep . . ."?

One of the reasons we worry about death is that there are so many loose ends and unfinished business in our lives. If you could put all your affairs in order and get ready to die and go to bed and wake up next morning just like the resurrection, and do this once a quarter, then once a month, then once a week, and then, by the time you are doing this every day, your affairs are permanently in order. This is not just the way to die, it is the way to live.

19

. . . .

BEATITUDES

Some folk have the mistaken notion that once you have been converted, have taken the preacher's hand and given your heart to Jesus, been baptized and numbered among the faithful, that you have it made. As a matter of fact, the person who is converted is in much the same situation in respect to the Church as the student is in respect to education who has just matriculated. It is not the end of something, but the beginning. That does not make him an educated man. Four years later when he graduates, he will have begun to realize all there is to know and what a small percentage of it he has mastered.

When you are converted and baptized, the important thing for the Church to do is to guide and direct you in your spiritual growth and development, which is something that goes on all your life long. The more saintly we become, the more aware we are of how far we have yet to go. The person who has no knowledge of God at all might indeed think of himself as a pretty nice guy, using the standards of the world as his yardstick. But the more advanced you are in your spiritual growth and development, the more painfully aware you are of how far yet you have to go.

The technical term in ecclesiology for the job I hold is the cure of souls. That defines any priest who is responsible for other people's spiritual welfare, to the point that God, on the Day of Judgement, will ask me, "Homer, where is Janet

Gilder? I was expecting her to show up here. She was your responsibility." The Greek word for cure of souls is "psychotherapy", oddly enough. This highly technical department of theology was developed on the basis of empirical observation and the practical experience of thousands of priests dealing daily with millions of souls. There grew up in the Middle Ages the habit of talking about three major stages through which the soul passes in its progress to God, and these were called the Purgative Way, the Illuminative Way, and the Unitive Way.

In the early Church, certainly by the beginning of the second century and probably even before that, when a person said, "I want to be a Christian," he was enrolled in what was known as a catechumenate class taught by someone called a catechist. The guy taking the course was called a catechumen. This class lasted anywhere from two to five years, meeting not less than once a week. During this time the person was not allowed to attend church with the congregation. He was not only instructed, but he was scrutinized, and when the catechist, usually a deacon in the congregation, judged him ready, he was brought to the church, baptized, and then for the first time was allowed to witness and participate in the Holy Communion.

One of the things that the catechist looked for in the catechumen were certain signs of spiritual growth and development. There were in particular three major spiritual crises which the person was expected to have passed through before he was judged ready for baptism. It is much the same sort of thing that Alcoholics Anonymous look for in alcoholics who come to them seeking help. If a man has not bottomed out, as they say, he is not ready for AA, and there are certain telltale signs in a man's attitude and his conversation that a well-trained AA person looks for to determine whether or not the man is ready for the AA programme. If he isn't ready, they won't waste their time with him. On the other hand, if he is ready, they will sit up all night, nights on end, working with him, helping him get over the shakes or whatever. In much the same way, the early Church looked for signs in a person to see if he was ready for the Christian religion and baptism.

We are going to trace the progress of the soul under a schema based on the nine Beatitudes given in the fifth chapter of St Matthew's Gospel.

"Blessed are the poor in spirit, for theirs is the kingdom of Heaven." It is blessed to have the kingdom of Heaven, but poverty of spirit is one of the prerequisites. Now even in a great deal of highly orthodox biblical commentaries, an effort is made to interpret this "blessed are the poor in spirit" in terms of other things that Our Lord says about wealth and money. "How hardly shall a rich man enter the kingdom of Heaven." "It is easier for a camel to go through the eye of a needle than for the rich man to enter the kingdom of Heaven." However, nowhere in the New Testament does Jesus say anything about material poverty being a good thing for its own sake. The "in spirit" in the Greek is what is called a dative of respect. "Blessed are those who are poor in respect to spiritual things." "Blessed are the woebegone." "Blessed are the dispirited."

There is a natural assumption that happiness is to be found in terms of our possessions and the use of other creatures, in material things. There was a baby boom immediately after World War II. These babies got older and there was a bulge in the population curve. A large number of kids all came into adolescence in the mid 1950s. Now what ordinarily happens sometime between sixteen and twenty-one is that it dawns upon a person that happiness does not consist of a new motorcycle. Life has got to have more meaning than just material things. And a whole lot of teenage kids made this discovery all at once. The result was the hippies, the flower children, who accused the grownups of being too materialistic. They had observed their parents working diligently and saving for a new car or a swimming pool, and they assumed, perhaps with some justification, that their parents thought that happiness was the possession of material things. They, in their new-found wisdom, knew that happiness is not in one's relation to things. This is the renunciation of the flesh.

Some people never go through it. You can find people in their seventies and eighties who still think that happiness is found in terms of bank accounts and things like that. Most people, fortunately, discover early on in life that it's not, and this discovery usually comes as a bit of a shock. It's the first really great spiritual crisis. They have a sense of having been deceived, if not by their parents, then by life itself. Usually this condition is momentary. "All the things I have worked for and looked forward to are a disappointment to me." A person goes to Jesus in this state and says, "Jesus, I've got the woebegones. I'm really upset about this." Jesus replies, "Lucky you. Only people who have gone through this ever find the kingdom of Heaven."

When you discover that material things will not make you happy, you have renounced the flesh. But it has to be a real gut experience, not just something you admit with your intellect. Some people, at this point, despair, turn to drugs or drink, and give up. But for those who refuse to give up, if happiness is not a Honda, what is it?

After a person has renounced the flesh, the next stage is

usually that of reformer or crusader of some kind. He says, "I am going to leave the world a little better place than I found it." I said that to my parents, and my kids said it to me. My grandparents heard it, and my grandchildren will say it to my children. Because there was such a large number of them discovering it all at one time, all of a sudden these innocent and peace-loving flower children became fiercely militant social reformers and went marching to Selma, Alabama, or the Pentagon. They were determined to take hold of the world and shake it down to its roots and refashion it into something that would be fit for human beings to live in. But they discovered that the world did not want to be saved. Revolutions are always fought by young people, by idealists. And if the revolution succeeds, they discover that the kind of leaders it takes to bring off a successful revolution are not the kind of people necessary to lead the new establishment. So the revolutionary leaders are thrust aside, or if the revolution fails, there sets in a period of disillusionment. As far as the young radical revolutionaries are concerned, they are very sincere, honest, and idealistic. And then they discover that the revolution doesn't work. The result of this is a very genuine sadness, and a rather pervasive sense of tragedy.

"Blessed are they that mourn for they shall be comforted." The word "comforted", here in the King James, originally meant strengthened, toughened up, not smoothed and consoled. This is the renunciation of the world. "I can't save the world and I am not going to try any more. It can go to hell if it damn well wants to." Imagine the disillusionment of the young people who left college in Michigan to go to Alabama and work for the civil rights of black people and were told, "Whitey, go home!"

The young idealistic revolutionaries become disillusioned and renounce the world. This crusade for the salvation of the world can be almost anything: Vietnam, women's rights, civil rights, and even Christianity. Back in the 1830s a movement swept over the churches in America and thousands of young men and women signed up for foreign missionaries under the slogan, "The world for Christ in our generation." Psychologically it was the same as burning down the army cadet building because you did not like the war in Vietnam. These revolutions frequently do accomplish something and leave behind a residue of good. But the revolutionary is always disillusioned.

This is the renunciation of the world. The person in this condition of mournful disillusion goes to Jesus and says, "I'm sad." Jesus replies, "Lucky you. You will be toughened up and this will make you strong." Again, at this point some people just give up. These spiritual crises are danger points, and people need help getting through them.

So what happens next? A person ordinarily says, "The world can go to hell if it wants to, but I don't have to go with it." And then he launches into some kind of self-development or self-cultivation programme, and he turns to yoga, or Zen Buddhism, or Transcendental Meditation, or even Christiantity. And his motive here is, "I am going to make myself into someone I can be proud of, or at least that I won't be ashamed of." The same kids that were so wildly revolutionary a short time before then turned to psychology, or astrology, or became followers of the Moonies or the guru. But when you discover that you can't guide and direct and manipulate your own development to the point that you can approve of yourself, that's the renunciation of the devil. Why the devil?

303

Precisely because that's the way the devil works. If you recall what he said to Mother Eve in the garden, it was, "Honey chile, you shall be a goddess." What each man wants in his secret heart is to be godlike, to be noble and heroic and splendid and glorious, and consequently, do-it-yourself programmes are strictly demonic. When you give up on that you have renounced the devil. Then, and only then, are you ready for baptism.

This purgation can be a profound experience or a rather superficial one, but nevertheless it is a very real experience in the lives of some people. It doesn't have to be as dramatic and public as it has been for a whole generation of young people. Some folk get stuck in one or the other of these stages and go through all their lives in the purgative state. What is underlying all three of these states is the effort to find meaning and significance for myself, to find my identity, without ever realizing that my identity is conferred upon me by my community. The real motive is to try to establish some sort of worth for myself whereby I can justify my existence in my own eyes.

Now when a person has finally given up on saving himself he says, "I can't do it. God, you do it." I am finally willing to turn my life over to God and let Him do with it whatever He wants. And this is "Blessed are the meek." Meekness is not Caspar Milquetoast, it is simply obedience. Moses was the meekest man in the Bible. This bearded cowboy walked out of the desert and in to Pharaoh and said, "Look here, King Pharaoh, you let my people go, or God and I will clobber you." Meekness is letting God run the show. This is the renunciation of the devil, and at this point one is finished with the Purgative Way. Not that you are going through the rest of your life without experiencing purgation. These three stages are not like grammar school, high school, and college, that when you leave one, you leave it completely behind. It is a question of which of these spiritual states is the predominantly characteristic one at any given time. You are in the Unitive Way from the moment God taps you on the shoulder and leads you to the faintest interest in Christianity. You are in the Purgative Way even a lifetime down the road when everyone else thinks you are very holy. But in this first stage of purgation what you experience subjectively is largely a sense of being emptied, cleaned out of self-will, illusion, falsehood, idolatory, and inadequate ideals.

A period of relative quiet comes after we have surrendered to Jesus and given up that senseless self-will and programmes for self-improvement and changing the world. All of a sudden we find that none of that is going to work, and we turn ourselves to God and become relaxed. It seems quiet, but it's actually a busy time because what is going on, of course, is that we are trying to make sense out of life in this world from God's point of view. We read our Bible, we meditate and reflect a lot, we pray a great deal, we think a lot. This is usually a stage in which religion is very rewarding and very gratifying. We go to church regularly and listen carefully to sermons. We are trying to see the world from God's point of view. This stage may last anywhere from three months to thirty years. "Blessed are those who thirst after righteousness." We want things to fit, to feel right. This is the kind of righteousness you get when you are putting together a jig-saw puzzle, and little by little more of the pieces fit and the pattern begins to emerge. You see what it is all about. Again, this is something that is going to go on for the rest of your life. There is a time in which this is a predominant activity, and you might seem at this time to be relatively indifferent to social evils and missionary activity. It seems, looking at it from the outside, that the person is rather selfishly preoccupied with his own soul.

The result of this is a succession of interior events which you can describe and say, "Oh, I see," or "So that's what that means," and "Of course, now I understand." Gradually there grows that mind in you which was also in Christ Jesus. There begins to be the business of seeing ourselves and seeing the world the way it looks to God, which is obviously the true way. While I will never fully see myself as God sees me, it is my job to approach that as much as I can. This is illumination, and the first thing that is illuminated is the mind. This is not something we do, but something that happens to us.

While we are perfectly content to go on learning, sorting things out, putting things together, and making sense of our lives, we begin to see that we are gradually being forced back into an active life, into the corporal and spiritual works of mercy. Poor people will knock on our door, people in trouble and in great difficulty. Potential suicides, runaway kids, marital messes, sick people, and all kinds of problem folk will begin to impinge on our lives in such a way that we are being forced to concern ourselves with them. This is the beatitude "Blessed are the merciful". It's not blessed are the kind and helpful, or the generous, or those who do good. It's blessed are the merciful.

Most of the people who come banging and crawling onto our doorstep are not very attractive people. Our natural inclination or temptation is to dislike them. Only as I remember that I, too, am not a very attractive person, and I can be and often am obnoxious and disagreeable, will I recall that Jesus loves this jackass who is here demanding my time, just as He loves me. What is happening at this stage is that the moral character is conformed to the moral character of Christ. This is putting faith into action. This is the Incarnation, the enfleshment of God's truth and reality, whereby we become like Christ. This is sharing in the passion and suffering of Christ so that our character is conformed to the character of Christ. It is the translation of the virtue of faith into the active virtue of hope. What we believe with our minds we now know with our hearts. Blessed are the merciful, the compassionate, the tender-hearted, and believe me, if you are going to engage very much in either the spiritual or the corporal works of mercy, you are going to have to be compassionate. There is a terrible danger when dealing with people who have made messes of their lives to feel smug, self-righteous, and superior because you haven't made a mess of yours. God's not going to let you do that. We have to approach our brothers and sisters in Christ in an attitude of mercy, knowing and remembering how much we need the mercy of God ourselves. This is the action of hope whereby we learn to love that at which we work.

Finally, "Blessed are the pure in heart." Remember that the human act which has integrity begins with an act of rational judgement and proceeds to an act of moral choice. When you practise virtue by forced acts of the will, finally the emotions are harmonized with the will and intellect, and you are in that blissful condition of which St Augustine said, "Love God and do as you please." When you're a saint, you can follow your impulses. I'm not there yet. My impulses are often quite contrary to my judgement and even contrary to my will. Twentieth-century man has elevated feelings far out of sight. Don't pay attention to your feelings, because they are deceptive and unreliable.

Think, and when you have come to a rational conclusion that is the best thinking you can do, then make a decision on the basis of your judgement, never mind how you feel. When you have done that over and over again and have disciplined yourself, the time will come when you will begin to love doing what is right. This is the purity in the heart of the beatitude. For they shall see God.

Now the seeing of God here is not the type of vision you would have if God appeared to you in the flesh. Rather, it is the kind of seeing that you say when you say, "Oh, I see." Having finally harmonized the intellect, will, and emotions, you see the hand of God in all things. St Paul says, "I live, yet not I but Christ liveth in me." The hand of God is revealed in the circumstances of our lives and we see that, so that in whatever happens to me I am aware of the reality, the presence, and the nearness and providence of God. Now, this is the end of the Illuminative Way.

Back in the Purgative Way, we were very gung-ho about civil rights and the poor, but notice that we talked about them in general terms. The Poor, The Oppressed. In the Illuminative Way, we are concerned not with The Poor, but with this poor person. Not with The Exploited, but with this particular victim of injustice. There is a concrete reality about it in the Illuminative Way. What I am really concerned with in the Purgative Way is myself, and the meaning that I can find for my life in the struggle for righteousness and justice. Here I have forgotten myself, and I am concerned with this particular victim of social injustice. Back in the Purgative Way I want to feed the hungry by getting the rich folks to give away three million dollars worth of groceries. In the Illuminative Way I open my pocketbook to feed this hungry child. I am not anxious to get anybody else to do it; I do it myself. If I don't have anything in my pocketbook, I take them home and open my refrigerator even if I have to go hungry myself. That's the Christian approach.

But even here, what God is concerned with is not feeding the hungry, but saving my soul, sanctifying my soul. God doesn't need me to feed the hungry, He proved that when He took five loaves and two fishes and fed five thousand people. He wants me to feed the hungry so that I will be happy.

Through the Purgative and Illuminative Ways God is concerned with redeeming me, but when I enter the Unitive Way, He is concerned with using me to redeem others. Sure, He can make use of wild-eyed egotistical radical teenaged revolutionaries, and they do do good. And He can use Christian souls in the Illuminative Way to go out and teach the ignorant and console the bereaved and feed the hungry. But the next beatitude says, "Blessed are the peacemakers, for they shall be called the children of God."

This is a technical scriptural term that needs a bit of explanation. We speak of the children of the prophets, which is a technical biblical concept which literally means someone who is carrying on the tradition of the prophets, in the same way that St Paul speaks of Timothy as "my son". The child of the prophets is a person in whose life one is able to see revealed the values and characteristics of the prophets. The children of Israel are those whose lives reflect the character of Jacob. And to be called the children of God refers to the Unitive Way. God Himself lives in their lives and characters. They are the peacemakers.

Peace is a by-product of right order, or justice. There are three ways the saint makes peace. First, he doesn't make waves. Through the Illuminative Way he has got everything straightened out and he lives in an ordered universe in which all of his priorities are straight. He is living his life so that he doesn't make unpeace. There is peace simply because there is no injustice. He doesn't do the sorts of things that make for disorder. Peace is the result of an overflow of the way he conducts himself in his day-to-day life.

The second way a saint makes peace is that, since he knows the right order and has peace in his own life, people seek him out for counsel. He makes peace by pointing out what things are for. Remember that sin is a reversal of ends and means, or a confusion thereof. The peacemaker will find himself more and more sought out for advice and counsel, and the result for those who follow his advice is that they will live in peace.

Finally, the third way in which a saint makes peace is that he has such a profound interior serenity that being in his presence makes you feel that everything is going to be all right. You can be very disturbed or upset and run into one of these saintly types and he refuses to get upset, so that somehow or other his interior peace communicates itself to you and you go away feeling more peaceful. God is in the business of redeeming and reordering a disordered society, and the peacemakers are those whom he principally employs in putting to order what sin has disturbed.

"Blessed are they which are persecuted for righteousness' sake." Remember that there are two kinds of people the world will not tolerate: the very bad and the very good. When you get to be very good, you will provoke hostility and resentment, and when you get to this point, you are being persecuted for the sake of righteousness. You are lucky, and I will show you why. God has a hankering for heroes. This is a rather exalted vocation, being invited to share in the redemptive passion of Christ. You begin that sort of thing simply by hanging on to your temper when you're provoked, putting yourself out just a little bit to assist someone who is a little bit less fortunate, stopping when you are driving on the highway to help someone change a tyre. You give up a little of your own time and your own convenience for someone else. This is not an enormous great crucifixion, and most of our crucifixions are going to be relatively small, but it is only as the cross of Christ is reproduced in our behaviour that we are going to benefit from it. Otherwise, we don't really accept Christ. To accept Christ means to accept inconvenience, hardship, privation, and even persecution.

"Blessed are you when men shall revile you and persecute you and say all manner of evil against you falsely for my sake. Rejoice and be exceeding glad for great is your reward in Heaven, for so persecuted they the prophets that were before you." Jesus was talking to His disciples. He couldn't very well say to them that if they experienced all that, then they were in the company of the martyrs, and St Francis, St Ignatius, and all the great Christian saints, because they hadn't lived yet, so he referred them back to the Old Testament prophets who were almost without exception persecuted. This refers to that special vocation of martyrdom. When you are persecuted for Jesus and identified with Him, this is the vocation of martyrs, who have always been the Christians par excellence. Martyrs are those people who give up their lives gladly and willingly for Christ.

Now take a deep breath and listen to this. There are only martyrs in Heaven. At the moment of our death we will have the opportunity to give our lives gladly and willingly into the hands of Christ, or we will go into eternity full of resentment and bitterness and rage. God is preparing us for that moment every time He asks us to give up five minutes of our time for a disagreeable neighbour. We are mortifying our vanity, our pride, our comfort, our convenience, and in the process we are growing holy. Any one of us may be called upon to be a martyr, and if we are, Jesus would say, "Lucky you." Back when you were fourteen or fifteen years old, you had dreams of being somebody great, splendid, heroic, and noble. Guess what, you were right. This is what God wants for you. Lucky you.

20

THE VIRTUES

Man is the only one of God's creatures that grows by an internal self-direction. An acorn, if you put it in the ground, will become an oak tree and it never does have to stop and think about where it's growing. Puppies grow up into dogs, eggs hatch into chickens without giving any thought thereto at all. But man is self-directed, and we largely become in this life whatever we set out to be. One of the most terrifying things about God is that He really does give us what we want. The trouble with most of us is that we don't know what's good for us.

Let's say it like this: if you ask a child, "What do you want to be when you grow up?", the only correct answer is "Grown up." It doesn't matter enormously whether I'm a tinker, tailor, soldier, sailor, butcher, baker, candlestick maker. What I really want to be when I grow up is grown up, a fully developed, perfected human being. The Church calls that a saint. So we're going to talk about the character of a saint in terms of virtues.

The way you acquire a virtue is that you've got to know what it would be like if you had it, what a person who has the virtue does in a number of different situations, how he behaves in a whole series of minor crises.

The virtues are defined as a disposition to act in accordance with right reason, with the truth, with reality. One virtue is distinguished from another virtue by what one

313

can have right reason about. There are eight categories: God, myself, my neighbour, things, circumstances, duties, bodily appetites, and sex. The virtues having to do with right reason about God are divided into three called the Theological Virtues: Faith, Hope, and Charity. The other virtues are called the Moral Virtues. These theological virtues correspond roughly to the three persons of the Trinity. Faith, Hope, and Charity conform us to the persons of the Trinity. Thus when you have fully perfected Faith, you are like God the Father, when you have fully perfected Hope you are like God the Son, and when you have fully perfected Charity you are like God the Holy Spirit.

Let's look at a couple of things Faith is *not*. Faith is not believing in a lot of doctrine. It is true that the whole range of Christian dogmatic theology is referred to under the broad general title of The Faith, but the virtue of Faith is not believing a set of doctrines. Neither is it believing that Jesus died and suffered for me so I won't have to.

Faith is that disposition of trust or confidence in God's providence such that one is put to work in obedience to God's commands. God created the universe and therefore He knows how it runs. He engineered it. As we've already pointed out, every one of God's commands is a direction for the use of the products, a prescription for happiness. God wants me to be happy and therefore He's told me how to conduct my life in this world so as to attain happiness. Certainly God is smarter than I am. Not only that, but God is benevolent. And therefore it behoves me to trust Him. If I have faith in God, I will obey God. As a consequence, there is no opposition between faith and works, as St James points out in his epistle. Neither is there any opposition

314

between faith and reason, since faith is a virtue and a virtue is a disposition to act in accordance with right reason. Remember, belief in God is *reasonable*. The Church has always insisted that "believing in God" is a moral rather than a intellectual matter.

Belief in God cannot be demonstrated coercively. It's not like believing that the square of the hypotenuse of a right-angled triangle is equal to the sum of the square of the other two sides. There are several evidences for a belief in God, but these are not coercive.

The alternative to believing in God, of course, is like Mother Eve in the Garden, being my own God, my own ultimate arbiter of right and wrong and truth and false-hood, so that while belief in God is really an intellectual belief, it involves an acknowledgement that God is bigger and smarter and better than I am. And He knows what's good for me better than I know.

If I have faith in God, I will set at work to obey God's prescriptions for happiness, God's commandments. Faith issues in obedience, but the moment a person sets out to obey God he gets in trouble. There are those who will lie to you and tell you that if you will do everything God tells you to do, you will be healthy, wealthy, and wise. Hogwash. It's not scriptural, in the first place. He whom the Lord loveth he chasteneth. Every branch that beareth fruit is pruned that it may bear more fruit. Jesus said, "Whosoever will live righteously shall suffer persecution." He said to His disciples, "In this world ye shall have tribulation." Don't think that by obeying God you can stay out of trouble. Trouble is the lot of man in this life. But it seems sometimes that when a person sets out to do right and obey God, that his troubles multiply.

And this is why. Remember, God desires exactly what

you desire. He desires our perfection. Now, what are the psychological laws of growth and development? Let's say that I'm a schoolteacher out in an old-fashioned one-room schoolhouse in the country, and I teach every subject from kindergarten to high school. One of the things I'm going to teach these little darlings is arithmetic. So in the first grade I begin to teach them simple addition: 2+2 = 4. 3+5 = 8. 2+10 = 12. That's hard for a little kid when he's first beginning. But I'm the teacher. Because I love that child, I will insist he learn his simple addition. I'll push him. I'll give him homework. I'll even give him a test. I may even keep him after school if I think he's not working hard enough at his homework. And he won't like it. I remember I didn't like it when I was in first grade. But the teacher insists, and after a while he begins to master simple addition, and it gets to be kind of fun. He gets a sense of achievement, and he begins to enjoy it. But if you keep on doing simple arithmetic long enough after you've learned how, it'll get boring, and you'll begin to lose interest. So the smart teacher – I'm a smart teacher – will allow the child to enjoy his simple arithmetic a little while. The kid enjoys it for a week or two, gets to show off to Mama and Papa at home how smart he is, but just before the subject begins to get boring, I'll slug him with subtraction, and once again he is cast down and disconsolate and depressed, that once again he's got to go to work and learn things strange and unfamiliar. And the process is repeated. He keeps on working at this and after a while he begins to master it and it gets to be kind of fun and he has a sense that he enjoys it, and about that time I hit him with the multiplication tables. And then after that comes short division, and then long division, and then I'm really going to throw him for a loop with fractions or decimals.

Now, I know that way out yonder, years in the future, lurking, lying in wait to pounce on this child, are trigonometry and calculus. You don't dare let him even suspect that there is differential and integral calculus waiting for him down the road years ahead, but they're there. And he's slowly moving towards these, and each new bite that he takes off is a little more than he can handle, and he's depressed, and he has to struggle with this, so that in the development of his mathematical life there are alternating periods of depression and elation, pleasure and discomfort.

The same thing is true of the spiritual life. God is a master teacher, and He gives us enough knowledge and insight and responsibility to tax our strength in the early and initial stages, and we are cast down, and then after a while we get to where we can handle this, and we get to feeling rather good about ourselves, and about that time we're overwhelmed again with either new insights or new responsibilities. There are in the spiritual life alternating periods of elation and despondency, called consolation and dry periods.

In the initial stages of conversion religion is fun. You enjoy saying your prayers, you enjoy coming to Sunday worship, you enjoy reading your Bible, you enjoy conversations about religion with religious people. It's fun, it's rewarding, it's gratifying, but it won't last. And after a while either one of two things happens. God may promote you to the next highest grade and load you down with additional insights, responsibilities, and disciplines, and it's hard for you once more, and you think, "Oh my God, I've lost my faith. It seemed so real and plausible before, but obviously I was mistaken." Or you may drift gradually into secularism. Your interest will wane and you stop saying your prayers and stop going to church and start sleeping in on Sunday mornings and mundane preoccupations demand your attention and you fall away from the Church.

The times of rich spiritual fervour are not the times of growth but the times of movement as a result of growth that took place during the dry period. Dry periods are times of spiritual growth, not times of consolation.

The way we get through the dry periods is with the virtue of Hope, which is the virtue of perseverance. If it makes sense to obey God, it makes sense to continue to obey Him. Hope is that virtue of continued obedience in the face of obstacles, in the face of apparent lack of progress, or perseverance in the dry spells. What you're supposed to do with a dry spell, of course, is to keep up all the religious practices you started under the influence of the period of fervour. This is why God sends you the fervour.

If Faith is the virtue that perfects the human intellect, hope is the virtue that perfects the human will. Hope looks down the road to the goal, and its character is perseverance. In the virtue of hope God is perfecting our moral character, building good habits. Remember that the human act that has integrity begins with a rational judgement about the truth. It moves from that to a moral choice. I will do what I know to be the truth.

Now a human act which lacks integrity, which is perverse, normally begins with the emotions, or emotion in response to some fantasy, some subjective condition. Wouldn't it be nice if . . . ? And then the will comes along and says, "Yeah, it sure would, let's do that." And then the intellect tags along behind and finds reasons for having done what we wanted to. We call that rationalization. The opposite of that is the supernatural virtue of hope.

Jesus said, "Where a man's treasure is, there shall his heart be also." In other words, what you work at you enjoy. Where you invest yourself, where you put your goodies, where you spend your time and your energy and your concern, that you will enjoy. This is completely contrary to what the twentieth-century secular man understands. He would turn it around. He would say, where a man's heart is, there would his treasure be. In other words, what you love you will work at. It seems as though that's the case, but bad psychology. The truth of the matter is that what you work at, you love. And I will give you several examples.

Why does a mother love her baby? What does the baby ever do for Mama? Let's just run briefly through a small catalogue of contributions the baby makes to Mama. First of all is morning sickness. She gets that for several weeks early in pregnancy, and she can't hold anything in her stomach. Then she gets sort of overweighted in front and has to walk funny to keep her balance and wear maternity clothes and be embarrassed when all the ladies in the supermarket give her what they call the stomach look, which is mentally counting up on their fingers and seeing how many months she has to go. And her feet hurt and her back aches – sounds like I've been pregnant, doesn't it? I've lived in the house with a pregnant woman six times. And then there is parturition, which if it is not pain, is certainly labour. But that's just the beginning, because she's got bottles to sterilize and diapers to wash and a 2 a.m. feeding and she has unremitting anxiety about where the toddler is. It forces a major degree of self-forgetfulness on a woman, and she loves the child and would die for it and why? Because she has invested herself in the child. Blood, sweat, tears, time, energy.

Where your treasure is, there shall your heart be. Notice how God works this. Faith – it is reasonable to believe that God loves me and intends my good and is smarter than I am so I'll do what He says. Hope – I'll keep on doing it even if I don't seem to be making much progress and it's all uphill. Finally, as a result there appears in my consciousness a sense of the preciousness of God – charity.

Charity is the love of God just because God is loveable. It's not charity to say I love God because He's so good to me. God is very good to me, but charity is not loving Him for that reason. Charity is loving God because He's good. It's sort of like the way you love Mozart. Mozart's good to me, I enjoy Mozart. But Mozart doesn't make me any richer or healthier, and it does take a certain amount of time. Similarly with God, you love God just for God's sake.

These are the three theological virtues, since they describe how we act in accordance with right reason about God. The moral virtues describe how we act toward the rest of the list: myself, my neighbour, things, circumstances, bodily appetites, and sex.

The first of the so-called moral virtues is Humility, or the disposition to act in accordance with right reason about myself. What is the right reason about me?

The Christian Church nowhere holds the doctrine of the supreme value of the individual, if one means the supreme value of me in my individuality. Being born is much more important than being born a Texan, great as that is. The most wonderful thing that ever happened to anyone has happened to everyone. One day we opened our eyes for the first time and saw the light of day. The most tragic and terrible thing that has ever happened to anyone will happen to everyone, and that is that we will one day close our eyes in death and step out into the great unknown. Being in love is more exciting than being in love with Alice. Being married is more of an adventure than being married to Dorothy. Everyone has seen the sun rise, and has thrilled to an electrical storm on a summer's night. The things that distinguish us from one another are quite superficial and trivial. I am handsome and you are homely. I am rich and you are poor. I am wise and you are foolish. I am a Democrat and you are a Republican. I am Queen of the May and you weren't even nominated. The first error people make about themselves is being excellently impressed with their own individuality.

There are three ways that one commits the sin of pride, which is the opposite of humility. One is to make oneself more important than anybody else, to be the centre of one's interest and one's world. Basically, regarding myself as the centre of my own interest makes me different and cuts me off and alienates me from anybody else. It causes me to be preoccupied with myself, with my own station in life, my own lot and my own circumstances. And it is easy to allow this to colour one's sense of values. The humble man, on the other hand, makes Christ his centre of interest, and in doing so he thrusts himself out on the periphery of life where he is aware of his kinship with all other men. I am not the most important thing in my life – Christ is.

The second way that man commits the sin of pride is to make himself his own standard of values. I don't really think that in order to be handsome you have to be six feet

321

tall and bald-headed. Of course, it helps. Everyone has a mental image of how he ought to be, and we judge ourselves and other people by this imaginary self, if we are not very careful. The humble man, on the other hand, takes Christ as his standard of values and judges himself and others by the standards of Christ. Humility is the curious, rare, and blissful ability to be clear-eyed and level-headed about oneself.

The third way that one commits pride is to try to be his own source of power. This is the person, for example, who will be delighted to help you with your homework, but never mind, he won't let you help him. He will do it by himself if it kills him. He is the guy who says he doesn't want to grow old and feeble and helpless and become a burden on other people, which may be kindness and charity, but on the other hand, it may be an unwillingness to admit one's dependence. The humble man relies on God for his strength, not himself, and as a result is much stronger. The proud man is a large fish in a small pond, a very interesting person in a dull world.

Boredom is frequently the sin of pride. A humble man is never bored. The humble man minimizes his own importance and magnifies the importance of everything else around him. He is a small fish in a very large pond, and a very ordinary person in an extraordinary, unusual, and exciting world.

An inferiority complex is a sin of pride, and so is a superiority complex, because in both cases a person is overly concerned and preoccupied with himself. God gave us our eyes to see things out there, and if you spend your time looking into your own eyes, all you will get is cross-eyed. It is the sin of pride to exalt oneself, and the sin of pride to belittle oneself. It is the virtue of humility to have no thought about oneself.

You don't like proud people. They are the people who will talk your arm off, tie you up for hours on end, talking about themselves with the most dreary recital of the most commonplace and ordinary events in their life which they have magnified out of all proportion; they confidently expect that their little odyssey is worthy of the pen of a Homer. Humble people, on the other hand, want to talk about you, they are interested in you. They like you and find you fascinating. What you don't realize is that they would be equally fascinated by a caterpillar, because having minimized their own value and importance, they have magnified the importance of everything else.

They are the people who have the remarkable capacity for being continually excited about anything and everything. The word comes from the Latin word *humus* which is the word for "dirt". It was applied originally by the Romans to their country cousins and means something like our English word "earthy", although it also carried the connotation of "yokel" or "country bumpkin". The country bumpkin comes to the State Fair of Texas and he goes out into the midway and stands in front of the Ferris wheel and says, "My God, look at that thing, it goes around and around and there are people sitting in them baskets up there, would you look at that thing?" The city sophisticate who has seen it all before goes strolling by paying no attention. Which one is having more fun? Humility is the beautiful quality of being able to find interest and excitement in ordinary things. It was one of the many things that Jesus surely had in mind when he said, "Except you be converted and become again as a little child, you shall not enter the kingdom of Heaven."

Humility is not something that you go out and deliberately cultivate. What you cultivate is charity. And you cultivate charity by practising the virtue of hope or perseverance, which comes from faith. Humility is the by-product of charity.

The second of the moral virtues is Benevolence. This is the disposition to act in accordance with right reason about my neighbour. The first thing to be noted about my neighbour is that he, too, can be seen under this dual aspect of his individuality and his common humanity. In his common humanity he is a thing of infinite worth and value. He can't do anything so despicable and so revolting as to deprive himself of my respect for his humanity. Even the most gruesome character is still a child of God, made in God's image, and someone for whom God died.

On the other hand, as an individual, he cannot grow to any height or virtue that would entitle me to trust him. The liberal humanist tradition dating back to the Enlightenment says that we ought to trust our neighbour, but the Bible says explicitly that you must not do it. When I meet a person for the first time I must say to myself, this is a child of God, a soul for whom Christ died, a creature of infinite worth and value, and if I turn my back on him, he is liable to stick a knife in me. And then I must turn my back on him. And if he does stick a knife between my ribs, I will not fall upon him and say how disappointed I am.

Trusting someone is a subtle form of moral blackmail. Everyone desperately needs approval and affection from his neighbour, and if I tell you that I trust you, what that means, of course, is that I am confident that you will behave according to my standards for you. If you don't, then I will be disappointed in you, and this is manipulating other people's behaviour. What I am supposed to do to you is love you, which is quite different. When I say that I love you, I am saying that you can stick a knife in my ribs if you like because I love you. To love someone is to live vulnerably, to expose oneself.

I mustn't trust you, because you are a sinner, and sooner or later you are going to sin. If I have taken that into account in advance, then it's not going to throw me when it happens. Trust or mistrust have no place in our personal relations.

Benevolence means that I will your greatest natural good, which is your freedom, which also means your freedom to sin. This freedom I must allow you includes the freedom to go to hell if you want to. But I don't have to go with you. I do, however, have to suffer the consequences of your sin if you choose to sin, and this is why I may not trust you. Benevolence includes the will which is the active desire for your good, and that necessarily involves putting myself to some trouble to accomplish or achieve your good, or to assist you in achieving it, all the time respecting and allowing the other person's freedom to goof it up.

The second thing benevolence means is that you are entitled to your good name even while it is wrong of me to trust you. In all instances I must give you the benefit of the doubt. For example, I come into a large room and see three of my friends sitting together at a table at the other end of the room with their heads together whispering and as I approach them, they hear my footsteps and look up and recognize me and fall silent and blush. What were they talking about? There are a number of possibilities. They might have been ripping my character to shreds, gossiping about me, slandering me, and here I have caught them at it, and they are embarrassed and fall silent and blush. That's one explanation. And it does explain the facts. Another possible explanation is that they were telling dirty jokes, and knew that I might disapprove, so they fell silent. And that would also explain the facts. Another possible explanation is that they were planning a surprise birthday party for me, and know that they can't continue to talk about it with me there, and realizing how I might easily misinterpret their silence, they fall silent and blush. I have the obligation if I practise the virtue of benevolence to put the best possible interpretation on other people's behaviour.

The third of the moral virtues is Generosity, the disposition to act in accordance with right reason about things. The opposite of generosity is covetousness. The first thing I should think about things is that they are the gift of God, and I should receive them with gratitude. So the first aspect of generosity is appreciation of things. the attitude of the Christian should be that of the small child on Christmas morning. We should experience a constant source of surprise and delight at the thing-ness of things, the muddiness of mud, the wetness of water. It's a wonderful appreciation of things.

The second quality of generosity is the intention to use things as their stewards, that is, to use things in accordance with God's purpose for them. Remember that there are no evil things, just the misuse of a good thing. We use cars to get from one place to another, and a good car is one that does that. It's not good stewardship to take inadequate care of the things God has given us.

The third quality of generosity is the ability to relinquish things without regrets. Our inclination is always to want to stop and glut ourselves on the present good, and we want to cling to the passing good, to eternalize the temporal. This is covetousness. It is a good thing to be a little baby. It is a better thing to be a child, and when the child comes into existence, the baby is gone. There is no way to go back, or cling to babyhood, or perpetuate the value of being a baby. It is good to be a child, but it is better still to be a young man. It is better yet to be a grown, mature man, but better still to be an old man. Our society cannot face this, but it is true. There are things you could do when young that you can't do when you're old. Your faculties are not as acute, your taste buds not as sharp, your hearing declines, and your agility is less, but there are compensations. A mellowness sets in, a sense of proportion and value. It's a good thing to be old, but it is a better thing still to have died and gone home to Heaven. A succession of goods are taken away from us in order that they may be replaced with a still better good. As we grow old and more of our intimate friends are no longer alive, our mobility is diminished and we are thrown more and more back upon God. I am forced to find my pleasures and delights not in sensual things, but in spiritual things, which are more valuable.

Generosity is that quality which enjoys things while we have them and releases them without regret when they are taken away. Every good thing that we have will be taken away. So, generosity is the acceptance of time, and the consequent loss of yesterday's goods. It is the turning loose of what is slipping into the past, and looking forward to what is coming next, and nowhere is this more important than at our death.

The virtue that has to do with circumstances is called Contentment, and it has to do with our attitude toward what happens. There are two kinds of circumstances: good ones and bad ones. Good circumstances are when we get what we want, and bad circumstances are when we don't get what we want. The virtue of contentment has to do with both kinds, of course, although more people go to hell through a surfeit of good circumstances. You will notice that good circumstances don't present themselves to us as intellectual problems. If I am walking down the street and find a $10 bill on the sidewalk, I do not beat my breast and say, "Why does this have to happen to me?" It's bad circumstances, or adversity, that makes this a problem. What, then, are the uses of adversity?

First, let's look at the use of good fortune. There is a great danger in thinking that God is rewarding me because I am so deserving. Look out for that; it doesn't necessarily follow. The response to good fortune is gratitude, the same as with good things. Accept it at the hands of God and return thanks to Him for it and make the appropriate use of it according to God's real purpose in your life. You accept responsibility for your blessings and talents. If God made you wise and gave you the opportunity to be learned, then you will have to do some of the thinking for the stupid folk, and you have to do it without despising them. The same thing is true of artistic talent, leisure, ability, wealth, or whatever good fortune God has bestowed on you. And you have to turn loose of it when the time comes. That time might well be an adversity.

You can offer adversity up to God either as an act of thanksgiving or an act of penance. If God lived next door to me and I were grateful to Him and wanted to show my gratitude, I might go mow His lawn. But God doesn't have a lawn for me to mow, but I have a lawn which is really God's, and I have to mow it. Mowing my lawn on a hot summer's day is something I regard as an adversity, and I can offer this to God either as an act of thanksgiving or an act of penance for my sins. Adversity can be offered up to God as a penance for sins that we get away with.

It can also be offered as an act of gratitude to God, of putting myself out for God in return for His generosity and kindness to me, not that I can ever pay God back. But if I have to mow my lawn on a hot summer day, there are plenty of reasons for offering it to God. When I am in love, the things that I sacrifice for my beloved I do not interpret as sacrifices.

The second thing I can do with adversity is to use it to build character. I can't acquire the virtue of patience unless someone imposes on me. Adversities come to me and they are opportunities to grow holy. No one is lacking in these opportunities. If I have to endure a toothache, I can offer this in union with Christ's suffering on the cross and it becomes an act of intercession. The voluntary enduring of pain, loss, hardship, and adversity can become a kind of prayer. It takes away the sting if it's voluntary.

If that sort of thing is imposed against our will, adversity is intolerable. But if it is something that we do voluntarily, it's completely bearable. Hundreds of thousands of ladies will diet for the sake of vanity who will not fast for the sake of their immortal souls. They can see the tangible fruits of dieting, but they can't see the intangible fruits of self-discipline or fasting. Adversity builds character. No one ever built bulging muscles by juggling marshmallows. Those who do not discipline themselves, God in His mercy will discipline through adversity. It is only by meeting and overcoming adversity that we grow strong.

The third thing you do with adversity is to make an adventure out of it. In the summer of 1937, when I was twenty-three, I went to Mexico to go to the university. There I met a *National Geographic* writer who was following the trail of Cortez from Vera Cruz to Mexico City and he asked me to go with him. This trail is not the way the roads and railroads go now. It went back into the mountains by footpaths. We were lost for thirty-five days in the Sierra Nevada on horseback without a change of underwear, a bath, and often without anything to eat, sleeping on dirt floors or wooden benches, getting rained on and having no dry clothes to change into, getting saddle-sore until we hardened up. I remember we climbed a pass called the Pass of the Name of God. My companion said that it was so called because people climbing this pass often invoked the name of God. We came out over this pass at about 10,000 feet over a beautiful sunlit valley which must have been two or three miles across, carpeted with small flowers of all colours, growing like moss close to the ground. We set out across this deserted place and as God is my witness, there was a shepherd. There was no one in sight for miles except this one man. He had his little shack and his sheep, and he was enthusiastically playing a marimba, making music all alone, playing for himself and his sheep. This trip was hardship and adversity, and it was marvellous. I would do it again in a minute. Anyone would delight in it, and grab a chance to do it.

When you're on a journey, afterwards you brag about your sufferings. Talk to hunters in Canada – they talk about how cold it was and how big the mosquitoes were, but they're bragging, because it was an adventure. What makes it an adventure is that you know it's not going to last. The good that comes, you savour it, not wanting to waste any of it. You enjoy it to the hilt. And the bad you laugh off, because it won't last, either. If the sun is shining, it might rain tomorrow. You can sit in your rocking chair on the front porch of the house in which you were born and never leave it, and things will happen to you, just like the things that happened to me on that trip to Mexico. If you have the notion that you are a pilgrim, passing through on a journey to Heaven, the whole thing will become an adventure.

Again, this is another offshoot of humility. The proud man takes these things deadly seriously and frets about them and worries about them. But one of the wonderful things about hiking through Alaska is that you don't know what's around the next curve in the road. If it's good, you suck all the juice out of it and thank God for it and laugh at it.

Any of you who are thinking about getting married, I will give you a quality to look for in a spouse that is one of the most important qualities that you can have in anyone you are going to live with in close quarters. If you tell your wife or husband that the washing machine has broken down and flooded one end of the house, the utility company has cut off the gas and the electric company cut off the electricity and the roof has sprung a leak and all the pot plants have frozen, and they fall down on the floor laughing, that's the person you want to live with. Saints do that and it's called contentment. It's also called detachment. It's allowing God to call the shots. It is turning each day over to God and seeing the will of God for me this day in the circumstances of my life.

St Francis de Sales says that is it better to eat what is set before you than deliberately choose the least palatable dishes because in the latter case you only mortify your appetite, and in the former case you mortify your will. So we mortify our wills by allowing God to plan our days. Most people will resent that because it will mean turning loose the reins. But it also means regarding all your life as a vacation trek through the Canadian woods, or through a strange city. We should simply regard each day as an adventure which God gives us, and we can turn adversity into a good thing.

The fifth of the virtues is Diligence, which is the disposition to act in accordance with right reason about our duties. If you are occupied with what other people owe you, you are not occupied with what you owe others, and this approach necessarily and inevitably tends to fragment and divide society into competing segments. However, if people are trained and conditioned and taught to think in terms of their duties, they will contribute to the centripetal force in society that holds everything together. Christian perfection consists in doing one's duty to the best of one's ability and to the glory of God, in that station in life to which it has pleased God to call one. One's station in life defines one's duties. It would be sinful for me to spend as much time with my nose in a book as a college student ought to. It would be sinful for him to spend as much time talking to people as I have to. A housewife and mother can sin grievously by spending an excessive amount of time on her knees in prayer in front of the Blessed Sacrament if by doing so she is neglecting her duties as a wife and mother.

It doesn't matter whether my vocation is Archbishop of Canterbury or plumber's helper, whether I am shovelling manure in a barnyard or writing a constitution for a world government, I should do whatever I do to the best of my ability and to the glory of God. Remember that each of these virtues is contained in the other, rather like a collapsible drinking cup, and if one has the previous virtue of contentment, it won't matter enormously what one does.

You can do anything to the glory of God. Every once in a while I wonder why I bother to write sermons. The congregation doesn't appreciate them anyway, and no one really listens. Then I think, okay, God is listening, and I'll write it for Him. That's a motivation you can always count on. You'll do a better job and have more fun. As a matter of fact, this is the basis for the ancient European tradition of craftsmanship whereby people insist on doing a very good job. It's awfully difficult to find workmen who take pride in their work, yet I am told that in some European cathedrals, if you erect scaffolding and get on the top side of the beams near the ceiling where no one but God will ever see it, you can find some of the most perfect and exquisite carving in the entire church.

Do your duty to the best of your ability and to the glory of God.

The virtue that deals with the bodily appetites is called Temperance, and it's quite simple. I have but one body with which to serve the Lord in this lifetime, and I will take care of it. Temperance is that virtue whereby I husband my resources and therefore I will eat enough but not too much, and get enough sleep but not too much. It is that virtue aimed at one's bodily health not for the sake of bodily health, but for the sake of the preceding virtue of serving God in one's station in life and doing one's duty. If I get sick with a bad cold, I can't do my duty. So I try to avoid catching a cold, not so I won't be sick, but so I can do my duty. The temperate person is not the person who is preoccupied all the time with his health. He is the person who is preoccupied with doing his duty. If I needed to hire a carpenter and there were two or three men who seemed to be equally well qualified, I think I would favour the one who took the best care of his tools. If his saw was well oiled and his chisels were sharp and he had taken the trouble to remove the blade of his plane so it wouldn't get nicked, it would indicate to me that he was the kind of craftsman who was careful about his work and wanted to do a good job, that he wanted his tools in good shape so he could do a good job. This is the virtue of temperance applied to the body.

The virtue that deals with sex is called Chastity. To be chaste means to be faithful in the disciplining of sexual appetites; consequently, people who aren't married don't have sex, and people who are married have sex only with each other.

There aren't any other possibilities. Sin has consequences, and the irresponsible use of sex has consequences of pregnancy and disease. The only remedy is the cultivation of this virtue, and no talk of safe sex is a substitute for the faithful obedience to the disciplining of our sexual appetites in the virtue of chastity.

The Christian is a person who is called to perfection, which begins with obedience. Christian perfection is achieved not by multiplying activities but by simplifying them. There is a process of paring away the dead wood, the unproductive activities, the unsatisfying loves. We begin with faith, which leads us to hope, which brings us to charity. At that point we will want to do what is right, and the moral virtues will follow.

LITURGICAL
PRAYER

For the past several decades the Church has been preoccupied with its role in the struggle for social justice, and
there have not been wanting voices which derided those
who would withdraw even momentarily from the world to
seek God in solitude and prayer. But ours is an incarnational
religion which gives place to both body and soul, to "all
things visible and invisible". The world is now taking its
revenge upon us for our neglect of things spir tual with
astrology, the occult, diabolism, Tarot cards and ouija
boards, and Zen and Transcendental Meditation and yoga
and foreign gurus, and strange sects which threaten us
(somewhat gleefully) with the end of the world. Like the
prodigal son, we fain would have filled our bellies with the
husks that the swine do eat.

It is high time we dusted off our long-neglected Christian
spiritual classics and teach men how to pray in a Christian
fashion. We do not have to go to Asia to find masters of the
interior life. There is a Christian way to pray, a way proved
by countless generations of the saints; in fact, it is this way of
prayer that has produced the saints, and it is available to us
today.

Christian prayer is not a gimmick to produce quick
ecstasies and raptures. Still less is it a device for wheedling a

reluctant God into seeing things our way, into giving us whatever we in our myopia decide would be good for us. It is rather a tedious work for dedicated souls who desire to grow holy. Prayer is not something for dilettantes.

However, prayer is supposed to be fun. Learning to know God is more fun than learning to know any great human being. A teacher can tell you about God, but coming to know God personally is something that every man does for himself, and he does it in his prayers. With prayer, we acquire the kind of knowledge that comes from spending time together in intimate conversation. Prayer is listening to God, for what He has to say to us is far more important than what we say to Him.

Your own personal prayer life begins at the Eucharist and grows out of that. Your most exalted personal prayers never lose their connection with the prayer of the community; you must return Sunday after Sunday to the altar, the place where prayer begins, at the representation of Christ's own total self-offering to the Father on Calvary. Prayer offered apart from that is not Christian prayer, because it is not prayer through Jesus Christ. Prayer at the Eucharist is an absolute minimum. And really, it is little enough. It means giving up to God an hour or two once a week on Sunday. Unless a person has the settled habit of regular attendance at the Eucharist every Sunday, he should not even think about learning to pray. This is where you start.

Then you could add the offices. Let me tell you a bit about the Divine Office and its background and history. The early Christians, of course, were Jews. When they met for worship they had a synagogue service, then a Eucharist. About the fourth century when the general moral level of the Church began to decline with the influx of uninstructed converts, a number of people in disgust retreated into the desert and became hermits, or formed themselves into little communities of lay people seeking, through prayer and meditation and solitude, to improve their conscious contact with God. They would go into the nearest town for Sunday Mass, but during the week, they would meet seven times a day for prayer services which all laymen could do.

For a thousand years, monastic spirituality was the normative model spirituality. When the English Reformation came along, monasteries were all closed by order of the king. However, Cranmer had a remarkable idea. "Why don't we aim for monastic spirituality for our lay people?" He took the Matins office and a bit of Lauds and a bit of Prime and put it together to make Morning Prayer. Then he took the Vespers office and a little bit of Compline and made Evening Prayer.

His idea – of course, it never worked – was that the whole village was supposed to gather in the church right after daylight and read together this essentially monastic office which was the old Jewish synagogue service, modified and given a Christian flavour by the addition of Christian hymns and prayers. Then they would have a Mass, then go out and eat breakfast and work all day. At the end of the day, they would gather back at the church to read the Vespers office. The church services would frame the day from daylight to sundown. Any village or congregation that did that for twenty-five or thirty years would produce a lot of holy people.

These offices are the reading of Scripture in the context of prayer. It is the same devotional material and the same devotional method which for 5000 years kept the Jewish people praying. They had a means of worshipping God that they could carry with them all over the world, and for sixteen centuries this is what shaped and fashioned, generated and formed Christian character and Christian spirituality.

The Prayer Book is designed so that if you read the offices every day, you read through the Old Testament once a year, the New Testament twice a year, and the Psalms twelve times a year. Think of what happens to your unconscious. There are whole portions of the Bible you will know by heart, without ever having attempted to memorize them, and all of this has taken place in the context of prayer.

Because we are baptized, our prayer is the prayer of the whole Church. We are members of a church; when we pray, the Church is at prayer. The Mass is the Mass of the whole Church said through the ministry of a few. Those few who come to early Mass tomorrow become the Church. Even when we don't go to Mass, if we roll out of bed and get on our knees and say our personal prayers, they too are the prayers of the Church. Somewhere else in our diocese and in yours, another parish church begins Mass a bit later. There is no moment, no hour of the day, in which somewhere around the surface of the globe the Mass is not being offered. Tomorrow when we say our personal prayers, we are being joined by Masses that are being said, and daily offices being read, in parish churches all over the world.

When God looks down from the parapets of Heaven and sees me at my prayers, He sees me as a member of a multitude of people at prayer. We can't pray alone. Even if we could select a moment in which we were the only person on earth in prayer, there are all the angels and archangels and all the company of Heaven, who are always praying and glorifying God. Even if they all stopped for breath at the same time, so that all the prayer in the world ceases except for ours, Jesus is praying. We are told He never ceases to make intercession for us where He sits at the right hand of God. My prayers to the Father go in union with the prayer of Jesus. It is through Him and by virtue of my membership in Him, my incorporation in His mystical Body, that God hears my prayers.

We pray out of a book because we pray in common, together. We are not individualists in this matter. The common prayers express the deep, fundamental spiritual needs and aspirations which are common to all. The familiar prayers are like familiar hymns because people are the kind of creatures they are, and the use of familiar prayers can often induce a mood of prayer, and can restore the troubled soul to the peace and calm most conducive to communion with God.

Our personal prayer life grows out of this deeper, common prayer life. The Prayer Book prayers express those deep human longings better than most of us could form in our own words, and we can either use those prayers or say nothing at all. About man's deepest spiritual needs most of us are tongue-tied. While it does not mean that prayers cannot be most intimate, we also pray out of a book because God is the kind of God He is, and a certain majesty and dignity should accompany our conversation with Him. The Prayer Book prayers are classics composed by great artists who have lived close to God and could say eloquently what all of us feel and cannot say.

When I was a child, I was taught that "canned" prayer, meaning those written by another and read out of a book or recited by rote like a parrot, were not prayers at all, but rather those vain repetitions which Christ condemned (Matthew 6:7). I was told I should pray in my own words, that prayer should be sincere and from the heart, unrehearsed and spontaneous.

I remember going to a youth group on Sunday evenings. The teacher would call on us in rotation to pray aloud. I was terrified. I remember many a Sunday afternoon I would rehearse in my mind and put together a prayer and try to memorize it so that I could stand up in front of the group and pretend that I was praying extemporaneously and from the heart. I knew that this was hypocritical and phony, but I had been told to say just what was in my heart, and my heart was empty. I listened to other people pray and I knew they were trying to do the same thing: thanking God for the lovely weather, our fellowship together, asking Him to bless the preacher and the foreign missions, and "to help us to serve Him and to please Him". The words might as well have been read out of a book because they certainly were not spontaneous and from the heart.

If I could have prayed what was in my heart, it might have gone something like this:

Good God, here we go again. I have been asked to pray and you know perfectly good and well that I don't know how to. Damn it. I hate the leader for calling on me and I hate You for letting her call on me. I feel like those other people are judging me and snickering at me for my clumsy and inarticulate praying. Some of them may be feeling sorry for me because they have been in the same situation. None of us is honest enough to admit it, so we will keep up this pretence of being pious. God, if You are there and can hear me, help me get through the next two or three minutes without making too much of a damn fool of myself. Damn it. Amen.

That was real prayer, not the silly drivel that came out of

my mouth when I spoke aloud. It isn't easy to pray. First of all, it's hard to talk to someone we can't see. It's sort of like talking to yourself. In nothing more than our prayers do we reveal the essential poverty of our spiritual life. One can learn to pray aloud well and eloquently, just like one can learn to debate, or do public speaking.

As a child, I was taught to tack on to the end of my prayers the phrase, "In Jesus' name" or "through Jesus Christ", but I was never told what that meant. When the Protestant Reformation did away with priests, the idea behind it was that the individual believer had free access to the throne of Grace, and everybody had a right to talk to God. No longer did you have to go through priestly channels. Well, there is free access to the throne of Grace, but the only channel you have to go through is Jesus Christ. My claim on God's ear is because I have been incorporated into Christ, God's presence in the Church. The Church is His mystical Body, and my prayer is, in fact, the prayer of Jesus Himself, and God always hears the prayers of Jesus. Since that is the case, then my prayer must be the kind of prayer that Jesus Himself would pray, or else I would be trying to force Jesus to ask for things that Jesus does not want.

Since you and I, being baptized and confirmed and belonging to a praying community, pray, we are commissioned, not just authorized, by the Church to say the Church's prayers, the prayers the Church wants said. Although we need to pray, that is not the primary reason we pray. We pray because God deserves to be prayed to. Prayer is a duty in the same way that sex in marriage is a duty. It is a duty in the sense that the right response when Aunt Susie brings little Charlie a gift is for little Charlie to say thank you. If he doesn't know how to say thank you, then his mother will say it for him, because Aunt Susie deserves to be thanked. She did not give the child the gift so that he would thank her. She gave it because she loved him. Her love and the gift which it sacramentalizes deserve some sort of response.

God has created us because He loves us, and we have all sinned and come short of the glory of God. God has overlooked our sin and has sent His own beloved Son to rescue us in the nick of time from slavery, lust, compulsions, phobias, and all kinds of horrid, dreadful things. He has given His life. It was a successful rescue, and there is something about that situation that imposes an obligation on somebody to say "Thank you." The Church is that committee that has pulled itself together and responded to the situation, to give praise and thanks to God for all His mercies and all His benefits. We do this because it is right to do it. We have been rescued and we appreciate it.

We pray out of a book because the soul, like the body, needs a balanced diet, and the Prayer Book, in the rhythm of the Church's seasons, gives us that well-regulated, balanced, spiritual diet which our soul needs for its optimum growth and health. Prayer is an art, like playing the piano. To tell the beginner to pray out of his heart without any instruction is like telling the beginning piano student to sit down at the keyboard and improvise. He just can't. If he tries, what comes forth is simply discord and noise. So you give him easy exercises at first, then later more difficult ones, and tell him to practise a little bit every day.

Prayer Book prayers are exercises from the Greek word *aschesis*, from which we get our word "ascetic". It simply means "exercising" which doesn't do anything but strengthen your muscles. We learn to pray by praying. What usually happens when a person starts out using the Prayer Book is that he outgrows is. Four hundred years ago at the time of the Reformation when printing with moveable type was still new, one of the first things printers did was to print little private prayer books called Primers. A primer is a pump-primer, a starter. All the great reformers like Luther, Calvin, and Knox, had been raised as children on these little printed primers, and they grew up to a point, which everyone will, sooner or later, when saying prayers out of the prayer book became a hindrance, not a help. That's when we can put the book aside and discover that we can pray.

These Protestant reformers could tell people, "Don't pray out of a book, just open your heart to God," because in back of each of them was thirty years of praying out of a book. This is like the piano student who is proficient enough to improvise lovely music. A person who has used the Prayer Book year after year frequently finds that his prayers become dry and empty. He comes to his priest and says, "Why don't I get more out of my prayers?" And the priest tells him, "It's time to put the book down." He tries it and soars like an eagle. He discovers it's a lot more fun to pray on his own.

Our Prayer Book prayers are kind of a springboard to commune with God in words or silences, as spirit to spirit, which comes out of the heart's depth. While prayer is multiform and complex and different in each soul, in essence all prayer is a response to the prior movement of God in that soul, the gradual growing accustomed to that other world, the gradual education of the faculties of the soul to the function of the other world. We still live in this world and still have all of our animal sense functions. But less and less do they obscure the things of the spirit as we grow in the spirit. Rather, all of our animal activities become more and more permeated by the Spirit. God is continually pressing upon us, willing us, calling us to Himself, but because we are earthbound and our faculties are dull and our understanding clouded, this relationship is one of becoming increasingly spiritualized. It is in slow and easy stages, little by little, daily, monthly, yearly throughout life. Usually the measure of this progress is so slight that we are not really aware of it. If we have been saying our prayers, receiving the sacraments, and participating in the life of the corporate public worship of the Church, we can compare ourselves with where we were ten years ago and see that we've been making progress.

It is a common mistake to equate or identify the action of God in the soul with emotions that accompany it. There may be none, as emotion is not spiritual at all, being something that we share with dogs and cats. Do not be in the least impressed with what are called "spiritual emotions". There is no such thing; it's a contradiction in terms. Emotions are always bodily things. What the ordinary person calls a spiritual experience or a mystical experience is very likely not mystical at all. Mysticism per se is a term designating an immediate, non-mediated experience of reality. In other words, if you can feel it, taste it, touch it, hear it, smell it, see it, it's not mystical. Mysticism bypasses perception. In religion there are often strange experiences through which we seem to see, hear, or feel things which are not objectively present to the senses – visions, voices, and so on. These may produce feelings of rapture or excitement, or perhaps even fear or dread. But there is no way of objectively verifying a mystical experience. All of the great saints and masters of the spiritual life tell us to pay no attention to these things. If mystical experiences occur at all, they are more likely to occur at the beginning or more rarely, at the very end of our spiritual development. The common mistake today is to seek such experiences and to identify them with an advanced state of spirituality. They may be purely psychological, or the result of unbalanced body chemistry, or hysteria, or the result of a crowd, or auto-suggestion. Where they are from God, they are for the sake of drawing the soul into an active life of prayer and worship.

It is a great mistake to go back and try to recreate these experiences over and over again. The Church is absolutely unanimous, and all the great doctors of the Church tell us that the only, the only test of the validity of a mystical experience is whether, afterward, you are nicer to your family and friends, whether there is a discernible moral improvement.

If you pray and don't feel a thing, that doesn't mean that nothing has happened. What does happen is that three days later you discover, to your astonishment, that something which last week would have annoyed and irritated you, you managed to rise above and deal with with equanimity and poise. That is where the effect of grace shows up.

Nearly twenty centuries ago God inhabited for a time this world, taking our nature in the womb of a virgin girl in Palestine. Even though He lived in this world, He lived with a life of that other world. He carried our nature through death into the full glare of that world's brilliant suffusion, and then revealed to His friends in flashes called the post-Resurrection period, His continuing presence with them, just beyond the edge of their bodily senses. He is here, in this room, in all of His glory. If we strain and squint, at times we can almost see Him. He continues to abide with His friends, lovingly watching over them and guiding them to Himself.

Prayer is our response to that unseen and beckoning presence, as we open up our minds and hearts to the presence of Him who loves us so much. It is the Church's belief that the Only One from beyond is not only by our side but actually pervades us, living in our spirit, uniting us to Himself in an intimacy that we cannot imagine, in a kind of mutual indwelling or mingling of spirits. We look outward at distant mountains or upward at the stars and are filled with awe at the mystery hovering over and in them. The same mystery is within us, even more mysterious and beautiful. I am more remarkable than a galaxy or a rainbow, and so are you. "If anyone loves me," says Our Lord, "my Father will love him and we will come to him and make our abode with him" (John 14:23). Also, "Behold, I stand at the door and knock. If any man hears my voice and opens the door, I will come in unto him and will sup with him, and he with me" (Revelation 3:20). Prayer is the way of opening the door. St Paul says, "I live, yet not I." My life is not really me, he is saying, but Christ's splendour, the majesty, the mystery, the beauty, the Beloved. The doctrine of the Church says that in every contract between God and man, God takes the initiative. One of the saints said, "You are seeking God? That is proof you have already found Him."

22

PERSONAL PRAYER

I don't believe that anyone ever became advanced in the
spiritual life who hadn't learned to regard prayer as a duty.
There are duties which are due to the circumstances of your
life, if you are married, for example, or are a parent, a doctor,
or anything else. Prayer is a duty that pertains to our status
as Christians. If we pray just when the spirit moves us,
human nature being what it is, there is going to be a good
deal of the time when the spirit does not move us. We start
praying and then the desire to pray builds up in us as we
pray, and we keep on doing it. We can't really trust our
feelings, so we decide that we are going to pray, and then
decide when, where, and what our prayers are going to
be. We get very explicit, and we make ourselves a rule of
prayer.

This rule is rather like a spiritual grocery list, like the list
you take to the grocery store so you won't forget what
you're out of. Most people have difficulty in finding time in
the day they can set aside for God. We are not really all that
different from all the generations that have gone before us.
It's a question of where our values and our priorities are.
Most authorities suggest the early hours of the day for
personal prayer before the burdens of the day begin to mess
up the schedule. They recommend we set our clock thirty
minutes early and avoid the rush of children off to school, or
the phone, or other demands. This is a good way to start the

day. The last thing before bedtime is not the best time to pray, because we are sleepy and might tend to skip our prayers, or not give our best attention to God. That doesn't mean you shouldn't say bedtime prayers, so that the last words on your lips before you fell asleep are words of prayer: "Into Thy hands, O Lord, I commend my spirit." However, we should not leave to bedtime the principal burden of our daily prayer. Find a time, either first thing in the morning, after lunch or supper, or whenever suits your station in life. If you can tie your prayers to something that you do at the same time every day, you will be much more likely to do them.

Ideally, we should try to have a particular place for our personal prayers where we will not be interrupted and which we can use every day, perhaps with a cross or crucifix on the wall, our books and other aids to prayer. Praying at the same time and in the same place every day becomes a conditioned response. One recommendation, if you don't have a place, is to use the dining room table. It's just about the right height and it also has suggestions as a family altar, since the altar in church is the dining room table of the church family. During family prayers your family can kneel around the family table.

As far as posture goes, you can walk, sit in a rocking chair, sit at a desk, kneel, whatever you want. The experience of millions of Christians over hundreds of years sort of settled on kneeling as the ideal posture for prayer, because it's not uncomfortable and yet it is not too terribly comfortable. Some people can pray while driving their cars.

Once we have the time, the place, and the posture for our daily prayers, we need to decide what prayers we are going to say. Make a list of the things you do now, like going to Mass and so on, and then another list of the things you would like to add. This list ought to be checked by your spiritual director, and now I'd like to talk about that.

Do you know anyone who has taught himself to play the piano without a teacher? Or a good athlete without a coach, or a play without a director? We human beings cannot be objective about ourselves, especially when learning a skill or a technique. We need what is sometimes called a "soul friend", or a person who has travelled the spiritual road and knows where it is leading. This is as true for the beginner as it is for the saint. We all need guidance and direction.

From time to time our coach will revise our rule. This will be necessary as we grow spiritually, and it also might be necessary if we change our lifestyles, such as get married, go off to school, or change jobs. We must remember that no two people are exactly alike. Doctrine is the same for all of us; sacraments are the same for all of us. However, in the mystical life we can't say that. Even if we go through the same stages of spiritual development, we go at different paces. This is why the office of spiritual direction is an art rather than a science.

Now I want to point out something very important about praying. A lot of people will go into the church and kneel down and spend a good deal of time in what they think is prayer, but it's really worry. Prayer first involves making contact with God. Even if I am going into the church to intercede for someone who is ill, the first thing I should do is place myself in the presence of God. I should pray first for an awareness of His presence. We need to make sure our lines of communication with God are open and flowing. We should have a sincere desire that God should have His way, and we should have trust and confidence in His love and mercy and omnipotence and providential care.

There is a certain normal progression in the types of prayer. We begin with formal, vocal prayer out of a book which we mentioned earlier, a primer. There will be days when you are absolutely dry, and you are relying on the spirit to move you and the spirit has gone fishing. That's what the primer is for, to call the spirit. On the days when the spirit is lively and active and ready in you, and you feel moved to informal vocal prayer, you will normally graduate from the formal prayers. You will discover that the Prayer Book has helped you phrase and formulate your prayers.

About the time a person begins to get going good on informal vocal prayer, he probably begins to make meditations, which is called discursive or mental prayer. When you really try seriously to meditate and you feel an interior call to some other type of prayer over a period of time, what normally follows is affective prayer, which is also called arrow prayer. Here you discourse with God in short phrases interspersed with periods of silence, prayer from the heart that comes spontaneously. Remember that religion is a love affair, and prayer is conversation between lovers. And we will usually find that our affective prayer will spill over into the rest of our lives, and that we are praying throughout the day, short interludes of intimate conversation with God.

Affective prayer will normally give place to the prayer of quiet in which we spend our time in prayer, and our heart is ordinarily by this time filled with such intense emotion and love that we can't find any adequate or appropriate words, so that we remain silent. It's kind of like when you and your best beloved are sitting side by side watching a log fire and she has her head on your shoulder and your arm is around her, and you are just sitting there watching the fire and not saying anything, just enjoying the fact of your closeness and intimacy.

The prayer of quiet gradually merges into contemplation, which is union with God where the soul is totally unaware of his physical surroundings. More about this later.

We need a balanced diet of prayer just as our bodies need a balanced diet of food – meat, vegetables, dairy products, cereals, and fruit. One particular prayer contains this balanced diet, and it is the prayer Jesus taught, the Lord's Prayer. It contains petition, intercession, confession, thanksgiving, praise, and adoration, and could be seen in terms of a ladder.

Petition is asking, and is the first rung. The conversation of a very small child with Daddy and Mama consists almost entirely of petition. "I want something to drink." "Can I go out and play?" Children do an enormous amount of asking their parents for things. This is childish, but it's not bad. Even if I am asking God to reveal to me His will for me, and give me the grace and strength to fulfil His will, even if I am asking God for help so that I can live my life to be pleasing to God, that is still asking for something. Jesus told us to ask. It is wrong not to ask. "Ask and ye shall receive. Seek and ye shall find." In the Lord's Prayer He told us, "Give us this day our daily bread." We are supposed to ask.

Next is intercession. Jesus told us to do it, so it must do some good. There are many ways we may intercede in prayer for others. While we are in the presence of God, we may gradually bring thoughts of that person into His presence. You can keep lists of people you want to pray for, or use arrow prayer when asked to pray for someone.

The next rung is confession. Our prayers change from "God give me" to "God *forgive* me". We have moved up a rung of the ladder to penitence. Some insight will be granted to enable us to see our soul as the bucket of worms it really is. We are overwhelmed with a sense of guilt and shame, and we go to God in deep and profound penitence, begging His forgiveness. One of the things that happens as a result of moving from petition to confession in our prayers is that our tendency to ask God for things diminishes.

First of all, we discover that we've been treating God like a celestial bell-hop. We have been taking God's assistance and divine mercy for granted. It begins to dawn on us, "What am I asking God things for? He knows what's good for me and He's loving me, and He's taking care of me. Why should I ask Him for anything?"

Then there comes a time when the principal burden of our prayer will be thanking God for all the mercies and benefits we have discerned in our life. Then we grow from thanksgiving naturally into the prayer of praise and adoration. The most important thing that we will ever say to God in our prayers is "I love you." And the finest answer we'll ever get to the best prayer we will ever pray is the conviction that God has whispered into our hearts, "You know, I love you, too." When we get to that point, we are home free. All of our ego hang-ups are solved, all of our need to impress other people or to be dependent on other people's affections or approval has disappeared. We really grow up at that point. We have climbed this ladder to praise and adoration, which is the most perfect kind of prayer.

On our way up the ladder, our prayers are self-centred.

"God, give me this because I want it." Then, "God, forgive me." Then, "God, thank you for what you have given me, or done for those I love." We only escape from self-centredness when we get to the top of the ladder where our focus, concentration, and interest is not on ourselves, but God.

Now we have to go down the ladder again, but on the other side, in which our prayers are God-centred. Each person climbs at different paces and with different strides. We might spend a lifetime getting to this point. But time is not important in relation to our spiritual journey. What is important is that we keep on trying, keep on with our balanced diet of prayer: petition, intercession, confession, thanksgiving, praise, and adoration.

After a time spent in praise and adoration as the principal part of our prayers, it will suddenly occur to us one day, "Hey, what if there were no God?" And we will thank God not for what He has done for me or what He might do for me, but for the fact that He is.

As we move down to the rung of penitence, there comes a maturity in our spiritual development when we begin to feel, as acutely and keenly as our own pain, the sins of the world. We will be far more concerned with the fact that God has been sinned against than the fact that we have sinned. As a matter of fact, the less we sin, the more we're going to feel genuine penitence for the sins of the world. We are thanking God for God, and we're being sorry that God has been sinned against, that there is such a thing as sin.

Finally we come back down the ladder like a little child, and after so many months and years of spending time in God's company we have learned to think like God. We have acquired a God's-eye view of reality, and we have learned to want what He wants and desire what He desires, feel what He feels, and have entered into the mind and life of God so that our desires and His are harmonized and lined up. Our prayers then become asking for what God wants. We go up the ladder with our interests and attention focused on ourselves, and we come down the ladder on the other side, and when we get to the bottom of the ladder we are powerful intercessors and things that we pray for usually happen, because by this time we do not ask amiss.

We say words when we pray, and the saying of those words tends to change our hearts, so that what is in the heart, the still point of the soul, begins to come around to and reflect the different meaning of the words of the prayer. The words of the prayers are addressed to us; what is addressed to God comes out of the depths of the heart. It means that the words are very important. If I want something and can verbalize it, it makes me want it more, unless verbalizing it makes me realize what a silly thing it is to want, and then I stop wanting it. But on the whole, when the prayers are good, the saying of the prayer tends to create the desire for prayer, the mood and interior disposition for prayer. The words are addressed to me, but the prayer actually takes place beyond the words, in the communion of my heart and God.

I am sure you have gone to church and as the preacher is droning on, your mind will wander off into something like wondering if you remembered to turn the fire off under the beans before you left home, or whether it is Tuesday or Wednesday that you have the doctor's appointment. If your mind wanders that way, then you very gently and patiently draw it back to the words of the liturgy or the words of the text. But sometimes the mind will wander off in the other direction, and you find yourself in a strange and mysterious fashion hearing the words but not hearing them, because your attention is focused on what the prayers are about – that is, on God Himself. You are having a contemplative, mystical experience. The words of the prayers are a kind of shield behind which your mind is free to concentrate on God. If this happens, of course, you would be silly to draw your attention back to the words. You have already accomplished what the words are there for, to establish between you and God the relationship of loving intimacy.

St Paul said we are to pray without ceasing. When we reach the contemplative stage there is an awareness of God in which God becomes sort of like Muzak, you know, always in the background, never entirely out of your consciousness. This is the state towards which our prayers should be leading us. We can become sort of God-conscious so that all we do, we do to please God, to give Him honour and glory. It doesn't make us absent-minded; on the contrary, it tends to increase our efficiency and our effectivenss when we are doing it for the glory of God. "To work is to pray." Work is offered as an act of prayer to God, and it can be. Washing a sink full of dishes or adding up a column of figures for my income tax return can be an act of prayer. It is a steady, continuous uninterrupted awareness of the presence of God with me and in my life.

Let's talk about aids to prayer, that prayer when you're not really paying attention to the words. I knew a good Baptist lady who would not be caught dead with a rosary in her hand, but when she cleaned house she would sing endlessly over and over again. "He lives on high, He lives on high, triumphant over sin and all its stains. He lives on

high, He lives on high, some day He's coming again . . ."
and on and on. She was doing a Baptist version of the
rosary. She was presenting herself with a rhythmical
stimulus that had sort of religious overtones and connotations behind which only she and God knew what was
going on in her mind. But I am sure that she was achieving
some sort of semi-contemplative interior state through the
use of singing this hymn over and over again.

A lot of people look at this and say, "Well, isn't that
what Jesus was talking about when He said, 'Do not use
vain repetitions as the heathen do and think that they shall
be heard for their much asking'?" Well, not at all, because
this is not a prayer asking for anything. It is essentially a
prayer of praise and adoration, and that is its motive and
intent. It's providing ourselves with a shield against
interior distractions. I don't know why it works, but it
does. Ask teenagers why they like to study with the radio
on. One example of this is the rosary, where you repeat the
Hail Mary over and over with the front part of your mind
in order to free the rest of it to be with God.

Another aid is the Jesus prayer: "Lord Jesus Christ, Son
of God, pray for us." This prayer has been popular for
generations in the East, in the Orthodox Church, and the
West has rediscovered this prayer in this century. It is a
prayer of stillness, using many repetitions of the phrase.
Sometimes the mind will be meditating on the Holy Name
and even go into contemplation. It is an excellent prayer to
use while waiting in line, driving the car, washing the
dishes, or at any time when the body is engaged but the
mind is otherwise unoccupied.

Then there is something called the *lectio divina*, or holy
reading. A short text from the Bible is chosen ahead of
time or the day before. It should be one that you have

studied and are aware of any background needed for understanding. Read the passage slowly, either aloud or silently. Let the words be a springboard to God. Sometimes you may achieve nothing; other times you may get only the meat out of the first sentence. However, you will want to chew or ruminate on this passage over and over again. The nice thing about this is that you can take it with you all day, returning to it again and again.

There are certain things in the life of the Church called mysteries, such as the doctrine of the Trinity, the Incarnation, and the Presence of Christ in the Blessed Sacrament. Birth is a mystery, death is a mystery, love is a mystery. Mystery in theological language is defined as anything that you cannot doubt but cannot explain. A murder mystery isn't a mystery at all, it's a murder problem, because when you finish the book and come to the last chapter, you know whodunit. A crossword puzzle is a problem, and there's nothing as uninteresting as a crossword puzzle that has already been worked. When you finish with a problem, you have exhausted the meaning there is in it. Mystery is something you could go on learning more and more about for ever, and never exhaust all the meaning that is in it. If you spend your entire life studying just one mystery, you will have learned a great deal about it, and you will have raised more questions than you've answered.

But being incomprehensible doesn't mean that you can't know anything about God. It just means you can never know everything about God. Prayer is one of those mysteries. We know that it works. I have no earthly idea why God answers some prayers and not others. Nevertheless, Jesus tells us to pray for one another and I'm going to suggest three possible ways in which that might make some sort of sense.

First of all, God has given us free will. There is a certain dimension of reality when you vocalize or verbalize something, so that vague, half-formed intentions or resolutions come into a degree of reality by being vocalized. With our free will we are simply making a decision and relaying a request to God. This is what I would like. If it's within allowable and legitimate limits, God may very probably grant it. That brings us right to the threshold of a much more profound and important aspect of the mystery.

God has made us co-creators. Our creativity is a participation, a share in the divine creativity, all the way from having babies to pulling a weed in a flower bed, painting pictures, composing or playing musical pieces, building houses, bridges, skyscrapers, decorating the guest room, or whatever. Man is creative, because he is like God.

God has also in the Atonement invited us to participate with Him as co-redeemers; the only thing in the long history of human sin and suffering that has ever stripped the mask of blindness from the face of sin is voluntary, innocent suffering. "Resist not evil, but overcome evil with good," said the Lord. "If a man strikes you on one cheek, turn the other cheek." "He that would be my disciple must deny himself and take up his cross daily and follow me." God has invited me to participate with Him in His enterprise of redeeming the fallen, sinful, wretched world to the peace and splendour of His loving intimacy.

Here is another instance of God inviting us to share with Him in His activity. One of God's activities is Providence. Nothing happens except by the active or permissive will of God. Within limits, God invites us to enter into and participate in His providence, so that our free choices really do make a difference. The whole course of human history from now until the return of Christ is different from what it would be had I chosen something different yesterday. It's a very small thing, and the difference a thousand years from now may be microscopic, but it's going to make a difference.

Under God, I am partially responsible for the course of history. This is not too hard to see. My choices shape that history. When I say that my prayers are a requisition on God's providence, it means that God honours and respects my choices as long as they are in the prescribed limits of His will, and to a considerable extent my choices shape and condition the future. I'll participate with God in His providential oversight of the future. Obviously, the closer I am to the mind of God in my own thinking, the more liberty I will have in this direction, and the more I can expect my prayers to be answered.

We are a spiritual unity, you and I, and what happens in my spirit influences your spirit. I don't understand this – it's another mystery – but I know it happens. We are members of one another. If one member suffers, all the other members suffer with it. If one member is honoured, all the other members rejoice, says St Paul.

This is what all the myths and fairy tales are about. It is the subject of every poem and every tragedy. It lurks behind every great piece of music or masterpiece of painting and sculpture. It looks at us through the eyes of our lovers and beckons to us in the lives of our heroes. It is the only thing we have ever really wanted. Christians call it God. Prayer is the way to know and to be united with it.

23

. . . .

MEDITATION

Meditation is the thoughtful, prayerful reading of the Bible or some other devotional work, and reflecting upon that reading. It begins when one has a basic grasp of the outline of Christian theology and a fair acquaintance with the Scriptures; that is, it begins when there is some Christian knowledge in the intellect. It is when the tongue is silent and the mind alone opens out its desires to God, pours out its love to Him, and inwardly embraces Him in love, or reverently adores and worships Him.

People make meditations all the time about non-religious things. In school, for example, in writing a research paper, you took a subject and thought your way through it, organized what you knew about it, compared two ideas together to get a third, arranged your knowledge in an orderly sequence, had sudden insights, compared what you had learned with what you already knew. You were meditating, but it was not a religious operation because you had not invited God into the operation.

There is some reading involved in meditation, but reading or study is usually purely intellectual. It is an accumulation of facts and involved analysis and distinction, and may or may not lead to synthesis; it is usually a process of critical systematic inquiry. Meditation engages our affections as well as our intellect, and is a more intuitive type of activity. It listens and waits on the Lord to give.

It is non-critical and cultivates openness and surrender to God.

We may read everything that is written about our favourite author, but until we sit down and talk to him over a period of time we really do not know him. When we first met our husbands or wives we were attracted to them, but only throughout the years of living close to them are we able to know their likes and dislikes, their weaknesses and strengths, because we love them. We may spend a lifetime reading the Bible, but as long as we are reading for content only, we are only reading about God the Word. We have not yet allowed the Word to come into our lives.

Reading puts us in contact with the Word, while meditation is the attempt to make the Word and the depths of its meaning completely our own by pondering, weighing, reflecting, considering, cherishing, savouring, and associating. Meditation thus makes the Word a living part of ourselves. It is ours to use, to give expression to our dialogue with God.

That is the theory or background. There are two kinds of preparation for making a meditation: exterior and interior. The exterior preparation includes time, place, and posture. You should find a time when you can be reasonably sure to be free from interruptions. You should find a place, perhaps a desk or a table or easy chair, where you can be comfortable. You can sit, kneel, or position yourself in any way that is comfortable.

The interior preparation involves detaching yourself from your immediate surroundings and the concerns of your life. Put yourself in the presence of God. You should already have selected the subject matter for your meditation. This can be the Bible, devotional books, hymns, anything like that. Then just be quiet for a bit. Put out of your mind the things that have been occupying your thoughts for the last hour or so. Ask God to be with you and help you in this exercise. You can say something like this:

"God, I know you are here with me. Maybe I don't feel your presence, but no matter. You promised to be with us always, even to the end of the world. I know you are here because you always keep your promises."

Say it calmly, confidently, either silently or aloud. Repeat it if you feel called to do so. If it helps, imagine Jesus sitting or standing beside you. Don't hurry with this part. Spend two or three minutes or more, just putting yourself in God's presence. Then say something like this:

"God, I am going to meditate on this passage. Please help me to understand whatever it is you want me to know from this passage. You are already in my soul, in my mind; don't let anything in me get in the way of hearing what you want me to know. Save me from trying to be smart or clever; let me just listen like Mary of Bethany to whatever you have to say to me."

Then re-read the passage you have chosen, slowly, pausing between your phrases. Maybe nothing will come into your mind. If so, don't be discouraged; at least you are reading the passage and getting its primary meaning.

Maybe the passage will suggest something to you, some related idea, some other similar passage of Scripture, something in your life or circumstances to which the words of Scripture apply, or some truth of theology that may take on a little more meaning. Chances are, for the first few times, or the first few dozen times, nothing much will happen. Don't worry. You have offered God that much of your time, and He will appreciate it. As you do it more often, you will get better at it.

Keep it up for as long a time as you have set, glancing at your watch only if nothing seems to be happening. If you are going strong and enjoying it, keep it up as long as you seem to be receiving input. When it seems certain that nothing more is coming and your assigned time is up, stop and think back over what has happened. Any insights or new ideas that come to you, repeat them, put them in some clear verbal form, or maybe even write them down. Some people keep a notebook for this purpose. You have spent some time with God, held conversation with Him, and perhaps learned something new from Him. Be sure to thank Him. It is only courteous.

Don't be in a hurry to leave and get on with your business. If some point in your meditation suggests something you ought to do, or might do during the rest of the day as an act of sacrifice or virtue, whatever the Spirit suggests, make a resolution to do that.

There will be distractions, as there always are when we try to pray. They come in many disguises, but they can usually be divided into two categories: those that are independent of our will, and those that aren't.

The distractions that are independent of our will are things like illness, lack of detachment, inadequately suppressed emotions that get in our way, or unsuitable direction. What you do about this is try to moderate the influence. Try to improve your health, and adapt your prayer to the circumstances in which you find yourself. Sometimes it is helpful to fix your attention on something like a crucifix.

Those distractions that we have some control over are lack of preparation before we begin, failure to consider the subject to be used, that sort of thing. These are things we can do something about, but not all at once. Make an effort to practise the virtue you want to acquire, and ask God to help you overcome the particular defect. Fight distractions of the mind directly by pulling the mind gently back on track when it begins to stray.

What we are doing in mediation is increasing our knowledge of God's ways under God's own instruction. This practice, employed daily for years, will immeasurably enrich our knowledge of God and of Christianity. We read the Scriptures, really listen to them, notice what they say, let them sink in. We have them in our memories for ready recall and application to our life situation. We inwardly and spiritually digest them, and let them become a part of us.

This is a kind of prayer. It is sometimes called mental prayer, or prayer with the mind. It is prayer because it is opening ourselves to God, allowing Him to instruct us, guide, comfort, and strengthen us.

Best of all, our love for God will increase. The will is moved by whatever the mind sees as good. As our intellect comes to know and understand God better, our affections will be stimulated to love Him more. Our faith will be strengthened and virtue will be acquired. But don't expect any of these fruits of meditation right away. God has a blueprint for our spiritual growth that is unlike that for any other soul. We want to go at His pace, not ours.

Along with our own meditations, we will want to become acquainted with the fruits of meditation in the lives of the saints and other advanced and articulate Christians. So we will begin the practice of spiritual reading. In our meditations we hold conversations with God, and in our spiritual reading we hold conversations between God, ourselves, and the saints. To what exalted company the Christian is invited! A certain man made a wedding feast for his son – you and me. What glorious conversation takes place around the table. These great works may be read simply as instruction, or they may be read thoughtfully, lovingly, and reflectively, or just for the sheer spiritual joy of knowing such friends of God and making them our friends. To put things in order: we want to learn to pray and here is how we do it:

1. Regular participation in the liturgy and the offices;
2. Regular use of a primer;
3. Solid foundation in dogmatic theology to provide a grasp of doctrine;
4. Increasing acquaintance with the content of the Bible;
5. Beginning practice of meditation and reading in spiritual classics.

When we have done that, we are beginners. But we have begun the most important journey we can take. It leads directly to God. Meditation can be fun, exciting, rewarding, and thrilling, but diligence and regularity are essential. The more generous we are with God, the more He gives back to us in grace. God is a gentleman, and He will never allow Himself to be outdone in generosity. What you will receive is reformation of character and increase of love.

24

· ·

CONTEMPLATION

It is the almost universal consensus among authors on the spiritual life, from the earliest Fathers to the present, that the height of Christian prayer is that state called contemplation. St Thomas says, "The purpose of work is to acquire leisure for contemplation." It is even said that all we shall do in Heaven is contemplation.

There is not only a state of prayer that can accurately be called acquired contemplation (i.e., an advanced state of prayer which man can, aided by grace, achieve by his own efforts), but there is also a kind of natural contemplation that is not religious at all. There is a perfectly natural state of attention that is properly called contemplation, and every normal person achieves this state fairly often, largely without thought or planning.

Infused contemplation refers not so much to the psychological or spiritual condition as to its content, the specifically religious or spiritual element of consciousness. Therefore, it would follow that the effort to achieve a contemplative state is an appropriate study in ascetical theology, and that a person can be trained, or can train himself, to enter into contemplation. Whether God will respond to intrude into consciousness an awareness of Himself and His presence in the soul of course cannot be contrived or controlled. But one can certainly dispose himself to a religious contemplation. Therefore we shall concern ourselves first of all with a description of the state of awareness that can properly be called contemplation, making use of the concepts and terminology of scholastic philosophical theology.

To begin with, contemplation is the exact opposite of concentration, or what is ordinarily referred to as concentration, an intense application of thought to an object. This is why, in the normal progression of the soul in prayer, we are taught that one sign of our readiness for contemplation, or that God is calling us to a higher state of mystical union with Himself, is the cessation of the effectiveness of that type of prayer called mental prayer.

In the popular language of today, when everyone is writing about the spiritual life, and when Christians are rushing out to learn about prayer from real or counterfeit gurus, it is customary to use the word meditation to refer to both meditation and contemplation. We prefer the traditional distinction, in which meditation implies an application of the active intellect to probe for the mystical meaning of Scripture, and contemplation the cessation of intellectual activity altogether.

Perhaps we can see this in an analogy. The artist, while painting a picture, is busily active, not only by applying paint to canvas, but also in continually criticizing his work and correcting it to bring it to perfection. But when he is finished, the purpose of the work is realized; then what you do with a picture is admire it, in the literal sense of "look at it".

So it is in the relationship of meditation to contemplation. Meditation involves the work of the intellect to bring one to a knowledge of the truth; when this is achieved the work stops. Then one simply admires it, gazes upon it, and enjoys it.

This is contemplation. In Heaven the soul will rest from its labours. This is the meaning of the beatific vision. The soul possesses in contemplative delight what in this life it has yearned for. The journey is at an end. Henceforward, we simply enjoy. The experience of contemplative prayer involves, first of all, a cessation of all thought, and secondly, a veiled and imperfect participation in all the timeless and purposeless bliss of Heaven.

Contemplation is a kind of apophasis. St Thomas says we know God by unknowing, a manner of uniting with God which exceeds the compass of our minds, when the mind recedes from all things and leaves even itself and is united with the super-resplendent rays of the divinity. For to understand that God is not only about all that exists but even above all that we can comprehend comes to us from divine wisdom.

This is the theological foundation of all that mysterious talk about dark nights, about the *via negativa*, all apophatic spirituality from Dionysius to St John of the Cross. Understandably, it is not popular in the twentieth century, with its fascination with science and nature and its demands for instant gratification of the senses.

Yet even the most sybaritic voluptuary contemplates, and if he reflects upon his own pleasures, will admit that the highest form of pleasure is in his contemplation.

My point is that between the highest forms of mystical contemplation and the ordinary, unintentional contemplation of ordinary people there is a similarity, even an identity, of psychological mechanism, and we understand the extraordinary and exceptional by its analogy to the ordinary and unexceptional. So we'll talk briefly about ordinary natural contemplation.

In this diagram you have two triangles joined at their apices, one on top of the other, and the lower one

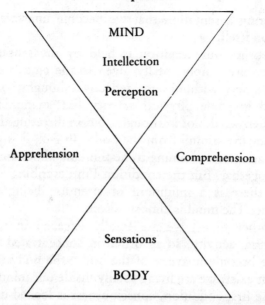

represents the body and its sensations. The intellect reaches down into the body to notice a sensation, it grasps it (apprehension) and draws it to itself and considers it. We are in touch with external reality through the body and its sensations.

Have you ever been kept awake by the ticking of a clock? Most nights you don't notice it, but it's there. We have the capacity for tuning out sensations, or tuning them in. Really hearing is paying attention to it and identifying it, and this usually results in our naming the sound or its source: "Hark, hark, the lark!" We hear the sound when the mind adverts to it, and we almost immediately take it up into the intellect and construct a judgement: "That sound is an aeroplane." Yet by receiving it into the intellect and considering it, we are to some extent withdrawing attention from the external object and considering it as an idea in the mind. We can in fact become so abstracted by considering a sensation that we become unaware of the sensation itself.

Sometimes our attention is held by the sensation, as when we are simply totally given to the enjoyment of a good dinner, without any reflective thought, or when engaged in some physical activity like swimming. The mind is engaged, not in thought, but in directing the body and receiving stimuli from the body. In fact, it is possible when eating or swimming to be thinking about something else altogether. But the condition I'm describing is one in which there is a minimum of attention being paid to anything. The mind is almost asleep.

At other times, we are totally engaged in reflective intellectual activity, so absorbed in concentrated thought that we become unaware of the body; the body might as well not exist; we are living totally inside our mind.

In the first condition, consciousness is locked up inside the body, our attention is absorbed by sensation. This is a condition experienced commonly while enduring severe pain, or great bodily pleasure, as in sexual orgasm, or strenuous physical activity like running a race. In the second condition, consciousness is locked inside the mind; it may be in problem solving, or in daydreaming, planning a vacation, rehearsing a speech, memorizing something.

There is a third mental state in which nothing is happening either in the mind or in the body, a kind of stupor, a vacuity of mind, a dullness.

And there is a fourth condition, different from any of the above, which is contemplation. In this state there is no discursive activity of the mind. We are not thinking about anything, yet the mind is fully awake and alert. This is the state in which we often listen to music or gaze with fixed attention at some natural beauty, soaking up sensations and impressions and enjoying them, just letting it happen, taking it all in. If we were to verbalize our consciousness at such times, it would probably come out something like, "Wow!"

In the diagram, the mind goes down to the apex of the top triangle to receive an impression from the bottom one, to grasp or apprehend something. Normally, we would immediately take this sensation back into the abstract realm of the intellect and identify it, think about it, and decide what, if anything, needs to be done about it.

In the top triangle, or in the bottom triangle, we are locked up inside ourselves, either in our mind or our body. Only at the tiny point where the triangles meet are we open to receive anything from outside ourselves. This is the point, and the only point, at which God enters consciousness. "Behold, I stand at the door and knock."

Contemplation is going to that tiny door and waiting, receiving, not retreating back into the intellect where we are in control, where we can impose meanings on things, and give them meanings that we choose. The point to note is that in intellectual activity there is no new input. We may get new ideas, but only by drawing out the implications of ideas we already possess. We have to go to the door, the apex, the still point, and pay attention to something in order to get the new input, new data, new experience. We will pass that door a hundred thousand times a day, in each instance making a split-second act of contemplation – you walk through your bedroom and notice a pot plant that needs water, a piece of clothing, a fluttering window curtain, a wrinkle in the bedspread, or hear the barking dog next door. You jerk these impressions quickly into the mind and dismiss them: the pot plant can go awhile yet without water, we'll attend to it later. We may, absent-mindedly, hang up the clothing, ignore the window curtain, straighten out the bedspread, mildly curse the barking dog, and go on about our business. But we have contemplated each of these for one-thousandth of a second.

In terms of psychological mechanics we do the same thing, only protracted, when we stand in the front yard at night and watch the approach of a thunderstorm, or admire the display of a bed of roses in bloom, or attend a musical concert, or stand in awe at the rim of the Grand Canyon. If in watching the thunderstorm we are engaged in thinking about electricity and wondering how we could harness such energy for the use of man, we have withdrawn our attention from the lightning and the clouds and retired inside our mind. The key to contemplation is admiration, from the Latin for "wonder". To look at something and simply admire it, enjoy it, delight in it, be awed by it, content that it should be – that is contemplation.

In this natural contemplation the active intellect is concentrated in the act of attending to something, and the result may be pleasure or dread. It's difficult for us, after two hundred years of rationalism, to accept the notion that contemplating is better than thinking things out. Yet whatever pleasure there is in thinking is the result of contemplating. For we can contemplate an idea, too. When you have solved a problem in mathematics and take pleasure in the solution, you have paused for a moment and turned from intellection and dropped into contemplation. Whenever we turn our attention to something and pause there, suspend discursive reason about it and just enjoy it, we are contemplating.

To stand at a window and watch with fascination the

slowly falling flakes of snow is a contemplative activity. To walk in the woods, soaking up impressions of light and shadow, gently waving grasses and branches of trees, noticing the subtle differences in shades of colour, listening to the noises of little wild creatures, smelling the moist earth and just enjoying it all – this is contemplation. To read poetry and be charmed by the turn of a phrase, the figure of speech, the progression and juxtaposition of ideas, the rhythm and cadence of the sound without analysing it, this is contemplation.

Religious contemplation may begin with simply pausing to grasp and apprehend some mystery of the faith, some doctrine like the Incarnation, some event in the life of Christ, when we just stand in awe and wonder and amazement at the love and beauty of God.

It leads us little by little to the contemplation of God Himself. Not some ideas about God, but God Himself. At this point the intellect is of no further use; love takes over.

There is a profound truth in Dante's *Divine Comedy*. Virgil, the symbol of reason, guides Dante through an understanding of hell and purgatory, but when he comes to Heaven, Virgil can go no further and turns back. Beatrice, the symbol of admiration and love, becomes his guide. The role of the intellect is to bring us to God; having arrived, we stop thinking about God and simply enjoy Him. All the activity of Heaven is contemplation, which is why all the activity of Heaven is pleasure and joy. There we cease from our labours, especially our intellectual labours, and just say "Wow!"

So it is with contemplation. No explanation of a great work of art, a great piece of music, a splendid view of distant mountains, can be anything but less than the thing itself. A mystical experience simply cannot be communicated in words. It cannot be shared with someone who has not had it. We can and will talk about it, endlessly, sometimes. But all we learn is that the mystics have had an experience that we have not had, and they find it entrancing, transporting, thrilling, captivating, delightful – and beyond description. It is beyond description because it is beyond the intellect.

Infused contemplation is that condition in which our openness is met with a response from God who receives us into Himself, bestows upon us the reality and awareness of His present love.

Although it is a natural experience we have had many times, and there are little tiny breakthroughs for fleeting moments that may well be unnoticed, when our first full experience of mystical contemplation occurs, it may take us by surprise. It may last only a moment. It may last, in advanced souls, for as long as thirty minutes or an hour. But ordinarily it comes and lingers only a few moments, and then either gradually or suddenly departs. Yet it still leaves the soul with a delicious sense of having been filled. There is certainty that one has been with God, intimately, surely, actually, really.

The experience is ordinarily not accompanied by visions or voices or ecstasies. It is a deep interior quiet that is filled with an ineffable sweetness and beauty. During it, time stands still, for we are in eternity, in God's time.

Even natural contemplation, such as that which some-times occurs when listening to music, is not something that we do. It is rather a cessation of all activity other than paying attention. In religious contemplation, there is an unmistakable quality of giveness, the experience of God coming to us rather than our going out in search of God.

Yet Jesus said, "Seek and ye shall find; knock and it shall be opened to you." One cannot manufacture religious contemplation, but one may desire it and yearn for it. At least one ought to know that such an experience awaits one and be open to it.

To achieve this pause or repose of the attention, one is greatly helped by bodily rhythm. Music is an excellent source for achieving natural contemplation. Another is the dance. Doubtless this is the great appeal of both these art forms. A rhythmic motion of the body, one in which each movement follows the previous one almost automatically without thought, allows the mind to become free, either to reflect on other matters, or just to repose in contemplative pleasure. Back in the time when poetry was read aloud, it was good, also.

It is doubtless for this reason that for ordinary folk, not instructed in the ways of prayer, the liturgy is the most common setting for the experience of contemplation. Our finest prayers are those in which we are not paying attention to the words we say.

This is what religion is all about. We spend so much time trying to help people that lots of folk know of no other purpose for the Church. But Jesus did not die on the cross to keep me financially solvent and make my wife do to suit me. He died to rend the veil of the temple and open the way for me to enter into the Holy of Holies, into the very presence of God.

This experience, or similar experiences, come often into the lives of layfolk during the liturgy. But it greatly helps if the liturgy is performed with this in mind.

Liturgy is supposed to be a vehicle for contemplation. Many priests, however, seem to think of it as primarily didactic and pedagogic, judging by the way they recite the words, with expression, like a recent graduate from a school of elocution. Perhaps the most offensive style is an affected folksiness. The correct method of liturgical reading is a somewhat monorhythmical pace, with just enough emphasis to preserve the clarity of the sense, a distinct and clear pronunciation of the words without rhetorical emphasis, so that the hearer can lose himself in the experience.

With better performance of liturgical celebration, there would surely be much more contemplative experience in the liturgy among the laity. One cannot help but wonder whether, with an awareness of the contemplative possibilities in liturgy, with better preparation, more attention to the music, and some instruction to the people of the possibility of contemplation, attendance at Mass would not increase noticeably. Certainly with people running off in search of TM and similar secular tactics of meditation, there is a hunger for this.

For all that, it is certain that for most contemplatives, the most common setting for the contemplative experience is in private devotions. But even here, the Christian needs instruction. It is the rare and advanced Christian soul (unfortunately all too often on his own without spiritual direction) who discovers that listening to God is more important than talking to Him.

. . . .

25

PRECEPTS OF
THE CHURCH

The precepts of the Church are what the Church expects of her members as a basic minimum standard. They go back to the Middle Ages, and there are six of them. Jesus summarized the Law and the Prophets by saying, "Thou shalt love the Lord they God with all thy heart, with all thy soul, and with all thy might. This is the first and great commandment, and the second is like unto it, thou shalt love they neighbour as thyself."

So there are three people we are supposed to love: God, my neighbour, and myself, in that order. Suppose somebody comes along and says to the preacher, "Okay, I love God, I love my neighbour, I love myself. Now what do I do about it?"

Of course, there is a vast, complicated response to that question, but we reduce it to an absolute, bare minimum in six precepts. Because I have a social self as a human being, and a private self as an individual, there are two things I do about loving God, my neighbour, and myself.

Remember, this is the minimum. The social part of loving God is to worship Him in church every Sunday and Holy Day. The private part is to prepare yourself for that worship. The social part of loving your neighbour is to support the Church, and the private part is to keep all personal relationships in the context of love. The social part of loving yourself is to make a Christian environment, and the private part is to strive for your own sanctification.

Let's look at it in a bit more detail.

Worship God in church every Sunday. Jesus commanded His disciples to "Do this in remembrance of me," and the Church accepts that as a commandment of the Lord. You do this, and you do it every Sunday and Holy Day of Obligation. It has been held for 2,000 years that to miss Mass on Sunday unnecessarily is a grave and serious sin. The Church expects those who are baptized and confirmed to be present at the offering of the Holy Sacrifice fifty-two Sundays out of the year. You worship God with your fellow man.

Now lots of people say, "I'm very religious, but I don't believe in the Church." What they're really saying is that they have a great love of God and a contempt for their fellow man. You don't love your fellow man if you don't come together with him at the most important and critical moment in which you and your fellow man are welded together in spiritual communion in the common worship and love of God.

I have been a priest a long time, and the devil has not yet quit trying to tempt me to a lack of faith. I'm quite sure that you, too, have been subject to the same sort of temptation. Is there really a God? Was Jesus Christ really anything more than just an itinerant Jewish prophet? Is there really any need for me to go to church? I am so tired, so sleepy, and I don't really want to get up and get dressed. Is it really worth it?

The national average for Sunday Mass attendance is about 30 per cent of the congregation. Those other 70 per cent are saying to each other, "Naw, it ain't worth it. Don't bother." But God has placed His reputation in your hands. These are people who will look at you and either find encouragement from you to commitment and dedication and discipline and adoration and worship and service and loyalty – or they will look at you and find encouragement to self-indulgence and self-serving. And just your presence at Mass on Sunday, the fact that you're there, is a statement you're making to everybody else who's there, that yes, it is worth it. I guarantee you, everybody in church next Sunday morning will have had an attack on his faith some time in the last month or six weeks. You know it's true, because it's true of you. One of the things that keeps your resolve at a high level is the fact that the other people in church who are there steadfastly, regularly, Sunday after Sunday, usually in pretty much the same pews, are making a statement to everyone else in the congregation that yes, it's worth it. It's important.

Communion is not only an act of uniting yourself with God through Jesus Christ, but an act of uniting yourself with everybody else who's united to Christ. It is an act by which we affirm an absolute moral commitment to love one another. It is the Mass that constitutes the Church.

There's a story about some Christians who were brought up before a magistrate in the days of persecution in the Roman Empire. Oddly enough, under Roman law it was not against the law to believe in the Christian Creed. You could believe anything you pleased. The Romans were very tolerant, as long as you got your religion licensed by the state. In order to get your licence, you had to burn incense before a statue of the emperor. Since the Christians wouldn't do this, they were an unlicensed organization. To the nervous and paranoid Roman government, this was tantamount to an open act of rebellion. Christians were not persecuted because they believed in Christ, but because they were regarded as a subversive threat to the stability of the Empire.

These Christians were up before the magistrate, and he was concerned whether or not they had participated in an unlawful assembly. He asked them, "Are you Christians?" And they replied, "Yes." And he said, "Have you attended the Eucharist?" The answer was, "We told you we are Christians. It's the Eucharist that constitutes a Christian." This was the mind of the Church in the third century. It never occurred to those people being tried for their lives before the Roman magistrate that they should deny their Christianity, or deny that they had been to Mass. It was two ways of saying the same thing.

In the early centuries of the Church, to miss Mass on Sunday was regarded as having repudiated one's Christian profession. You just didn't bother to come back, unless you came back by way of confession and received absolution.

There are three things that excuse Sunday Mass attendance. One is when you're sick in bed. The Church doesn't define how sick you have to be. It would be rather ridiculous to say, "You have to go to Mass if you have a fever of 102°, but if it's 102.2°, you can stay home." A good rule of thumb is that if you're sick enough that on a Tuesday you wouldn't go to work or to school, you're probably sick enough so that you needn't go to church. A doctor friend of mine once said, "Half the world's work is done by people who don't feel very good." Not feeling very good is not really an excuse not to go to church. But if you're really sick, stay home. And if you're sick enough that you stay home on Sunday, you may call the priest and he will be delighted to bring you your communion. It isn't part of your obligation to receive communion at home if you can't go to Mass on Sunday, but it is your privilege.

So one of the things that excuses you from Sunday Mass attendance is when you're sick. One of the things that does not excuse you is when you've got out-of-town guests, or when you were out late Saturday night. Sorry about that.

The second excuse for missing Mass on Sunday is when there's no Mass to go to. Obviously, if you're cast away on a desert island, you can't go to Mass on Sunday. There is a sort of practical rubric of common sense here which depends on the availability of transportation. You can travel longer distances to go to Mass if you've got a car than if you walk on foot or ride a burro. There are places in the mountains of the northern Philippines where Episcopalians will travel on foot all Saturday afternoon, a distance of maybe eighteen or twenty miles through the jungle to get to the nearest town where a Mass is being celebrated. They will spend the night, go to Mass, have lunch, and spend all Sunday afternoon walking home. They will do this fifty-two weekends out of the year. That's devotion.

The third thing that excuses Mass attendance is what is called the conflict of a notable work of charity. For example, if you have somebody in your family who's sick and needs a nurse, and if you left them alone to go to Mass they might get worse, obviously you don't go to Mass. If you're driving to Mass on Sunday and there's an automobile accident and somebody needs to take an injured person to the hospital, and if you did it you'd miss Mass, then you just miss Mass. The Church in her mercy and wisdom and common sense has decided that this exemption also applies to people who have to work on Sundays in jobs that have something to do with public service, such as nurses and doctors, pharmacists and even taxi drivers, airline pilots and flight attendants, policemen and firemen and so on. There are a host of jobs that are really necessary to keep the machinery of society geared up and moving, and require people to work on the weekends. However, if that is your situation, it is your duty to go to your priest and say, "Father, can you say a Mass for me at some time I can go?"

Theoretically, there ought to be only one Mass in one parish on any one Sunday. The Holy Spirit dwells in the *full assembly of the saints*. It mutilates the unity of the congregation to have two or three separate congregations, which is what happens when you have multiple Masses on Sunday. If you get into the habit of going to the 8:00 Mass, you can belong to the same congregation for twenty years and never meet the people who are in the habit of going to the 10:00 Mass. You can't very well have a close intimate Christian family and a community of love that way. Nevertheless, most churches have more than one Mass on Sunday, and in spite of what I'm saying, will continue to have separate congregations. But we ought to make an effort to go to the principal Mass of the church on the Lord's Day, the parish Mass, the *missa pro populi*.

Now we come to Holy Days of Obligation. There are five of them, and they are set by tradition and were determined by popular devotion, by people just like you.

The five traditional days are Christmas; 1 January, which is the Feast of the Holy Name; 6 January, which is the Feast of the Epiphany; Ascension Day, which is a Thursday and always forty days after Easter and slides

along the calendar as Easter does; and 1 November, which
is All Saints' Day. Easter is not a Holy Day of Obligation
because it is always a Sunday anyway. To this list I would
have to add Ash Wednesday. These days everybody seems
to want to go to Mass on Ash Wednesday and get those
ashes on their foreheads. If you were to ask most people in
this parish if Ash Wednesday is a Holy Day of Obligation
they would say, "Oh, yes," but it's not, in the sense that no
committee of theologians ever said so. Ash Wednesday is a
privileged *feria*, not a Day of Obligation or a feast of the
Church.

I think Ash Wednesday has become an almost obligatory
day for Mass attendance because twentieth century people,
as a people, suffer from a morbid, neurotic guilt complex.
More people come to Ash Wednesday than to the
Christmas Midnight Mass. I think this is because the Ash
Wednesday service says something, it speaks to where we
hurt, it responds to a spiritual need that vast numbers of
people have. Popular devotion determines these Holy
Days of Obligation.

The first part, then, of the social part of loving God is to
worship at the Eucharist every Sunday and Holy Day
of Obligation unless prevented by illness, unreasonable
distance from the church, or the conflict of a notable work
of charity.

What do I do because I love God and am a private
individual? When I receive my communion, this is my
personal, intimate act of loving union with God, and I need
careful preparation before, and thanksgiving afterward. I
don't just walk into church and say, "Oh, this is
communion Sunday," and receive communion. I anticipate
what's going to happen, and prepare myself by meditation
and reflection and prayer, preferably the night before. If I

can't do it Saturday night, I get to church early enough on Sunday to do it then. It might be a superficial cursory preparation, but we ought to make some kind of preparation. And the reason for that is quite simple.

The sacrament works because God works it. There is always an effect of the sacrament. What that effect is depends on the interior subjective disposition of the recipient. The greater our faith, the greater our love of God, the greater our determination, the more clear our intention to serve God, the more love we have for our neighbour, the more deeply penitent we are for our sins, then the more effect the grace will have in our soul. If you receive communion, for example, with your heart and mind bent on evil, the power in the sacrament will strengthen your will for evil. It really will. St Paul says if you receive it unworthily, you purchase for yourself a greater condemnation. If your will is sort of vaguely directed toward God, it will be strengthened in a vague way. But if you have a deep and intentional love of God and an intentional desire to serve Him, the grace of the sacrament will strengthen your intention to serve God. Spend some time, perhaps a minimum of ten to twenty minutes, thinking about what you're going to do at Mass. You are preparing to meet God face to face, and you ought to be ready. You also ought to say thank you afterward. We have an interesting custom in most Episcopal churches, and that is as soon as the candles are put out, the organist plays a few different notes as a signal to everybody that the service is over, and everybody all at once gets up and moves into the centre aisle, struggling to the exit door, and greeting one another and making conversation. That's not good. It creates a serious hubbub. When Mass is over, each person ought to remain on his knees until he has finished his own private thanksgiving, and get up and go out quietly so as not to disturb somebody else who prays longer. If people are in church saying their prayers, you don't want to disturb them.

Now, what I do because I love my neighbour and am a social being is support the church. This is commonly misunderstood as having something to do with parish finances. It's not. We are a family, and we have a primary loyalty to one another as a family. My mother was an old bat, and I can say that, but you can't, and I don't want anybody else to say that. I love my mother, I know her faults, and I will fight to defend her good name. The church is our mother. Boy, do I know her faults. I could start right now and talk till midnight about the faults of the church, but I'm not going to talk to outsiders about the faults of the church. We should have a filial loyalty to our mother, the church. That means also we should have the same filial loyalty to one another. The support of the church means loyalty to the family community. It's a primary community. You forgive one another's sins, you carry one another's burdens, you protect one another's good name. It's very important.

There is another level of meaning when we talk about the support of the church, and that is that we should do our share of the work that goes on around here. This is home and we should feel at home, and make ourselves at home. My wife is relatively short, and in cleaning, she rarely if ever sees the top of the refrigerator. She just doesn't see it. Every once in a while, it will get to me, and I will go get a sponge and soapy water and go clean off the top of the refrigerator. Nobody has to tell me to do this; it's my home and I want it looking nice.

Now if you come up here and the windows need

washing, you don't have to ask the priest for permission to wash your windows, because it's your church. We've got acolytes, altar guild, choir, Sunday School, parish suppers, and work parties in which we mow the lawn, mop the floors, patch the sidewalk, and do the work that needs doing around here. Support of the church means *doing our share*, being willing to serve in some capacity. Before I came to this parish some years ago, we didn't have a choir, and after the first few weeks a number of people asked me, "Father, when are we going to have a choir?" And I would answer, "When you are willing to give up one night a week for choir practice." When you come to church here on Sunday morning and listen to those people making beautiful music up in the choir loft, does it ever occur to you that they've given up a couple of hours every Wednesday night to come to choir practice? That is the support of the church.

What makes us members of this community is that we break bread together on Sunday morning and together eat the body of Christ and drink His sacramental blood. That makes us a community. There are those people who are devoted and committed, and volunteer for the jobs that are there. Anyone can belong to that little clique that runs things if they want to, if they have a sense of dedication and commitment, and a feeling that they have a responsibility here. Two people doing altar work get done twice as fast. Well, not really, because they stop and talk. But it's more fun.

This support of the church because I love my neighbour and am a social being also involves, of course, bearing my proportional share of the burden of the cost. The technical norm here is the tithe, one tenth of my disposable income. I wouldn't be honest or fair with you if I didn't mention that in biblical times the tenth that went to the temple not only went to the preacher, kept the temple roof in repair, paid for the incense, and so on, but the temple also performed a number of civic functions that are now performed by the government and paid for by your taxes. Public education came out of the tithe, as did medical services and legal services, so I would not insist that one-tenth of your income is an absolute moral obligation. It certainly is an act of great devotion, and I have never known anyone who tithed regularly who regretted it.

A number of years ago there was a widow here in the parish with small children who had a job which enabled her to come home shortly after the kids got out of school. When summer came and school was out, she was faced with the task of hiring someone to babysit her children. She came to me and said, "Father, I made a pledge to the church and I want to tithe, but I can't do that and hire a babysitter. What shall I do?" I said, "Let me ask the vestry." We took it up at the vestry meeting and got a beautiful answer from them. They said, "Tell her to continue to tithe, and we'll pay for the babysitter." Now that's really the Christian answer.

The motive for giving is not to support the church. God's got plenty of money. The main reason for giving is to express our gratitude to God. The other reason is to discipline our appetites.

Next, what I do because I love my neighbour and am a private person is that I strive to keep all my personal relationships in the context of love. And as an absolute irreducible minimum, it means that I go to confession when in grave sin. Obviously, if I have sinned against the community, I will go to the community and apologize. There is a certain amount of sensitivity to the good name of the Christian community, and when I have misbehaved in some scandalous fashion, I owe an apology to the community, in order to keep myself and my relations to my fellow man in the context of love.

What I do because I love myself and am a social person is to strive to achieve and maintain a Christian marriage, a Christian home life, and a Christian family life. It is my duty to myself as a social being.

Because I love myself and I am a private being, I strive for my own sanctification. Now if you love someone, you want the very best for them. If you're a rotten, no-good, no-count parent, a blind and foolish parent, you will want an easy life for your children, to see that they are pampered and get everything they want. If you are a really loving parent, you will want your children to be holy, to be strong, stalwart, mature, moral, responsible individuals, to be saints. You want them to be wise, disciplined, able to say no to their whims and appetites; you want them to be reasonable, logical, kind, generous, humble, loving, and chaste.

So if you love yourself, you strive for holiness yourself. It's a lifelong, continual, never-ending process of moral and spiritual growth and development. By and large, what this means is that there are conflicts arising on a fairly regular basis between what I ought to do and what is comfortable and convenient to do. Ordinarily, it's a pretty good rule of thumb when facing a moral decision that what's right and what you ought to do is what you want to do least.

In order to do what you ought to do instead of what you want to do, you have to be disciplined. You have to have the habit of allowing your mind and your will to govern your feelings and your bodily appetites. And this is largely about as much as I can tell you in a nutshell about the whole Christian moral life. It's doing what's right, instead of what's convenient and pleasant. The Church gives us a little miniature gymnasium exercise in moral discipline, and so what I do because I love myself as a private individual is to keep the Church's laws of fasting.

First let me distinguish between abstinence and fasting. Abstinence has to do with the kind of food eaten, not the quantity. When you abstain from certain foods it means that there are certain kinds of foods you don't eat. Fasting has to do with the amount of food.

Normally, the Church abstains from the flesh meats of warm-blooded animals like pork, chicken, beef, turkey, bear meat, buffalo meat. Fish and crustaceans are exempt; you can eat fish or shrimp or lobster or crawdads. You abstain on all Fridays of the year except those in the season of Christmas and the season of Easter. In addition to the Fridays, the Wednesdays together with the Fridays in Lent are days of abstinence from flesh meats. This is a mitigation of a much more severe discipline in the Middle Ages, when the forty days of Lent was observed as forty days of abstinence and fasting, and you abstained not only from flesh meats, but from all animal by-products, such as eggs, milk, and cheese.

Actually, the prohibition against meat was really a prohibition against having a party. Throughout most of the Church's two-thousand-year history and in large parts of the world today like South America, Southeast Asia, lots of places in Africa, meat is not a part of the common daily diet of ordinary people. They don't have refrigeration, and they don't have a handy supermarket full of chickens already cut up. If any meat is going to be eaten, it is going to be killed or purchased at considerable sacrifice, and therefore meat was reserved for special occasions. So abstinence from meat on Friday, the weekly anniversary of the death of Christ, is a prohibition against observing Friday as a festal day. On the other hand, your big Sunday dinner is a very Christian institution. Sunday is a holy day. If there is any day of the week on which it is right and proper to have a party, to have a dance, to celebrate, it's Sunday. If there is any day of the week on which it is inappropriate to have a party, it's Friday.

Fish is exempt from the prohibition because at the time the rule was promulgated, fish was not regarded as a festal dish. It wasn't something you served guests. As you know very well, fish must be kept refrigerated or it'll go bad pretty quickly, and the ways of preserving fish with salt don't produce a main course at a festival dinner.

Fasts are distinguished between strict fasts and moderate fasts. The forty days of Lent are moderate fasts, and it's during Lent that you diminish the quantity of the food you eat. Sundays in Lent don't count, though, but on the forty weekdays of Lent, you eat two half-meals and one whole meal. A light breakfast, a light lunch, a normal supper, that sort of thing. The days of strict fast are at the beginning and end of Lent, Ash Wednesday and Good Friday, and these are observed by a collation in the morning, that is, one solid and one liquid, like a glass of milk and a piece of toast, or a cup of coffee and a doughnut. No lunch, and a half-meal at supper which contains no flesh meat. You're supposed to get hungry on a day of strict fast.

There are three reasons for fasting and abstinence. First, it reminds us what day it is. There are meats I never really get hungry for except on Friday. Seems like every Friday morning I want old-fashioned country pork sausage for breakfast. Fast and abstinence mark the day, and help you remember what happened on that day, and therefore can be an aid to devotion. You could accomplish the same thing by putting your left shoe on your right foot and your right shoe on your left foot, and every time you took a step you'd remember Jesus died for you on Friday. The abstinence is not really enough, you see. You should abstain from flesh meats *and* remember that Christ died on Friday.

The second reason for fasting and abstinence is that it is something I can give to God. It's an offering I can make to God when I give up that second egg for breakfast, or give up meat on Friday, when I eat less and go hungry. God has given me so much, and of course, there's nothing in the world He needs. So the only thing you can do is give something up. It's an offering to God either as an act of thanksgiving or an act of penitence for our sins.

The third reason is that it's an act of discipline. In times of moral crisis, we need to be in the habit of subjecting our passions, our bodily appetites, our whims, our desires, our inclinations, and our comfort in favour of doing what is right, but perhaps inconvenient, so the Church has set up a little arbitrary, artificial act of sacrifice as a training device. You go down to the YMCA or the health club and you see people working out with exercise equipment, and it looks pointless, purposeless. But who knows when you will need that strength?

Once when I was about fifteen years old, my mother and I were driving back from Oak Cliff and crossing the old wooden trestle bridge over the Trinity River on Forest Avenue, and right ahead of us a car turned over, a Model A coupe, and a man was pinned under the car. Mother stopped the car and I got out and ran toward the car. I remember very distinctly that on the left-hand side of the road was a little grocery store and a filling station. Three or four men came barrelling out of the filling station and grocery store, and there were some houses nearby, and in a matter of seconds, there were eight or ten people gathered around this car. Somebody took charge, a little community formed, and somebody said, "The three of you get over here, and the three of you over there, and when I say 'Three,' let's lift." And we got in place and he said, "One, two, three – " and we lifted that car and pushed it off the man. I don't remember it being particularly heavy, and the adrenaline was flowing excitedly. So I exercise to build strength, not because in and of itself it has any particular value. But when you lift a car off a man who's been pinned underneath, there's some point to the exercise.

If you're going to build strength, you need to lift a little bit more weight than is comfortable. You only build muscles by straining muscles, but you don't want to overdo it. A little at a time will build muscles, so when you need muscles, you've got 'em.

A weekly self-denial of abstinence and a Lenten fast will build moral muscle. You don't acquire moral strength without moral exercise. And the abstinence and fasting are small, self-imposed disciplines, something that we can experience and feel, in which the body is conditioned to obey the intellect and the will. And the intellect and the will are conditioned to command the body. You do this in little ways, on a regular basis. You never know when you're going to face a crisis and have to make choices between what's right and what's pleasant, and our fasting is a way in which we can train and discipline ourselves in the matter of making difficult moral choices, by doing things that are really not all that difficult, but by doing them on a regular basis.

So the sixth precept then is to keep the Church's laws of fasting and abstinence. Remember, I said these things were the minimum. It's not for a moment suggested that these are all that a person ought to undertake. One ought to read one's Bible, say one's prayers, engage in the corporal and spiritual works of mercy, fight against his besetting sin or other vices he might have, and pray for and practise the acquisition of all the virtues. One ought to continually throughout life be educating oneself in the theology of the Church and the knowledge of the Holy Scriptures. There are a vast number of things that one can do. Most of these extra spiritual activities should be undertaken after consultation with one's spiritual director, parish priest, or some wise old Christian friend. One of the absolute sure and certain things is that a Christian in social isolation is a Christian in spiritual difficulty, and that's a fact. An absolute, undeniable fact.

God love you,
Padre